AMERICAN LABOR, CONGRESS, and the WELFARE STATE, 1935–2010

AMERICAN LABOR, CONGRESS, and the WELFARE STATE, 1935–2010

Tracy Roof

The Johns Hopkins University Press
Baltimore

MT

The Johns Hopkins University Press
2715 North Charles Street
Baltimore, Maryland 21218-4363
www.press.jhu.edu

Library of Congress Cataloging-in-Publication Data

Roof, Tracy.
American labor, Congress, and the welfare state, 1935–2010 /
Tracy Roof.
    p. cm.
  Includes bibliographical references and index.
  ISBN-13: 978-1-4214-0086-0 (hardcover : alk. paper)
  ISBN-13: 978-1-4214-0087-7 (pbk. : alk. paper)
  ISBN-10: 1-4214-0086-3 (hardcover : alk. paper)
  ISBN-10: 1-4214-0087-1 (pbk. : alk. paper)
    1. Labor unions—Political activity—United States—History.
2. Welfare state—United States—History. I. Title.
HD6510.R66 2011
322'.20973—dc22   2010047699

A catalog record for this book is available from the British Library.

*Special discounts are available for bulk purchases of this book. For
more information, please contact Special Sales at 410-516-6936 or
specialsales@press.jhu.edu.*

The Johns Hopkins University Press uses environmentally
friendly book materials, including recycled text paper that is
composed of at least 30 percent post-consumer waste, whenever
possible. All of our book papers are acid-free, and our jackets and
covers are printed on paper with recycled content.

12/28/11

CONTENTS

PREFACE

When I first began this project, I was interested in why rising income inequality went largely unaddressed in the political system. This led me to the question of which groups were most likely to push these issues on the national stage, which quickly led me to the labor movement. After reading a wide range of critical assessments of the American labor movement, particularly those dealing with the decline of the power and influence of organized labor, I initiated my own research into why labor had failed in pushing for a more comprehensive welfare state that could have mitigated worker insecurity and income inequality. I found that organized labor repeatedly pursued a range of policies addressed to these issues throughout the postwar period, but it was routinely thwarted at one stage of the legislative process or the other, even during periods when scholars considered labor to be much stronger than it is today. The project thus came to focus on the hurdles organized labor faced in the legislative process and how labor leaders attempted to overcome them, with occasional successes, but more frequent failures. I became a lot more cognizant of and sympathetic to the necessity of compromise in the American political system that has so frequently frustrated the ambitions of both the Left and the Right in American politics and often created inefficient or ineffective public policies.

Many people have made this long project possible. I would like to thank all of my colleagues in the Political Science Department at the University of Richmond, especially Jennifer Erkulwater and Dan Palazzolo for their scholarly engagement and advice on numerous chapters and Sheila Carapico and Andrea Simpson for their encouragement and help in navigating the publishing process. I would also like to thank Deb Candreva and Doug Harris, who have provided crucial advice since graduate school. I would like to thank Ira Katznelson, who on short notice provided valuable comments on several chapters at the end stages of the manuscript preparation, as well as the anonymous reviewers who provided many helpful suggestions. I would also like to thank Henry Tom and Suzanne Flinchbaugh with the Johns Hopkins University Press for their professionalism and efficiency. The archival research was made possible by travel grants from the Harry S. Truman Library Institute and the Lyndon Baines Johnson Foundation. The project was generously funded by several faculty research grants from the University of Richmond's School of Arts and Sciences. I also gained invaluable insight into the legislative process from my fellowship in the office of Senator Tom Harkin through the American Political Science Association's Congressional Fellowship Program. Finally, I would like to thank my mom, Billie, and my dad, Rick, for their enduring support and my two little girls, Clara and Lucy, who never fully understood why Mom had to spend so much time at the office. Finally, I owe the most to my husband, Mike, without whom I could have never completed this book.

AMERICAN LABOR, CONGRESS, and the WELFARE STATE,

1935–2010

Introduction

The Senate and therefore the Congress of which it is an equal part are too often too late with too little to meet the rapidly developing problems, needs and opportunities of an age of atomic energy, automation and a Communist expansionism that is bent upon and has repeatedly announced its intent to take over the entire world. We can ill afford continued minority rule. National welfare, strength, security and survival require the establishment of majority rule.

Walter Reuther, president of the United Autoworkers Union, 1957

Unfortunately, the fate of much good, constructive legislation in Congress is too often determined not on its merits but by horse-and-buggy era rules, procedures, and traditions which enable a conservative minority to block or delay action.

"Labor Looks at Congress," AFL-CIO, 1963

The Senate is distorting democracy. They've set up a system that does not represent what the American people want—and not just on health care. It sets the stage for America to be unable to meet the challenges on everything from jobs to energy to trade to foreign policy.

Andrew Stern, president of
the Service Employees International Union, 2009

On election night in 2008, no one was more elated with the victory of Democratic presidential candidate Barack Obama than the activists in the labor movement. After three decades of attacks on the welfare state and pro-labor policies, labor leaders saw the 2008 election as an opportunity to turn the tide in public policy toward a more activist government committed to the security of American workers. They hoped a unified Democratic government might finally make progress on policy goals sought by organized labor since the 1940s, including labor law reform, universal health care, and policies to create more jobs at better wages. Although breakthroughs would prove possible, as during the Truman,

Johnson, Carter, and Clinton administrations, the institutions of the legislative process would continue to challenge labor's ability to accomplish its goals. The fight over health care reform in President Obama's first year in office proved to be a roller-coaster ride for labor that perfectly illustrated both the emerging prospects and enduring obstacles to significant policy change.

This book makes two main interrelated arguments. First, it argues that institutional obstacles in the legislative process, such as the filibuster, have restricted labor's influence and repeatedly frustrated labor's efforts to further the postwar liberal policy agenda of economic security and pro-labor policies. Second, it argues that labor responded to these obstacles to its legislative agenda by moderating its demands, pushing the Democratic Party to the left, and working for congressional reforms to empower the majority in the majority party to control the legislative process. In these efforts the labor movement helped shape the contours of the American welfare state, the contemporary legislative process, and the party system in the postwar period. These slowly evolving changes created the legislative context that made health care reform possible in 2010, just a few years after it appeared that both liberalism and labor had reached postwar lows in political influence.

The fate of health care reform depended on whether a compromise could be reached that would attract the 60-vote supermajority necessary in the Senate to overcome an inevitable filibuster. At the opening of the 111th Congress, the Democrats' Senate majority stood at 58 votes, with the Senate race in Minnesota still undecided and a couple of Democratic senators in very poor health. A handful of these Democrats came from conservative states where labor and other liberal groups have limited influence. The battle over the administration's first priority, a near trillion dollar spending bill to stimulate the flagging economy, suggested the challenge ahead on health care. Despite overwhelming support and party discipline among Democrats in the House and the Senate and a big push by organized labor to get the bill passed, three Republican moderates were able to significantly scale back and alter the contents of the stimulus package as their price for supporting cloture. Following this model, Senate Democrats engaged in months of futile negotiations with a handful of Republicans to reach a compromise on health care reform. The dynamic appeared to shift when Republican senator Arlen Specter of Pennsylvania declared himself a Democrat and the undecided Minnesota Senate seat was finally awarded to Democrat Al Franken after an extended court battle. The Democrats finally reached the magic number of 60 for the first time since the mid-1970s.

After almost a year of negotiations, both the House and Senate passed versions of health care reform on party-line votes. But before a legislative compromise could be struck between the two chambers, Republican Scott Brown won a special election for the Senate seat of Democrat Ted Kennedy, the legendary labor ally and advocate of universal health care, who died in office of brain cancer. With the loss of one Senate seat, health care reform—and liberals' entire legislative agenda—was suddenly thrown into limbo. Ultimately, the Democratic leadership was able to work out a deal between the House and the Senate on a measure that could be taken up under a special process for budget-related matters known as reconciliation—a process that was not subject to Senate filibusters. After a series of dramatic votes in the House and Senate, the final bill passed the Senate 56–43, with three Democrats joining every Republican in voting against it. Once one of the most influential advocates of a single-payer system, organized labor clearly did not get all it wanted in the heavily compromised bill. But the 2010 reforms made the most progress in covering the uninsured since the adoption of Medicare forty-five years earlier. Yet the monumental struggle over health care pushed other labor priorities like labor law reform to the back burner, where they were likely to remain with the Democrats' loss of their supermajority.

As this volume demonstrates, the policy battles of the first year of the Obama administration are just the most recent examples of an important but often overlooked limitation on labor's political power and on the most ambitious goals of American liberalism more broadly. In a political system characterized by the separation of powers, checks and balances, and numerous protections for the minority, reformers need to have a very high level of support across a range of political institutions in order to produce significant policy change. This study examines the effect of the legislative process on the ability of reformers to expand the social safety net for workers through the lens of organized labor, which has been the most influential, most enduring, and best-organized advocate of these policies in the postwar period. It is focused on the efforts of organized labor to shape national public policy, largely under the leadership of the AFL-CIO. But in tracing these efforts, it recounts the much larger story of the fate of the postwar vision of American liberalism that labor shared with a broad range of groups including civil rights organizations, liberal religious groups, and liberal policy advocacy organizations. Many of the insights of the following chapters can be applied to this broader movement and indeed to any group or movement trying to pursue significant policy change.

Contrary to the claims of some of labor's critics, the national leadership of the labor movement has spent the past seventy years trying to build a social safety net to protect both unionized workers and the unorganized. As in other Western countries, organized labor became the leading advocate of a workers' welfare state centered on a full-employment, high-wage, and high-consumption economy secured through government spending and tax policies, economic planning, regulation, and policies fostering unionization. Workers would gain additional security from generous government insurance programs for retirement, unemployment, disability, and health care. Limited versions of all these programs have been adopted and gradually expanded, but the safety net in the United States is considerably less comprehensive than the protections in other advanced industrialized countries. While most of these countries institutionalized and expanded their welfare states in the early postwar period, proposals for similar programs stalled in the United States as a conservative coalition of Southern Democrats and Republicans used institutional veto points in Congress, including the House committee system and the filibuster threat, to slow or stop the expansion of a workers' welfare state. Issues considered during the reconversion years, like full-employment policy and universal health care, have appeared over and over on the policy agenda. But policy advances have been largely symbolic or incremental, leaving labor's broad policy goals unmet. In other areas, such as reforming labor law, there has been consistent gridlock.

Organized labor has not taken these defeats lying down. Since the 1940s the labor movement and its liberal allies have tried to reform and reorient the political system to improve the prospects for labor-backed public policies. Convinced that many of the labor movement's policy priorities would never be passed by Congress without changes in the American party system and the legislative process, labor strategists took a leading role in a labor-liberal coalition early in the postwar period that sought to realign liberal forces into the Democratic Party and expel conservative Democrats. Toward this end, the coalition focused on the legislative struggle for civil rights and pressuring Democrats to pursue congressional reforms to empower the non-Southern wing of the party in Congress.[1] The long-term effects were exemplified in the 111th Congress (2009–11). The passage of near-universal health care reform, one of the cornerstones of the postwar liberal agenda, was the culmination of a decades-long transformation of the American political system that the birth of the modern labor movement helped set in motion. Despite legislative wrangling, Democratic unity on congressional votes reached near record highs, and the majority in the majority party had much more control over legislative outcomes than it did the first time a universal health care proposal was considered, during the Truman administration. But while the administration, congressional leaders, and reform advocates reached a compromise on health care that every single Democrat in the Senate could support after almost a year of effort, the need to pass the final bill through reconciliation after the Democrats lost their supermajority made it clear that conservative minorities still had considerable power in the legislative process to obstruct many of labor's goals.

The policies associated with this postwar vision of a workers' welfare state did not stall simply because the public was fundamentally opposed to them, because labor leaders were too conservative or divided, because union membership was too small to affect the outcome, or because the Democratic Party was insufficiently supportive of liberals' goals, all commonly cited explanations. While some of these factors have no doubt come into play in various policy battles in the postwar period, the one constant across them all has been the high hurdles posed by the institutions structuring the legislative process. These institutions include major features of the American political system, such as the constitutional separation of powers, the system of checks and balances, the varying electoral bases of representation for the House, Senate, and president, and congressional procedures such as the House committee system and the Senate filibuster, which together have made it very difficult for labor to leverage its power effectively in the policy-making system. As a result, organized labor and its liberal allies have often had to settle for watered-down policies and to spend a great deal of time and effort trying to change the rules of the game in the political system. The institutional obstacles to the passage of liberal policies—and labor's response to them—have received little attention in the study of organized labor. Yet they are central to understanding the political involvement and limited policy accomplishments of the labor movement in the past, the present, and the future.

Common Explanations for Labor's Political Failures

Most of the literature on organized labor's political activity coalesces around one of two themes—the unique weakness of the Left in the United States compared with other advanced, industrialized countries or the failed strategies of labor leaders. Both of these literatures fail to fully explain the political influence and policy accomplishments of organized labor in the postwar period because they do not take into consideration the obstacles in the legislative process that labor confronted.

American Exceptionalism

The limits on organized labor's political influence are often tied to the unique weakness of the Left in the United States. For more than a century, scholars have attempted to explain this "American exceptionalism," which has prevented the development of an enduring socialist or social democratic party, a strong labor movement, and a more comprehensive welfare state as occurred in other Western countries. This body of literature has produced dozens of possible explanations, but most are tied to ideological and political factors.[2] Scholars such as Louis Hartz and Seymour Martin Lipset argue that Americans share a distinct national ideology shaped by faith in the individual, low levels of class consciousness, and a commitment to laissez-faire capitalism.[3] This underlying "American creed" is believed to have made American workers less interested in unionization and collective social struggle and more suspicious of the government, socialism, and social democratic policies. Other American exceptionalist explanations emphasize the political impediments to a viable labor or socialist party. For instance, winner-take-all elections discourage voting for less-established third parties because voters fear their votes will be wasted and their least-preferred candidate will win. Third parties also have difficulty getting on the ballot, and leftist parties have historically faced repression. Moreover, since the emergence of the two-party system in the mid-1800s, the Democrats and Republicans have managed to co-opt the popular issues of third parties, quickly robbing them of their momentum. The result has been a system with two dominant parties that have often downplayed class issues in favor of building cross-class coalitions based on ethnic or other appeals.[4] These appeals effectively divided working-class voters and prevented them from becoming a powerful political force that could be mobilized by labor unions.

While these theories point to important differences between the United States and other countries, they have a number of limitations. The ideological explanations ignore a history of violent industrial conflict characterized by bloody clashes of employers with workers and their communities.[5] This history belies the notion of a complacent working class uninterested in collective struggle against inequality. Many American values like egalitarianism and commitment to democracy have been quite radicalizing under the right circumstances, and labor activists have often appealed to them. Since they are embedded in enduring characteristics of American political culture, the ideological explanations are also static.[6] They do not account for the rise and fall of workers' movements from the Knights of Labor to the Congress of Industrial Organizations, or the periods of significant demand for government expansion such as the Progressive Era and the New Deal.

Like the ideological explanations, the political explanations also have a number of problems.[7] The comparative evidence suggests that it is possible for a labor party to gain power in countries with dominant two-party systems, such as Great Britain. Third parties even managed to build some political power in the United States at the local level in winner-take-all elections. More important, these explanations assume that workers can gain power only through a third party and that co-optation of third-party issues by the dominant parties cannot work to labor's advantage. The permeability of American political parties and their varying regional identities has almost served as the equivalent of a multiparty system that has allowed new issues to be absorbed into the dominant two-party structure.

Both the ideological and party-based explanations are particularly poorly suited to the political conditions that emerged in the 1930s and 1940s. Much of what was exceptional about the United States changed during this period. Americans clearly questioned unregulated capitalism and demanded a larger role for the government. The country elected and reelected Franklin Roosevelt and Harry Truman, two presidents who denounced "economic royalists" and greedy corporations and campaigned on promises of an expansive government ranging from public works spending to national health insurance. A class cleavage in voting developed and grew stronger over this period, and the national Democratic Party cultivated its ties to the working class.[8] A labor party never gained strength, but the national Democratic Party endorsed an agenda very similar to that of reformist social democrats in other countries. Moreover, one of the missing ingredients in earlier periods of reform—a powerful labor movement committed to political action—finally came onto the political stage and grew to represent more than a third of the nonagricultural workforce by the conclusion of World War II.[9] In many states, the unionization rates exceeded those of other Western countries with strong labor movements, but unions' penetration outside heavily industrialized areas in the Northeast and Midwest and on the West Coast was uneven. Although labor leaders considered third-party politics, they decided their interests would best be served by joining in a labor-liberal alliance committed to working through and transforming the

Democratic Party.[10] With all these changes, many reformers thought the United States might catch up with or even surpass Europe in the development of social welfare policies.[11] But after the foundations of the welfare state were laid in the early years of the New Deal, the agenda of welfare state expansion bogged down in the late thirties and forties, and organized labor faced a growing political backlash. Despite the broad transformation of the political environment, the policy proposals of labor and liberal reformers met growing opposition in Congress. Theories of how American exceptionalism has constrained the labor movement do not adequately explain these developments.

Labor's Strategic Failures

Many of the studies that focus on the postwar evolution of labor within the United States attribute labor's failures to misguided leadership. Critics of the labor movement on the left argue that labor leaders made strategic decisions during the late 1930s and 1940s that doomed the labor movement to failure and decline.[12] These critics suggest that labor leaders missed an opportunity at a critical moment in American history to push for broad-scale social change. Instead of taking advantage of the transformative potential of widespread rank-and-file worker militancy in the 1930s and 1940s, labor leaders undermined it by choosing to work within the labor relations system established by the government and allying with a Democratic Party that failed to deliver pro-worker policies. Third-party or independent labor politics might have posed a real threat to the power structure, but instead labor leaders entered into what one labor critic terms a "barren marriage" with the Democratic Party.[13] Labor was credited with some level of influence and political success during the Great Society years, but observers stress that even then labor was more successful in pursuing general welfare legislation like Medicare and the War on Poverty programs than legislation targeted at benefiting organized labor.[14] The implication is that if labor leaders had decided to challenge the power structure instead of being co-opted by the Democrats, the United States would have taken a different path and labor would be in a better position today.

Since the late 1960s, each legislative failure has been viewed as further evidence of labor's political decline and the futility of labor's enduring support of the Democratic Party. Republican administrations from Richard Nixon through George W. Bush were believed to be disastrous for labor, but critics of the labor movement's political strategies argued that things were not much better under

Democratic administrations.[15] The failure of even watered-down proposals for labor law and health care reform during the administrations of Jimmy Carter and Bill Clinton, when Democrats controlled both the White House and Congress, supposedly revealed labor's weakening influence within the Democratic Party and politics in general. Observers argued that the Democrats had become beholden to business and centrist, suburban middle- and upper-middle-class voters at labor's expense.[16] The Democrats still counted on labor's support, but the party took this support for granted. Thus many activists and scholars of the labor movement continue to believe that labor should pursue independent or third-party politics or that labor should demand more from Democratic leaders in exchange for its support. In terms of public policy, critics of the labor movement have argued that labor has been too quick to compromise on issues like health care reform and that as a result it has failed to build an effective progressive coalition capable of producing far-reaching change.[17]

The Importance of the Institutional Context

Most critics of the labor movement's political strategies fail to fully recognize that American legislative institutions virtually require concession and compromise and limit labor's leverage. All reformers must operate in a political system that was set up at the time of the founding to make legislating difficult. Because of the framers' concerns about what Madison termed the "mischiefs of faction" and the "tyranny of the majority," the Constitution established a fragmented legislative process across the House, the Senate, and the president—all elected in different ways, by different constituencies, at different times.[18] This process makes it difficult for popular majorities to make effective demands on the government.[19] The small states and slave states also insisted on protections for political minorities through equal state representation in the Senate and the structure of the electoral college, which further complicate majority rule. The Great Compromise, which was necessary to get the Constitution ratified, cast a long shadow over American public policy, making the national government less responsive to the interests of urban, industrialized areas.[20] The U.S. Senate is the only upper house among the governments of advanced, industrialized nations that is coequal to the lower house in its legislative powers, and it is the most skewed toward the representation of areas with small populations.[21] This bias has reduced the political influence of organized labor because more than half of all union members have consistently been located in five to six populous, heavily industrialized states and many states in the South and rural West have very low levels of unionization.

Independent of the framers' intentions, Congress later developed rules and procedures that further fragmented power in the political system and gave additional protections to minority, often sectional, interests. For much of the postwar period, this diffusion of power was supported by four institutions: (1) the congressional committee system, (2) the House Rules Committee, (3) the seniority system, and (4) the Senate filibuster. Congressional committees evolved to take on most of the work of negotiating and writing legislation. The Rules Committee became an independent gatekeeper and a force in shaping legislation because it controlled which bills would come to the floor, what amendments could be offered, and how floor debate would be structured. In order to minimize intraparty power struggles, seniority also became the norm in selecting committee chairs and filling seats on prominent committees. Because Southern Democrats faced no party competition through the 1960s, they gained seniority and assumed a disproportionate share of chairmanships. In the Senate, the filibuster provided the most protection for minorities, requiring two-thirds, and after reform three-fifths, of the body to cut off debate. All four factors interacted to empower a conservative coalition of Southern Democrats and Republicans in the legislative process from the late 1930s through the mid-1970s. The first three factors have declined in importance over time because of institutional reforms pushed by labor and other liberal constituencies. However, even the reformed filibuster remains a powerful obstacle to majority rule, party responsibility, and many of labor's legislative priorities when the Democrats control the Senate.

There is a growing literature on the role of political institutions in shaping policy outcomes and the influence of interest groups. Comparative research demonstrates that fragmented political systems are associated with policy stability and smaller welfare states.[22] This literature suggests that the United States has a more limited welfare state because it has the most fragmented political system with a federalist as opposed to a unitary structure, a presidential as opposed to a parliamentary government, a bicameral rather than a unicameral legislature, and single member legislative districts rather than proportional representation.[23] As a result it is more difficult for majorities, especially narrow majorities, to produce policy change. Looking at the effectiveness of doctors in opposing national health care in several European countries, Ellen Immergut demonstrates that a larger number of veto points where policy proposals can be obstructed empowers interested minorities to stop reforms. She argues that it is not necessarily the variance in the policy position of the groups but their differential access to veto points across various political systems that shaped the viable options for health reform in each country.[24] Sven Steinmo and Jon Watts have applied the same logic to the repeated failure of health care reform in the United States.[25] But the impact of veto points on the influence of groups varies with the groups' agenda. Groups like organized labor that favor an activist government and a comprehensive welfare state will have a tougher time achieving their goals.[26] The weakness of organized labor is often cited as an explanation for the small size of the American welfare state, but labor's power is limited by its opportunities in the political system.

Labor has a hard time enacting its agenda, even in periods of Democratic control of national institutions, because a number of veto points in the American legislative process can be overcome only with supermajorities. Formal theorists such as Keith Krehbiel, David Brady, and Craig Volden have emphasized the role of supermajoritarian institutions such as the Senate filibuster and the presidential veto in producing persistent gridlock in the American legislative process.[27] Based on the assumption that legislators' policy preferences on any particular proposal can be represented along a single continuum, they argue that the "pivotal players" who determine whether a bill will become a law are the senators who reflect the potential 60th vote to invoke cloture, or the House and Senate members at the two-thirds mark in the more unlikely case of overcoming a presidential veto. Absent large ideological majorities, rare in American politics, the pivotal players tend to be centrists and often represent the minority party in the chamber. For legislation to pass, the pivotal players must prefer the proposed change to the status quo, which encourages moderation. As Brady and Volden note, "When a policy advocate suggests a change so major that supermajorities are difficult to achieve the change will be stopped by a filibuster or veto. To build the needed coalition for cloture or a veto override, compromises will need to be struck."[28] Given labor's geographic concentration, noted above, it is unlikely that the pivotal 60th senator necessary to break a filibuster of a liberal initiative will come from a state with substantial labor union membership, even in a Democratically controlled Congress. It is even less likely that labor will have much influence over the 67th senator necessary to overcome a Republican president's veto of a liberal initiative. But on the flip side, labor may well have influence over the 41st senator necessary to block a conservative initiative in the Senate or the 34th senator or 145th House member necessary to sustain a Democratic president's veto. Thus it is very difficult for labor to get favorable policy changes but comparatively easy to defend favorable provisions that have already made it into law. This dynamic also makes labor's success highly contingent on Democratic Party discipline, since labor cannot rely on constituency leverage in enough states to build supermajorities. But absent substantial Democratic supermajorities, party discipline does not necessarily make legislating labor's priorities more likely. As Nolan McCarty, Keith Poole, and Howard Rosenthal argue, the polarization and rising unity of the parties in recent decades have expanded the range of policies subject to gridlock, which has combined with other changes in the political system to make it more difficult to pass measures that might address rising income inequality.[29]

Although labor scholars rarely make reference to these literatures, they help explain the political strategies and limited success of organized labor. American political institutions dictate that labor politics—and the politics of reformers in general—is the politics of compromise, incrementalism, and navigation of an extremely complicated policy-making process. Although labor leaders are often criticized for being too conservative or for caving in policy battles, their flexibility is in fact a rational adaptation to the demands of the political system.

The nature of the legislative process places labor strategists in the very difficult position of balancing idealism and the merits of a policy with the nuts and bolts of assembling a congressional majority, or supermajority as is typically the case. Because they know they will need to make concessions in any particular policy battle, they have to demand more than they are willing to accept. But they also need to educate and mobilize union members behind a policy position without encouraging the membership to become so wedded to a proposal that anything else looks like a failure. Straddling these multiple objectives can be daunting, and the labor movement itself is often split on the best strategy to take in any particular battle, which further compromises labor's success. Thus labor leaders are vulnerable to charges that they have made strategic missteps because it is so difficult to thread the needle through Congress.

But it is not clear that another political strategy on the part of organized labor would have produced more favorable results. Even if a viable labor party had developed in the forties (or later), labor would have faced the same institutional obstacles to comprehensive welfare state legislation. Particularly since the 1960s, the problem has not been the commitment of *most* Democrats to the policy priorities of organized labor but rather the power that labor's conservative opponents have been able to wield in the American legislative process— even when the Democrats control the presidency, the House, and the Senate.[30] The social democratic model of labor influence in which the labor movement allies with a labor party in pursuit of favorable public policies, common in other Western countries, is simply not as effective in the United States because the majority party cannot always deliver on its program, given the fragmentation in the political system. Under these constraints, the labor movement and other liberal reformers have not been able to build a comprehensive welfare state, but the incremental expansions of government regulations and programs like the minimum wage, Social Security, Medicare, and the recent health care reform law reflect important achievements.

Labor, Congress, and American Political Development

Much of the work on the impact of institutions on public policy reflects an approach known as "historical institutionalism," which this book shares. Although prominent in the study of comparative politics, historical institutionalism is also widely represented in the study of American political development (APD), which is focused on understanding the evolution of the American political system and politics. As Karen Orren and Stephen Skowronek note in their survey of the APD field, "The claim of the 'new institutionalists' is that institutions do not merely express or reflect or deflect elements in their political surroundings. Institutions participate actively in politics: they shape interests and motives, configure social and economic relationships, promote as well as inhibit political change."[31] Institutions have had a profound impact on the development of organized labor.

But some institutions have been more prominent than others in structuring labor's political activities in different time periods. William Forbath and Victoria Hattam demonstrate that the resistance of the courts to economic and social legislation in the late 1800s and first decades of the twentieth century encouraged the AFL to turn to collective bargaining over political mobilization behind pro-labor legislation that would likely be invalidated by the courts.[32] During the Progressive Era, federalism played a role by concentrating many labor reformers' efforts on the states.[33] As a consequence of these factors, the mainstream of the labor movement entered the Depression era with limited national policy goals and a limited infrastructure for political action. However, the growing activism of the federal government and the emerging deference of the Supreme Court to the elected branches on economic and social regulation over the course of the 1930s opened a world of possibilities for labor's political action. But as labor turned to the national legislative arena, it encountered a different set of institutional impediments to its agenda in Congress.

It is impossible to understand the evolution of organized labor's political activity since the late 1930s without examining its interaction with Congress and the party system that structures congressional organization. APD scholarship has provided valuable insights on the executive branch and the courts in the public policy process, but perhaps because of the early focus on administrative capacity and state building, far less attention has been given to Congress.[34] In one of the few studies in APD on labor and Congress, Sean Farhang and Ira Katznelson demonstrate how congressional institutions empowered conservative Southern Democrats to thwart labor's aspirations for social democracy in the 1930s and 1940s.[35] But the story does not stop there. The Great Depression and World War II unleashed social forces, including an ambitious labor movement, that could not long be accommodated by the existing institutional order in Congress and the party system.

Labor has often been dismissed as a force in contemporary politics, but this book argues that organized labor has played a largely unrecognized role in changing both the party system and the legislative process. The long-term consequences of these changes are at least a partial explanation for the growing party unity and polarization in Congress observed by a range of political scientists in recent decades.[36] In the language of the literature of American political development, the period from roughly 1935 through 1948 was a "critical juncture" in which strategic choices on the part of the labor movement set the political system down a certain path. The growth and activism of the labor movement and its alliance with the national Democratic Party fed a growing schism in the party that was not resolved until conservative Southern Democrats finally left. The next three chapters describe labor's rising frustration with the power of conservatives in the Democrat-controlled Congresses that labor helped elect over the forties, fifties, and sixties. Labor and its liberal allies in and outside Congress responded by trying to undermine the bases of Southern conservatives' power by pushing for civil rights and congressional reform, as described in Chapter 4. It would take decades, but eventually the Democratic Party realigned toward its labor-liberal wing and became more disciplined in Congress, as elaborated in Chapters 5 and 6. Of course labor alone did not produce these changes, and there were numerous factors at work. But it is hard to imagine they would have unfolded in the same way without labor's participation in the process.

This book ties together the study of labor, the study of Congress, and the study of American political development by bringing more attention to the push and pull between Congress and organized constituencies over the postwar period that produced significant changes in Congress and the party system. It focuses on why labor failed to accomplish its policy objectives, as well as the consequences of these frustrated efforts for the American political system. Historical institutionalists have emphasized the durability of institutions and outlined the processes that lead to the persistence of institutions long after the forces that led to their rise have dissipated.[37] But institutions are always subject to challenge and rarely static. Thus an emerging concern among historical institutionalists reflected in this study is to explain why, given their status quo bias, institutions change.[38] One of the most common explanations has been a theory of "punctuated equilibrium," in which institutions are thought to be stable for long periods and then undergo rapid change because of dramatic external shocks, only to return to a new equilibrium.[39] The changes in both congressional institutions and the party system described in this book are much more gradual, dynamic, and often unpredictable as labor and its liberal allies have taken advantage of evolving opportunities and confronted unforeseen obstacles in trying to open up the legislative process to their policy goals.

Case Selection and Method

This study takes a close look at labor's efforts to pass favorable public policies in the postwar period in four policy areas: labor law reform; full-employment planning; workers' income security programs including the minimum wage, unemployment compensation, and the expansion of Social Security to include disability insurance; and universal health care reform. These four policy areas were chosen for two reasons. First, they were central to the workers' welfare state organized labor hoped to construct in the postwar years, and the limited accomplishments in these areas illustrate the exceptional nature of American public policy. Second, tracing developments in these four areas over time illustrates the varying degrees to which institutional configurations have influenced policy outcomes. In labor law, institutional protections for political minorities have produced a long period of stalemate in which neither labor nor its opponents have been able to pass legislative changes since the late 1950s. In full-employment-planning policy, there have been two major efforts in the 1940s and 1970s in which conservatives used their control of institutional veto points to force concessions that gutted the substance of the bills, resulting in largely symbolic, ineffective legislation. In the workers' income security programs, reformers repeatedly secured incremental expansions of coverage and benefits, but the compromises necessary to overcome conservative obstruction watered down reform. The minimum wage has often lagged behind inflation, and unemployment compensation has not been reformed to meet the needs of a changing workforce.

In health care reform, the impact of institutions has varied over time. From the 1940s through the 1970s, a major obstacle to universal health care was the lack of a consensus approach that could hold the support of labor-liberals and attract a legislative majority. Fragmentation in the legislative process and on-going changes in the health care system made this task more daunting. But by the 1990s, institutions emerged as the key stumbling block, with the need for supermajority consensus required by the filibuster posing a seemingly insurmountable obstacle in a highly partisan environment. The impact of institutions comes through most clearly in the way that health care reform finally passed. It was only achieved with a 60 vote Democratic supermajority in the Senate, use of the special reconciliation procedure, and significant compromises that produced a final bill far removed from labor's ideal approach.

Although the labor movement is composed of a broad array of organizations, this study focuses on the AFL, CIO, and AFL-CIO, which have taken the lead in coordinating labor's political action, in pursuing these policies.[40] This focus overlooks some of the divisions and diversity in the labor movement. For example, the minimum wage has been more important to unions in low-wage industries, and unions like the United Auto Workers (UAW), and more recently the Service Employees International Union (SEIU), have been more active on health care policy. There have also been divisions over policy approaches with some unions steadfastly arguing for a single-payer system while others were more willing to compromise. But in general, the mainstream of the labor movement has worked toward common goals in each of the four policy areas this study focuses on, and the AFL-CIO has been central to these legislative efforts.

The following chapters provide detailed accounts of the movement of representative policy proposals through the legislative process. This approach is useful because many scholars have looked only at outcomes—whether a policy proposal becomes a law or not—and thus have missed the impact of various institutional obstacles on labor's power. Because so many proposals are killed, stalled, or compromised in the legislative process, it is easy to jump to the conclusion that labor is weak or the Democrats have not been committed to labor's goals. But looking at the trajectory of a proposal from its conception through each step in the process yields more nuanced conclusions. It becomes clear that labor often had majority support at many points in the legislative process, even though a proposal never made it into law because of minority obstruction. Close analysis also reveals how and why ambitious proposals are scaled back on their way to becoming law.

To reconstruct the battles over these legislative proposals, this volume has incorporated evidence from labor and presidential archives as well as contemporary press accounts. Information from the labor archives reveals the strategies labor leaders developed to try to get their policies enacted and the compromises they were willing to accept. There is also considerable evidence of the intense frustration labor leaders felt with institutional obstacles and their efforts to try to circumvent them. Information from the presidential archives, particularly those of President Carter, show an administration that worked far harder for some of labor's priorities than is commonly recognized. Although every Democratic president has been blamed by pundits and labor activists for insufficient commitment to liberals' policy proposals, in many instances evidence from the archives suggests that the presidential administrations were just as frustrated with their own inability to move Congress as labor leaders were.

Plan of the Book

The following chapters trace the changing political and institutional context shaping labor's legislative influence from the birth of the modern politically active labor movement in the 1930s and 1940s through the period of conservative ascendancy under the George W. Bush administration, with more limited attention to labor's early experience under the Obama administration. The first two chapters look at labor's interaction with Congress during the heyday of the conservative coalition. The third chapter examines labor's policy accomplishments and failures at arguably the peak of postwar liberalism during the Great Society years as the power of the conservative coalition started to wane. The fourth and fifth chapters deal with labor's efforts to change the political environment to make it more hospitable to liberal legislation and the immediate consequences of these reforms. The final two chapters look at the period from the 1980s through the present as the reforms of the previous decades continued to reverberate through the political system.

Chapter 1 outlines the transformation of the labor movement from the New Deal through the early postwar period and the impact of this transformation on the political system. Labor union membership surged as a result of favorable government policies such as the National Labor Relations Act (NLRA), wartime mobilization, and competition between the AFL and CIO. But the growing power and ambition of the labor movement provoked a political backlash that led to the rise of the conservative coalition of Southern Democrats and Republicans in Congress. This coalition sought to limit labor's power, ultimately amending the NLRA with the Taft-Hartley Act. Truman's veto of Taft-Hartley and his support of civil rights going into the 1948 elections solidified a labor-liberal-Democratic alliance that would continue to challenge the power of conservative Southern Democrats in the party.

Chapter 2 focuses on the conservative coalition's use of institutions in the legislative process to fight pro-labor and welfare state policies in the early postwar period. Conservatives often held congressional majorities during the 1940s and 1950s, regardless of which party controlled Congress. But liberals' influence in the legislative process was further restricted by the conservative coalition's power on a number of important congressional committees, including the House Rules Committee, which it used to shape legislation ranging from Truman's full-employment proposal to minimum wage bills. Truman's proposal for national health insurance never came out of committee. Not only could labor not get Congress to repeal the Taft-Hartley Act during this period, but labor's congressional allies were outmaneuvered on the House floor in the passage of an antiunion corruption bill known as Landrum-Griffin. At a critical juncture in American and labor history, labor was unable to translate its growing power in the economy and society into favorable public policies.

Chapter 3 demonstrates both the opportunities and the limitations on labor's political influence in the postwar period as the conservative coalition was temporarily overwhelmed by the substantial liberal congressional majority elected along with Lyndon Johnson in 1964. This chapter analyzes the decade-long struggle against conservative resistance to get Medicare passed, as well as multiple efforts to improve the minimum wage. But the conservative coalition was more successful in fighting other proposals, such as national standards for the unemployment insurance system and labor's top goal of repealing a provision of Taft-Hartley known as 14(b), which was defeated by a filibuster. This chapter suggests that, even at the height of postwar liberalism, labor did not have the supermajority support necessary to pass some of its top policy priorities.

Chapter 4 focuses on labor's efforts as part of a larger labor-liberal coalition to permanently undermine the power of the conservative coalition and re-orient the American political system. The two main strategies in this effort were support for (1) the enfranchisement and legal empowerment of African Americans to facilitate the realignment of the Democratic Party and (2) congressional reforms to empower the majority in the majority party in Congress to control the legislative process. With the passage of the Civil Rights Act of 1964 and the Voting Rights Act of 1965, African Americans in the South finally gained political rights that would change the politics, if not the ideology, of the South. Over the course of the 1960s and 1970s, a series of congressional reforms chipped away at the power of committee chairs and seniority in the House and the cloture threshold required to end filibusters in the Senate. These changes would interact to transform the political system over the next three decades.

Chapter 5 looks at the early impact of these reforms, which initially resulted in disarray in the legislative process and destabilization of the Democrats' electoral and governing coalition as the party realigned. During the presidencies of Republicans Richard Nixon and especially Gerald Ford, the presidential veto became a powerful weapon against labor-backed legislation. However, labor's agenda continued to falter into Democrat Jimmy Carter's presidency. As the conservative coalition declined in both size and influence, the obstacles to labor's legislative agenda in the House committee system virtually disappeared. But the filibuster, as the last refuge of conservatives, became far more prominent and was used to gut the Humphrey-Hawkins full-employment proposal and kill a labor law reform package. Although health care reform seemed inevitable with Carter's election, no congressional committee could arrive at a politically viable compromise that could also maintain the support of labor, and the effort gradually lost momentum. Despite congressional reform, stalemate continued on many of labor's legislative priorities.

Chapter 6 focuses on the impact of the demise of the conservative coalition and the rise of party polarization on labor's political influence from the 1980s through the eve of Obama's election as the reforms of the 1960s and 1970s continued to reshape the political system. During this period, congressional Democrats became more supportive of organized labor as conservative Southerners left the party and African Americans helped elect a few liberal Southern Democrats. However, the loss of support in the South made it much harder for Democrats to win control of the White House and Congress. During the two years of Democratic control of both during the Clinton administration, labor once again saw priorities like health care and labor law reform go down to defeat. The power of the majority party leadership grew in the House, which worked to further labor's priorities. But the filibuster emerged as the major obstacle to labor's agenda. Throughout the rest of this period, under the Republican administrations of Ronald Reagan, George H. W. Bush, and George W. Bush and under Republican control of Congress, labor discovered that it too could benefit from the filibuster and Clinton's veto threats. The government moved to the right, but labor and its allies were able to defend policies like Social Security, Medicare, and even favorable labor law provisions from conservative attacks.

The final chapter concludes with a discussion of what organized labor—and reformers in general—can reasonably expect to accomplish in the legislative process, with particular attention to the Obama administration and labor's prospects for the future. When unionized workers reflected more than a third of the workforce in the early postwar years, labor could not translate its numbers into commensurate influence over legislation because of the structure of the party system and the legislative process. Over the past sixty years, the Democratic Party has realigned toward its liberal urban wing and is now strongest where labor is strongest. Liberals also exert more influence in the legislative process. But the supermajority consensus necessary to overcome the filibuster is difficult to reach on most issues on labor's agenda, especially in a more partisan and polarized Congress. There are occasional breakthroughs, such as the passage of health care reform in 2010 that will greatly increase Americans' access to health insurance. But legislative accomplishments will always be incremental and limited. This makes the organization of more workers paramount in building a more equitable society.

1

The Rise of Organized Labor and the Conservative Coalition

The American labor movement was transformed in the 1930s and the 1940s, setting in motion a series of changes that would reverberate in the American political system for decades. During this period, which spanned the presidential administrations of Democrats Franklin Roosevelt and Harry Truman, a class cleavage emerged in the American electorate, workers gained legal recognition of the right to organize in the National Labor Relations Act, unions grew to represent a third of the workforce, and most of the labor movement became active in Democratic Party politics. Consequently, labor gained an unprecedented role in the American economy and government.

This chapter examines the rise of organized labor and its consequences for the Democratic Party and congressional politics. The emergence of an ambitious, pro–civil rights labor movement created a backlash that split the Democratic Party between labor-oriented liberals and conservative Southern Democrats, who feared labor's challenge to the political economy of the South. Starting in the late thirties, conservative Southern Democrats joined their ideological allies in the Republican Party to rein in the power of organized labor, culminating in the passage of the Taft-Hartley Act in 1947. The conservative coalition was most effective when it controlled legislative majorities. But even when it did not, members used legislative institutions like the House Rules Committee to undermine the interests of the labor-liberal wing of the Democratic Party. These tensions came to a head in the 1948 election when Truman ran on issues that appealed to labor-liberals but alienated the South, such as the repeal of Taft-Hartley and civil rights. At a critical moment for both labor and the Democrats, Truman's actions ensured that labor would stay with the Democratic Party, instead of leaving to form a labor party. But the conservative coalition would continue to challenge labor in Congress.

The New Deal and the Transformation of Organized Labor

The Great Depression and World War II spurred the growth of a more diverse and politically active labor movement. The New Deal marked a major turning point in the history of organized labor. Franklin Roosevelt was elected in 1932 by an overwhelming margin and brought the working-class voters of the Northeast and the industrial West into the Democratic coalition. Yet organized labor had not been a major player in the election, and it was unclear how unions would fare in the Roosevelt administration. In his first two years in office, Roosevelt walked a fine line between business and labor, straining his relationship with the American Federation of Labor (AFL).[1] However, FDR's support for labor rights won him a great deal of support in the labor movement. The core of the early New Deal was the National Industrial Recovery Act (NIRA), which targeted the negative economic effects of cutthroat competition among firms by encouraging industrial codes for production levels, wages, and prices. A controversial provision recognized workers' rights to join unions and bargain collectively. The NIRA spurred successful organizing drives in 1933 in industries such as coal, in which the United Mine Workers (UMW) under the leadership of John L. Lewis circulated flyers telling miners that the president wanted them to join the union. But the National Labor Board, which was established under the act, was too weak to implement the labor provisions, and many employers continued to ignore the law. A wave of industrial unrest, often characterized by bloody confrontations of workers with police and employers over the issue of union recognition, spread in 1933 and 1934.

The labor crisis fed a sense of urgency that something needed to be done. The liberal Democratic senator Robert Wagner of New York proposed legislation to create a more powerful independent labor board capable of enforcing workers' rights to join unions. Supporters argued that the bill would foster industrial peace and improve the economy because unions would redistribute wealth from corporate profits to wages, increase consumer purchasing power, and reduce the likelihood of cyclical depressions. Reluctant to alienate business, FDR initially refused to endorse Wagner's legislation, and it languished in Congress in 1934. However, the continuing industrial crisis renewed interest in the legislation the following year in a Congress fortified with newly elected liberals.[2] After extensive debate in committee, Wagner's National Labor Relations Act (NLRA) easily passed the Senate in May. Shortly thereafter, FDR threw his support behind the bill.[3] Within days of FDR's announcement, the Supreme Court ruled a major portion of the NIRA unconstitutional, leaving the administration with no labor policy and no way to spur wage growth.[4] Labor leaders called for strikes in industries in which the collapse of industrial codes resulted in wage reductions and longer workweeks, redoubled their efforts to pass priority legislation like the NLRA, and pledged to lead an effort to amend the Constitution to clearly stipulate the government's authority to regulate social and economic conditions.[5] In spite of opposition from the National Association of Manufacturers and other business groups, the NLRA passed the House with limited debate and was signed into law on July 5, 1935. The legislation recognized workers' rights to join unions and participate in collective bargaining, forbade company-run unions, established election procedures for workers to choose union representation, and empowered the National Labor Relations Board (NLRB) to enforce the act.

The Rise of the CIO

The passage of the NLRA in 1935 escalated an ongoing debate over organizing that led to a split in the labor movement and the mobilization of new segments of the labor force. As the International Workers of the World had done decades earlier, dissidents in the AFL argued that the labor movement's future depended on organizing the growing ranks of unskilled workers in the mass production industries. But old-line unions favored organizing along craft rather than industrial lines and were reluctant to commit resources to the challenging task of organizing unskilled workers, who were in a weak bargaining position with employers. Lewis, the charismatic and irascible president of the UMW, emerged as the leader of a rival group that emphasized the power of organizing all workers in an industry into one union. Lewis felt the NLRA offered an opportunity to unionize the largely unorganized mass production industries along industrial lines. Several months after the bill's passage, Lewis and his allies formed the Committee for Industrial Organization, which later left the AFL to become a rival labor federation, the Congress of Industrial Organizations (CIO). In less than two years the CIO grew to more than four million members.[6] Although the CIO only briefly eclipsed the AFL in membership, it forever changed the labor movement by mobilizing new groups of workers and taking a greater role in politics.

The CIO invested unprecedented resources in organizing industries such as steel, rubber, and auto production and used radical tactics that capitalized on the growing militancy of rank-and-file workers during the Depression. Faced with intense employer resistance, the CIO's United Auto Workers (UAW) resorted to the sit-down strike against General Motors early in 1937. In the first of a wave of sit-down strikes that would sweep the country, autoworkers occupied two Flint, Michigan, plants and refused to leave without union recognition. GM finally capitulated. Three weeks later, the CIO's Steel Workers Organizing Committee (SWOC) gained recognition from U.S. Steel, which had used every tool available for decades to thwart unionization. CIO militancy spread to a range of workers from meatpackers to shop clerks. The rivalry encouraged the AFL to sink more resources into organizing, including the organizing of low-skilled and unskilled workers, and the AFL actually surpassed the CIO in growth by the end of the thirties.[7] Total union membership almost doubled from 1935 to 1937.[8]

As part of a broader social movement for equality, CIO activists embraced workers of all races and ethnicities. Although the AFL was rhetorically committed to the equal treatment of blacks, it did little to suppress discrimination within its own ranks, particularly in the South. In contrast, the CIO organized whites alongside blacks and became a strong supporter of civil rights legislation. CIO unions targeted industries dominated by black workers such as meatpacking, hired black organizers, set up headquarters in black neighborhoods, and pressed blacks' particular grievances against employers. After touring Southern states in 1941, Harold Preece, of the National Association for the Advancement of Colored People (NAACP), referred to the CIO as a "lamp of democracy."[9] The CIO also targeted industries with ethnically diverse workforces, which led the CIO to stress what historian Lizabeth Cohen terms a "culture of unity" in order to minimize ethnic rivalries often exploited by employers.[10] CIO union halls fostered a new level of socializing across ethnicities in a number of communities during the 1930s and 1940s.

The CIO was also more committed to political mobilization. While the AFL had been rather passive in elections, the CIO plowed money into campaigns and made well-organized efforts to mobilize its membership at the polls.[11] CIO leaders, like Sidney Hillman of the Amalgamated Clothing Workers, saw politics as central to labor's future.[12] Lewis and Hillman persuaded George Berry of the AFL's Printing Pressmen's Union to join them in forming Labor's Non-Partisan League (LNPL), which raised a million dollars for Roosevelt in 1936.[13] Although the LNPL was formed explicitly to support Roosevelt, CIO leaders had grand plans for it. Hillman noted in a speech on the activities of the league, "The interest of the country as well as of labor demands a realignment of all progressives into one party, and the basis for that kind of realignment ought to be the organization of labor in the political field."[14] As the rivalry between the AFL and the CIO intensified, Berry pulled out of the LNPL, but many AFL unions continued to work with it. Some AFL leaders remained skeptical about the utility of political action, but as they watched CIO leaders like Hillman develop a close relationship with the Roosevelt administration, they felt it necessary to defend their interests. In fact, the CIO put so much effort into the 1940 and 1944 elections that many argued the Democratic Party was "captured" by the CIO.[15] This drew the AFL toward greater involvement in politics over the next decade.[16] Labor's growing interest in politics was also reinforced by the intricate involvement of the government in labor issues during World War II.

Labor's Wartime Gains

The NLRA spurred far-reaching changes in the labor movement, but organized labor continued to face widespread employer opposition and limited government protection that hindered further growth until the onset of World War II. The Senate's La Follette Civil Liberties Committee investigated employers' anti-union practices from 1936 to 1940, exposing widespread use of violent and illegal tactics. One of the most flagrant examples occurred when police hired by Republic Steel fired on a protest march outside its Chicago factory in the 1937 "Memorial Day massacre," which killed ten union sympathizers and wounded more than fifty. The White House proved an unreliable ally to labor. Roosevelt's refusal to send troops to evacuate the factories in the sit-down strikes at GM was viewed as a sign of his support for union growth. But when Roosevelt, weary with the lack of resolution of the steel crisis, said of employers and the union, "A curse on both your houses," it was viewed as a sign of his waning support for unionization.[17] The notoriously antiunion Ford Motors also remained impervious to the UAW, and Ford's private police continued to assault union organizers and sympathizers with little government intervention. Across a range of other industries organizing efforts stalled. The momentum behind union growth appeared to be waning when World War II changed everything.

Defense mobilization gave labor new leverage against employers. The fifteen-month period leading up to the attack on Pearl Harbor in December 1941 produced 1.5 million new union members.[18] As the economy approached full employment, organizing drives and pent-up wage demands precipitated a wave of more than four thousand strikes in 1941. Eager to sustain production, many employers finally came to the table. The Little Steel firms, including antiunion stalwart Republic Steel, one by one recognized SWOC over the course of 1941, transforming the position of labor in the steel industry. Strikes for UAW recognition at Ford threw the manufacturer into disarray, and managers finally agreed to a certification election, which the UAW won overwhelmingly.[19] Membership in AFL unions such as the Teamsters, the International Association of Machinists, and the Carpenters also surged because of defense mobilization.

Union growth was fed not only by improved economic conditions but by the government's wartime policies. After the United States' formal entry into the war, leaders of both the AFL and the CIO agreed to a "no-strike pledge" in light of the national emergency. The National War Labor Board (NWLB), composed of representatives of the public, labor, and management, supervised industrial relations for the duration of the war. Labor leaders were expected to cooperate in the defense effort by restraining workers' wage demands, disciplining the rank and file, and maintaining uninterrupted production.[20] In exchange, the board pressured employers to recognize and bargain with unions. Cooperative unions were also offered "maintenance of membership" arrangements in which new employees in unionized firms automatically became union members and unionized workers had to remain members for the duration of a contract. Eventually the board even ordered employers to withhold union dues from paychecks.

Union growth brought organized labor unprecedented economic and political power. Union membership grew more than 50 percent over the course of the war to more than fifteen million in 1945.[21] Organized labor represented more than a third of the civilian labor force.[22] CIO unions penetrated almost every area of the industrial economy, and the AFL continued to expand. Although organized labor still faced considerable challenges and had barely broken into certain areas of the economy or the South, it was hardly the underdog of the early Depression years. Labor's mobilization in elections and participation on the war boards also brought a new level of political influence. Labor leaders became what C. Wright Mills termed in 1948 the "new men of power," joining business leaders and politicians as part of the power elite.[23]

Rising Opposition to Labor

The invigoration of organized labor from the passage of the NLRA in 1935 through the conclusion of the war led to a split in Congress and in the Democratic Party on labor issues. The overwhelming majority of non-Southern Democrats continued to support organized labor during this period, but increasing numbers of conservative Southern Democrats and Republicans became critical of the labor movement.[24] The NLRA passed with substantial support across the Democratic Party and the entire Congress. Though Democrat Millard Tydings of Maryland, a handful of Southern Democrats such as the legendary Senator Harry Byrd of Virginia, and several Republicans publicly criticized the legislation, there was no sharp regional or partisan cleavage in the roll call vote. The bill passed the Senate 63–12.[25] Eighty-one percent of non-Southern Democrats supported the bill, compared with 73 percent of Southern Democrats and 54 percent of Republicans.[26] The House passed the NLRA on a voice vote with no record of the distribution of support. However, in a roll call vote several days earlier, most Southerners supported extending the provisions in the NIRA that dealt with collective bargaining, wages, and hours, suggesting there was Southern Democratic support for New Deal labor policy in both the Senate and the House.[27] As in other New Deal programs, agricultural and domestic workers were excluded from the protections of the NLRA to minimize Southern resistance.[28] While some Republicans were progressives who generally supported New Deal programs, the Republican opposition was likely muted by the party's substantial losses in 1934.[29] But the limited debate surrounding the passage of the NLRA soon gave way to intense criticism of the act and the labor movement.

Much of the growing opposition stemmed from the CIO's tactics and perceived radicalism. While many in Congress voted for the NLRA because they wanted to empower organized labor, others supported it out of desperation to calm industrial unrest.[30] Some feared that if something was not done, more radical forces might gain power and capitalism itself might be threatened.[31] But as noted above, the legislation initially did little to stem high-profile strikes or radicalism. CIO unionists resorted to the controversial sit-down tactic because employers refused to comply with the law, many because they expected it to be declared unconstitutional. Conservatives viewed the sit-down strike—in which workers effectively took over a plant, refused to work, and refused to leave—as a radical violation of property rights. Conservatives were also alarmed by the CIO's willingness to use Communist organizers and the influence of Communists in many CIO unions, a factor that was later exploited in a series of congressional investigations.[32] Although David Plotke argues that the discrediting of business and conservatism muted opposition to the passage of the NLRA, increasingly negative public opinion regarding labor in the late 1930s emboldened these forces. Polls showed that a third of the public had a less favorable view of labor in the wake of the sit-downs and more than half favored making sit-down strikes illegal and using force to remove the strikers.[33] Polls also suggested that the public thought the NLRA actually caused the surge of sit-downs.[34]

While conservatives in both parties shared these concerns, Southern Democrats had additional fears. Conservative Democrats felt the CIO had become an adjunct of the New Deal because of the CIO's extensive role in the 1936 elections and the presence of many bureaucrats favorable to the CIO in the NLRB and throughout the Roosevelt administration. Conservatives feared organized labor might take over the Democratic Party, which had been the base of Southern agrarian power since the Civil War.[35] When FDR refused to intervene in the wave of sit-down strikes in 1936 and 1937, intense friction developed between Roosevelt and Southern Democratic congressional leaders and even Vice President John Nance Garner, who was a Texan.[36] Southern congressional leaders became particularly strident when the CIO launched organizing drives in Southern textile mills. Eugene Cox (D-GA) proclaimed, "I warn John L. Lewis and his Communistic cohorts that no second-hand carpetbag expedition in the Southland under the banner of Soviet Russia . . . will be tolerated."[37] The South attracted textile mills and other businesses away from the Northeast because of its low wages and pliable workforce, and many Southern leaders did not want this advantage compromised by unionization.

Most important, Southern leaders were alarmed by the CIO's interest in unionizing black workers and its support for integrated locals and civil rights. In their study of growing Southern opposition to labor during this period, Farhang and Katznelson note that, by the 1940s, "in the mind of the Southern legislator . . . labor had become race."[38] The two issues had been braided together. Race was not an issue when the NLRA passed because most AFL unions in the South represented skilled white workers and adopted local racial norms. They did not challenge the Southern caste system. But even though the CIO never made much headway in the South, it represented a threat Southern conservatives could not tolerate. With the CIO's growing commitment to civil rights and political action, unionization in the South reflected a dual threat to the economic and political power structures that supported most Southern politicians. As a result, Southern Democrats moved to the right on labor issues.[39]

The Rise of the Conservative Coalition and the House Rules Committee

As the New Deal progressed and labor's influence grew, Southern conservatives felt increasingly threatened by the challenge of urban liberalism to Southern dominance of the Democratic Party. Signs of Southerners' loss of influence accumulated. The Southern states' shrinking percentage of the Democratic electoral college vote in the Roosevelt landslides demonstrated that a Democrat could comfortably win the presidency without the support of any Southern states. The 1936 Democratic convention removed the requirement that the presidential and vice presidential nominees receive the support of two-thirds of the delegates, a provision that had effectively given the South a veto over the nominee. The following year, the Southerners' preferred choice for majority leader of the Senate lost by one vote following Roosevelt's intervention in the race.[40] Southerners were further alienated by Roosevelt's unprecedented intervention in local politics in his ultimately unsuccessful efforts to "purge" five conservative Democrats in the 1938 primaries. Moreover, as the federal bureaucracy expanded, many Southern Democrats became more concerned about a growing federal government that might move beyond doling out money to the underdeveloped region to intervening in racial matters and the South's political economy. Southern Democrats, who had once shown the greatest party loyalty on roll call votes and supported most of Roosevelt's social and economic policies in his first years in office, increasingly found common cause with Republicans and defected from the party line.[41]

The conservative coalition began to take shape in 1937 when support for labor, Roosevelt, and much of the New Deal agenda faltered. Alarmed at what they perceived as Roosevelt's power grabs and his threat to the separation of powers, conservatives came together to undermine FDR's plans to pack the court with New Deal supporters and reorganize the executive branch. But conservatives were joined in their opposition to these proposals by a diverse group in Congress in terms of ideology and region.[42] The conservative coalition that would control Congress over most of the next three decades emerged more clearly on labor issues. Unsuccessful votes to outlaw sit-down strikes and investigate the CIO in 1937 reflected a new pattern of support among conservative Southern Democrats and Republicans. After failing to appear on a single vote in 1933, the conservative coalition appeared in 9.1 percent of House roll calls in 1937 and showed up with increasing frequency in subsequent years.[43]

The House Rules Committee emerged as the conservative coalition's most important institutional power base.[44] The Rules Committee serves as a gatekeeper, reporting bills from the substantive committees for floor consideration, setting the limits for debate, and controlling which amendments can be offered, including full substitutes for original bills. Prior to the late 1930s, the committee had largely served as the instrument of the majority party leadership, and members voted the party position even if they did not personally support the legislation. But the emerging regional and ideological split, driven in large part by conflicting views toward labor and Roosevelt's agenda, changed the norms of committee members. Three Southern Democrats, Cox of Georgia, Howard Smith of Virginia, and Martin Dies of Texas, were appointed in 1931, 1933, and 1935, respectively, when the party was relatively unified, and all appeared to be loyal Democrats.[45] But by 1939, all three ranked among the most conservative Democrats in the House, and they were joined that year by William Colmer of Mississippi, who moved to the right after his appointment. All four were strongly antilabor. Eric Schickler notes that from 1939 to 1952 "the Rules Committee consistently included three to five Democrats who scored among the most conservative 10 to 20 percent of party members."[46] This group often allied with the Republican members to control the committee. The seniority system made it very difficult to remove these members after it became clear they gave conservative policy positions priority over the national Democratic Party's interests.[47] Conservatives used the Rules Committee to undermine labor in three ways: blocking measures labor supported, pushing to the floor measures labor opposed, and launching investigations of labor organizations and agencies administering labor policy.

The blocking potential of the Rules Committee became apparent in the legislative battle over the Fair Labor Standards Act (FLSA). The FLSA, which eliminated child labor, set a maximum workweek with overtime pay, and established a federal minimum wage, was a high priority of the Roosevelt administration, the AFL, and the CIO, although there were divisions over the specifics.[48] While most Republicans were opposed in principle to government regulation of wages, many Southerners worried that a minimum wage law would compromise the region's low-wage advantage and minimize wage differentials between whites and blacks. This was precisely the goal of labor leaders, who wanted to reduce wage disparities between regions, industries, and firms and between nonunionized and unionized workers. Moreover, as historian Steven Fraser suggests, labor leaders like Sidney Hillman, the leader of the CIO's Textile Workers Organizing Committee, viewed fair labor standards legislation as key to a three-part "Southern strategy" to "overturn the South's prevailing social and political order" along with unionization and the presidential purge of conservative Democrats.[49]

These concerns prompted a number of Southern Democrats to reject party loyalty on the FLSA. Despite a provision for regional wage differentials and the exclusion of much of the workforce, 45 percent of Southern Democrats sided with 93 percent of Republicans in a failed effort to stall the bill in the Senate.[50] Knowing the popular legislation would likely pass on the House floor as it had in the Senate, Southern Democrats joined Republicans on the Rules Committee in refusing to report the bill. In a rarely used or successful parliamentary maneuver, supporters obtained the necessary 218 signatures for a petition to discharge the bill from the Rules Committee directly to the floor in a special session of Congress called by Roosevelt in 1937. But the bill was narrowly defeated when conservatives were aided by the AFL's opposition to a provision in the version of the bill that came up for a vote. A compromise with the AFL was worked out, but supporters again had to discharge the bill from the Rules Committee in the 1938 session. The FLSA ultimately passed with large margins in the House and Senate, but only after compromises were incorporated that significantly weakened the bill. Southern senators, who threatened to filibuster if regional wage differentials were not in the final bill, were appeased with a provision allowing some flexibility in the application of the minimum wage.[51] Furthermore, only one-fifth of workers were covered by the FLSA because many categories including agricultural labor were excluded.[52]

The FLSA was to be the last major piece of New Deal legislation. Its legislative trajectory demonstrated two emerging problems for labor: the defection of Southern Democrats from the party line on labor-related issues, and the ability of Southerners in alliance with Republicans to use congressional institutions to block or water down legislation. As Democratic representative Maury Maverick of Texas (whose liberal family inspired the term "maverick") defined the problems in response to action on the FLSA:

> Two questions are now brought to a head. One is technical, and the other of national social importance. The one is the highhanded behavior of the Rules Committee. The public cannot understand these technicalities; all it wants to know is whether the Democrats deliver the goods, or not. And unless Democratic leadership and the party gets a system, including rules, where its pledges are fulfilled it will be repudiated, as it should be. The other point is the South. The South is for the good old time virtues, but is not averse to taking a few billions of gold from the Federal till for the TVA, for cotton subsidies, WPA and others. . . . But when a general bill is offered, the South is liable to pull Thomas Jefferson from the grave, and swear it's coddling the people.[53]

Conservative Southern Democrats would support federal government programs that redistributed resources to the region but oppose those they thought threatened the South's political economy. As Poole and Rosenthal point out in their comprehensive analysis of congressional voting, the vote on the FLSA marked a departure from voting among Democrats on labor issues earlier in the New Deal. A new division appeared between Northerners and Southerners signaling rising economic conservatism among Southern Democrats.[54] Robert Fleck's analysis of the House votes and constituency data reinforces Poole and Rosenthal's conclusions and further finds in distinguishing among Southerners that "representatives from low-turnout Southern districts, where the political system gave low-wage workers little influence," were more likely to turn away from the New Deal.[55] Although conservatives on the Rules Committee did not prevent the FLSA from passing, they demonstrated the capacity to undermine the priorities of the national Democratic Party by exploiting House procedures and the leadership's inability to enforce party discipline.

Political scientists Schickler and Kathryn Pearson find that the conservative coalition on the Rules Committee not only blocked legislation favored by liberals from reaching the floor but also forced conservative proposals to the floor over the opposition of Democratic leaders.[56] Fifteen of the forty-four such initiatives they identify from 1937 to 1952 dealt with labor-management relations, and several others dealt with farm labor. They included amendments to the FLSA, provisions to limit strikes, and other changes to the NLRA.[57] Suggesting how important labor issues were in consolidating the conservative coalition, most of the first measures Rules forced to the floor dealt with labor. Schickler and Pearson note that "the committee crafted rules that made possible the consideration of broad, conservative antilabor substitute bills that had not even been approved by a legislative committee and that otherwise would have been ruled out of order on germaneness grounds."[58]

The Rules Committee also had jurisdiction over investigations that conservative members used to harass organized labor and the executive agencies that enforced labor laws. The House voted against a Rules resolution to investigate the sit-down strikes in 1937, but Dies's House Committee on Un-American Activities (HUAC) took up the issue the next year. When the new Wages and Hours division of the Labor Department set up to enforce the FLSA came to supervise compliance in the hosiery mills located in Representative Cox's district, he requested a congressional investigation of the Labor Department division and the NLRB. Representative Smith, an intense opponent of the Roosevelt administration and organized labor, used Rules to launch the "Smith Committee," a panel he chaired that hounded the NLRB for two years and managed to link the board, the CIO, and Communist radicals in the public mind.[59] HUAC also investigated the CIO's ties to Communists during the war. Many of the antilabor bills that Rules pushed to the floor were never taken up by the Senate, but the House investigations fed negative attitudes toward labor that contributed to growing congressional support for antilabor legislation.

The Road to Taft-Hartley

Just as the war effort gave labor new leverage with employers, events during the war and reconversion period created an opening for labor's critics in business and Congress. They sought to curtail the organizing rights recently granted under the NLRA, while the Roosevelt and Truman administrations struggled to manage the conflicts between labor and management, and labor leaders struggled to balance the demands of their members with the need to maintain government and public support. The dislocations of the postwar period complicated these tasks, and a public backlash against the Democrats made possible the passage of the Taft-Hartley Act in 1947, which labor leaders termed the "slave labor law." The legislative battles over labor demonstrated the growing power of the conservative coalition and the deepening rift between the Northern and Southern wings of the Democratic Party.

Defense Mobilization and Efforts to Regulate Labor

Defense mobilization heightened the stakes of labor issues. The wave of strikes in 1941, many in defense-related industries, angered critics of organized labor who accused "radical" unions of subverting the defense effort just as Communist unions in France contributed to the nation's fall to the Nazis by hindering defense production.[60] Red-baiting of CIO unions became a common activity in Congress. While the administration tried to gain labor's voluntary cooperation in the defense effort through various mediation boards, conservatives in Congress sought to force it. Labor's critics pushed right-to-work legislation for defense industries that would effectively prohibit union security arrangements. They also called for antistrike legislation ranging from outright bans on strikes in defense industries to mandated "cooling off" periods before a strike could begin. Although such legislation passed repeatedly in the House, it all died in the Senate Education and Labor Committee. In the wake of the Japanese attack on Pearl Harbor, a similar wave of bills to regulate unions was proposed but failed to pass as labor's supporters tried to impress upon conservatives the need to enlist organized labor as a willing ally in the defense effort. However, the bargain between labor, government, and management became increasingly strained as the war progressed.

A series of strikes by the coal miners and conservative gains in the 1942 congressional elections precipitated the first successful attempt to amend the Wagner Act to curtail unions' power and tactics. Wartime inflation led government mediation boards to hold wages below what workers would have been able to obtain in a free market given the shortages of labor and high corporate profits. Combined with ineffective controls on prices, workers' frustration with restrained wage growth grew intense. Wildcat strikes unauthorized by union leaders rose in 1943 and again in 1944 when the Allies' victory seemed secure. Lewis, who had withdrawn his support of Roosevelt in the 1940 election and pulled the UMW out of the CIO, never agreed to the no-strike pledge. He was very critical of government intrusion in labor-management relations during the war and repeatedly called the coal miners out on strike. Lewis became a national symbol of labor's irresponsible use of its newfound power. Conservatives in Congress, emboldened by public disapproval of Lewis and the miners, pushed the Smith-Connally Act, named after its Democratic sponsors, the consistently antilabor Smith of Virginia and Senator Tom Connally of Texas, who had actually voted for the NLRA eight years earlier. Also known as the War

Labor Disputes Act, the legislation allowed the president to seize industries central to the defense effort that were threatened by strikes, required NLRB-supervised strike votes and mandatory cooling-off periods, and restricted union political activity. Roosevelt vetoed Smith-Connally because the administration feared it would antagonize labor and jeopardize production. But his veto was overridden by Congress—the first of FDR's vetoes to be overridden since the beginning of the war. The highest level of support came from Southern Democrats, with 92 percent backing the bill in the House (compared with 77% of Republicans and 17% of non-Southern Democrats) and 88 percent backing the bill in the Senate (compared with 82% percent of Republicans and 31% of non-Southern Democrats).[61]

The Problems of Reconversion

Tensions during the reconversion period were heightened by conflicting expectations on the part of business, labor, and Truman, who assumed the presidency after Roosevelt's death near the end of the war. Although some business leaders supported unions' rights to collective bargaining, most wanted to curtail union power, particularly in areas where they felt management's prerogatives had been undermined during the war. Labor's most ardent foes in the business community saw the reconversion period as an opportunity to eliminate the labor movement's gains since the onset of the Great Depression. In contrast, labor expected its sacrifices during the war to be rewarded.[62] Labor leaders tried to suppress strikes and workers' demands, but the rank and file grew restless by the end of the war. Workers were apprehensive about the future economy, overburdened by inflation, frustrated by union discipline and the no-strike pledge, and eager for wage increases and a whole new standard of living denied over the course of the war and the Depression.

The Truman administration, eager to avoid unemployment and inflation while converting production to meet pent-up consumer demand, tried to navigate these conflicting expectations, and it would repeatedly be drawn into the conflicts between management and labor in the postwar years. After victory over Japan, President Truman called a Labor-Management Conference in November 1945 with the intention of resolving the most pressing labor relations and economic issues for the reconversion period. The conference dragged on for three weeks but reached few compromises on how to achieve a smooth reconversion. Before the conference's unsuccessful conclusion, a number of strikes began that initiated the largest strike wave in the nation's history. In the year following V-J day there were 4,630 strikes involving roughly 5 million workers and a loss of more than 120 million workdays.[63]

Important players in the Truman administration believed employers would be able to increase wages without raising prices because of accumulated wartime profits. The administration erroneously expected that wage increases would be negotiated without production interruptions.[64] Instead, the process of collective bargaining broke down. Eager to end government price controls, business after business insisted they could not increase wages unless the administration allowed for an increase in prices. Labor leaders were convinced that employers, many of whom were protected from losses in the reconversion period by special federal tax laws, were intent on breaking the power of unions and determined to provoke strikes in order to precipitate "economic chaos."[65] Essentially, the loss of production during strikes was being subsidized by the government, and proposals to terminate the tax provisions were tied up in congressional committees.[66] Two high-profile strikes in the steel industry and against General Motors in late 1945 and early 1946 epitomized these tensions, and their resolution ensured continued inflation and public dissatisfaction.

The steel strike was the first to be settled, and it signaled the end of effective price controls. Demanding government approval of a substantial price increase on steel before it would engage in collective bargaining with the United Steelworkers, the steel industry refused to accept the terms suggested by a fact-finding board appointed by Truman. After a series of internal struggles within the Truman administration, the president ultimately conceded to a price increase double what the head of the Office of Price Administration had originally offered in exchange for the industry's acceptance of a sizable wage increase. The settlement would ripple across negotiations in every industry.

In the contemporaneous GM conflict, Walter Reuther, the head of the GM division of the UAW, called what would become one of the longest strikes of the reconversion period. Trying to tie labor's demands to the public interest, Reuther insisted that GM could offer a sizable wage increase without an increase in prices. Recalling one of the problems of the Great Depression, insufficient consumer demand, Reuther argued that redistributing large corporate profits to wages and keeping the price of consumer goods low was central to achieving a high-production, high-consumption, high-employment postwar order and an improved standard of living for the average American. When GM insisted to Reuther that it could not afford to increase wages without raising prices, Reuther demanded that GM open its books to the union and the public to prove its inability to pay. GM refused, and both sides settled into intransigence as the strike of more than two hundred thousand workers dragged on. In December, the Truman administration appointed a fact-finding board that made suggestions for a settlement. The union eventually endorsed the recommendations, abandoning its larger goals, but GM continued to refuse the terms. Influenced by the steel settlement, the 113-day strike was ultimately settled with a similar wage increase and administration approval of an increase in product prices.

The conclusion of the steel, GM, and other contemporaneous strikes had a number of consequences. The Truman administration's effort to stabilize prices through the reconversion period was effectively abandoned. Inflation spiraled out of control, and many unions returned to the bargaining table before the end of the year to demand more wage increases. Industry leaders argued that higher prices were driven by unions' wage demands. Labor leaders argued that higher prices were driven by corporations' quest for higher profits.[67] Business won the public relations battle. As the reconversion period progressed, both the media and the public increasingly blamed price increases on what they perceived as the unreasonable and well-publicized demands of labor unions.[68] Reuther failed in his bid to associate organized labor's goals with the public interest. These events helped set the stage for the passage of legislation to curtail labor's power.

The Postwar Strike Wave and the Case Bill

In addition to the problem of inflation, politicians and the public grew increasingly frustrated with production interruptions that threatened reconversion and the stability of the national economy. Coal and railway strikes in particular fed this mood. Lewis again called the mineworkers out on strike over the coal operators' refusal to help fund a union-administered health and welfare fund. Both the UMW and the mine operators declined Truman's offer of arbitration. Because shortages of coal threatened the reconversion of industrial production, Truman, utilizing authority granted in the Smith-Connally War Labor Disputes Act, which was still in effect, seized the mines and established a compromise under government operation. The Truman administration was also forced to intervene in a dispute between the railroad operators and the multiple unions of rail workers. Truman seized the railroads and established a settlement with two of the unions. However, two other unions held out and called a strike, effectively against the government, that brought a virtual collapse of the nationwide rail transportation network. An exasperated Truman seemed to share the view of labor's most ardent critics. Government negotiators arrived at a compromise just as Truman went before a joint session of Congress to request emergency legislation to empower the president to prevent strikes that threatened the national economy. In a game of political brinkmanship with organized labor, Truman proposed the Temporary Disputes Settlement Bill, which among other things would have allowed the president to draft strikers, a proposal backed by two-thirds of the public.[69] Although the bill passed overwhelmingly in the House, the Senate refused to act, in part, ironically, because of the opposition of Republican senator Robert Taft of Ohio, who would become the archenemy of organized labor because of his role in the passage of the Taft-Hartley Act.

Despite the growing hostility to labor and the circulation of numerous legislative proposals to amend the Wagner Act and curtail the power of unions, no major bill became law in the 79th Congress (1945–46). After the failure of the Labor-Management Conference in late 1945, Truman called for legislation requiring a thirty-day cooling-off period and enabling the president to appoint fact-finding boards in labor-management disputes that threatened the "national public interest." Neither management nor labor would have been compelled to comply with the board's recommendations, but both railed against the proposal. Ultimately legislation even more objectionable to organized labor, a bill introduced by Republican congressman Francis Case, was substituted for the administration bill, a move facilitated by the actions of the conservative coalition on the Rules Committee.[70] In February 1946, the Case bill passed the House 258–155 and, after several months delay, the Senate 49–29, hours after Truman's speech to the joint session of Congress in conjunction with the railroad dispute. The Case bill incorporated several ideas that had been circulating around Congress for years, including the establishment of a sixty-day cooling-off period before strikes or lockouts, a provision to allow unions to be sued for contract violations, denial of Wagner Act protections to employees who participated in wildcat strikes or violated union contracts, and a prohibition of secondary boycotts in which unions force their employer not to do business with another employer, typically one that is resisting an organizing drive. All of organized labor again expressed intense opposition to the bill, and mail urging a veto poured into the White House.[71]

The passage of the Case bill precipitated a debate within the Truman administration over whether the president should veto the bill and highlighted a growing rift within the party over how to handle labor. Some advisers suggested that labor had nowhere else to go but the Democratic Party and that, by not signing the bill, the president might alienate middle America. But many labor relations specialists suggested that the bill might do more to foment industrial unrest than to prevent it.[72] The president was also urged to veto the bill by pro-labor Democrats in Congress who saw labor's support as crucial to the party.[73] Ultimately, Truman decided to veto the bill. The House barely sustained the veto, with almost all Republicans and ninety-six Democrats, eighty from Southern states, voting to override. Five Southern Democrats, under party pressure, switched from voting in favor of the bill to voting to sustain the veto, which averted an override.[74] Labor's allies in the Democratic Party narrowly managed to save labor from unfavorable legislation once again. Although a number of scholars have questioned the value of labor's relationship with the Democrats during this period, it is rather remarkable that most Democrats remained committed to labor in spite of the antilabor tenor of public opinion at the time.[75]

Even though these proposals did not become law, they had an effect on the labor movement. A report to President Truman by CIO president Philip Murray detailed conservative efforts to amend the NLRA from 1937 to 1946. Murray argued that many of the proposals were introduced to keep labor and its congressional allies on the defensive, even though they had little chance of becoming law. Murray observed:

> A basic aim of the sponsors of these bills has been to use the legislative process itself as a means of smearing labor and of artificially stimulating resentment against trade unions. The program of this group has become and continues to be a war of nerves to soften up or neutralize progressive opposition to antistrike legislation through a constant stream of restrictive bills. This program of misrepresentation in the form of bills also had other more immediate objectives. It was designed to frighten workers away from trade unions, to cheat labor of the fruits of Federal labor legislation, to force the labor movement to operate in a constant state of crisis and thus to dissipate its time and energy in defending itself. Finally, by attacking labor as a whole, this group of legislators encouraged large groups of American employers to attack the unions of their own employees. This group of legislators used the legislative apparatus to promote disregard of Federal labor laws and to keep alive hopes of repealing them.[76]

The attacks in Congress as well as the overwhelmingly critical stance of the news media on organized labor shaped public opinion and fed the momentum to revisit the NLRA that ultimately resulted in the passage of the Taft-Hartley Act after the Republicans took control of Congress in the 1946 elections.[77]

The power of organized labor became a major issue in the 1946 campaign. The strike wave and Washington's seeming inability to control it contributed to public anxiety over inflation, severe housing shortages, and a dearth of consumer goods following years of sacrifice for the war and more than a decade of sacrifice in the Depression. The Republican congressional candidates capitalized on this sentiment by nationalizing the 1946 elections around a common theme. The Republicans used the slogan "Had enough?" and promised to fight the "Three C's"—"Communism, Confusion, and Chaos"—of Democratic rule and the existing labor law.[78] This message was highlighted by Lewis's threat just before the elections to call another coal strike. Truman himself blamed Lewis for the outcome of the 1946 elections.[79] Scholars such as Michael Goldfield, Frances Fox Piven, and Richard Cloward have argued that worker insurgency forced the government to make concessions in the mid-thirties including passage of the NLRA.[80] Many scholars have also celebrated worker insurgency during the war and reconversion periods,[81] but it hurt labor's political position. Voter turnout was low, and voter turnout of labor union members was particularly down.[82] The Republicans won control of both houses of Congress for the first time since the Depression set in. In the House, Republicans gained a majority of 246–189, and 109 of the Democrats came from Southern states. Republicans gained a 51–45 majority in the Senate, with roughly half of the Democratic seats held by Southerners. Liberal congressional forces were decimated.

Although elections are a blunt instrument in the United States and rarely reflect the endorsement of particular public policies as much as unhappiness with present conditions,[83] conservative Republicans viewed the result of the 1946 election as an opportunity and even a mandate to reverse New Deal public policies. Moderate Republicans did not necessarily share the view that most of the New Deal should be revisited, but there was widespread consensus that New Deal labor policies should be amended. This was also a priority for many of the Southern Democrats returning to Congress. Dozens of measures to amend the NLRA were introduced in the first few days of the 80th Congress, and hearings were held in the early months of 1947.

Representative Fred Hartley Jr., chairman of the House Committee on Education and Labor, and Senator Robert Taft, chairman of the Senate Committee on Labor and Public Welfare, with the assistance of National Association of Manufacturers (NAM) lobbyists and other conservative Washington lawyers, hammered together proposals circulating since the introduction of the Wagner Act into comprehensive legislation to scale back the power of unions. The Hartley proposal, considered to be the harshest toward labor, passed the House by the large, veto-proof margin of 308–107. The Taft proposal, which omitted some of the House bill's more antilabor provisions because the Republican majority in the Senate was not as large and not as conservative, also passed with a veto-proof majority of 68–24. As in the House, the majority of Democrats who voted in favor came from Southern states. Hartley intentionally played up the House bill as harsh and the Senate bill as mild.[84] If the conference committee moved in the direction of the Senate bill, Hartley reasoned, this would make it easier to sustain veto-proof supermajorities on the conference compromise.

Provisions of the Taft-Hartley Act

The purpose of the Wagner Act had been to protect workers trying to organize from employer abuses and to encourage unionization. From the time of its passage, critics of the act felt that it went too far by shifting the balance of power in favor of unions and placing individual workers, employers, and the public interest at the mercy of power-hungry union leaders. The expressed goal of labor law reformers was to level the playing field between unions and employers and guarantee workers protection from unions as well as from employers. Labor's friends saw the reform proposals as an effort by business and its conservative allies to reverse union advances and give employers new tools to fight unionization.

The Taft-Hartley bill had a number of goals. In an effort to tame an NLRB that many considered to be biased toward unions over management (and the CIO over the AFL), the board was restructured to administer a more legalistic, adversarial process in the enforcement of labor law.[85] As part of an effort to ensure managerial prerogatives, supervisors were no longer allowed to unionize. To handle strikes classified as national emergencies, the president could trigger a fact-finding process, obtain injunctions against strikes, and order cooling-off periods. Jurisdictional strikes, which tended to occur when an AFL and a CIO union were both fighting for recognition in the same firm, were prohibited. In an effort to force national unions to control the wildcat strikes of their locals, unions could be sued in federal courts for violation of contracts and held responsible for the acts of their agents.

Taft-Hartley included several provisions to expand the rights of members in their unions. Dues check-offs had to be voluntary. Unions were required to make annual financial reports available. Employees and employers could petition for decertification elections to remove a union as the recognized bargaining agent. To protect individual workers and to make it harder for union organization to take hold, the closed shop (whereby only union members could get a job in a bargaining unit) was forbidden. The union shop, whereby new employees had to join a union or pay their share for collective bargaining services, which was often negotiated in collective bargaining contracts, would require a separate vote by the membership to take effect. States were also permitted to pass right-to-work laws that prohibited the union shop. Another important provision that was rhetorically aimed at protecting the rights of individual union members, but clearly intended to tame unions' growing political power, was a prohibition against union contributions to candidates in federal elections from union treasury funds.

Many of the provisions targeted union organizing efforts. One measure prohibited secondary boycotts in which, for example, workers in a third-party unionized firm might refuse to handle products from a firm targeted by an organizing drive in order to encourage the targeted firm to recognize the union. Employers were guaranteed free speech rights to counter an organizing campaign, a provision that was increasingly utilized by employers to wage elaborate and effective antiunion campaigns among their employees. To gain the protections of the NLRA, union officials had to sign affidavits testifying they were not Communists. Part of the rising red scare, this provision was also aimed at eliminating some of the most aggressive organizers and created internecine battles within a number of CIO unions.[86]

Truman's Veto

Under the new Republican-controlled Congress, the final version of the Taft-Hartley Act—unlike the Case bill, which included many of the same measures—passed by veto-proof margins of 320–79 in the House and 57–17 in the Senate. It was a rout for organized labor, which lobbied aggressively against the bill. As Taft-Hartley moved to the White House, the labor effort intensified. Labor leaders argued that Taft-Hartley would result in endless litigation, precipitate more industrial unrest, and lead to an employer attack on unions, wages, and working conditions that would push the United States into another depression. Unions organized large rallies against the bill across the country, including a high-profile event in Madison Square Garden. The AFL alone was alleged to have spent more than a million dollars to shape public opinion.[87] Spurred by the efforts of the AFL and the CIO, more than three-quarters of a million pieces of mail and telegrams, the vast majority urging Truman to veto the bill, poured into the White House.[88] Other liberal groups, including religious organizations and the National Farmers Union, joined labor in opposition. Increasingly tied to the labor movement, Democratic Party regulars outside the South also lobbied Truman to veto the act.[89]

Taft-Hartley precipitated the same debate within the administration over a veto as the Case bill. All but one of the prominent labor relations experts whom the Truman administration asked to comment on the bill recommended he veto it.[90] However, the administration was concerned about the political ramifications. Many advisers pointed out that the elections had been a mandate against unions. Others countered that the elections revealed frustration with other postwar issues and could not be read as a mandate on labor law. Southerners emphasized that the party might fall apart just over a year before the presidential election if Truman vetoed the act. Advisers again argued that organized labor had nowhere else to go and that Truman needed to hold on to the conservative wing of the party by not issuing a veto. Still others argued that while labor might not go to the Republicans, its members might stay home as they had in the disastrous 1946 elections. The Democratic National Committee chairman warned that Truman's failure to exercise the veto might give former vice president Henry Wallace an issue on which to build his third-party movement.[91] Truman was faced with choosing between two wings of his party in a situation in which there was no compromise.

Truman decided again to side with labor and the liberals by vetoing Taft-Hartley. He issued a stinging veto message, calling the bill "unworkable" and "discriminatory" against labor. Hours later, the House voted to override, 331–83. A short filibuster started in the Senate, and at one point it appeared that Truman had just enough votes to sustain the veto. There were even plans to summons the ill Senator Wagner (D-NY) from his deathbed and to fly Senator Elbert Thomas (D-UT) back from Europe if their votes would have been decisive in sustaining the veto. However, support slipped, and the veto was finally overridden 68–25. The regional division was again apparent with Southern Democrats and Republicans voting overwhelmingly to override Truman's veto. Most of the support for upholding it came from non-Southern Democrats. Only four Southern Democratic senators voted to uphold the veto, the liberal Claude Pepper of Florida, the senators from Alabama, where the United Steelworkers union was strong, and a member of the Senate Democratic leadership from South Carolina. There was even less support for labor among Southern Democrats in the House where only a dozen voted to sustain the veto.[92] Even though the Republicans controlled Congress, Southern Democratic support was crucial to the veto override. Thus, the shift in the attitude of Southern Democrats toward organized labor since the passage of the NLRA made its amendment possible.[93] The NLRA had not been repealed, but the national labor law no longer reflected the position that unionization and collective bargaining should be fostered as a matter of public policy.

Waning Union Growth and the Enduring Problem of the South

The rate of union growth declined the year after Taft-Hartley passed, and by the mid-1950s union density began to fall.[94] Most Southern states and a number of rural Western states quickly adopted right-to-work laws prohibiting the union shop, which made it more difficult for fledgling unions to solve collective action problems.[95] There is some debate about the effect of the legislation on union growth, but it is clear that the law offered new tools to antiunion employers, who would become experts at using the provisions of Taft-Hartley to fight unionization drives. On the fifth anniversary of the law a UAW memo cited numerous studies showing that, particularly in the South, Taft-Hartley was "being used more and more by anti-union employers to prevent organization of their plants or to crush unions where they already exist."[96]

It isn't clear that Southern unionization would have taken off in the absence of Taft-Hartley, but the law certainly made an inhospitable environment even more so.[97] The CIO and AFL had launched major Southern organizing drives in 1946.[98] As part of the CIO's Operation Dixie, affiliates like the Textile Workers Union of America (TWUA) plowed money and staff into organizing the large Southern textile mills. But three years later, the CIO membership in the Southern states at four hundred thousand was virtually the same as it had been at the beginning of Operation Dixie.[99] The effort was formally disbanded in 1953.[100] Union density in the South lagged considerably behind that in the rest of the country, with an average of 17.1 percent of the nonagricultural workforce unionized among Southern states, compared with a national average of 32.6 percent.[101]

There are no firm conclusions as to why the Southern organizing drives failed. Race, religion, an oppressive social order, hostile local politicians and policies, violent resistance to unionization by companies and police, and the inadequacy of the CIO's financial commitment and organizing strategy are all viable explanations.[102] The economic position of the South intensified the effects of all these factors. The weak and largely unindustrialized Southern economy dating from the Civil War fed antiunion attitudes. Employers and the community leaders determined to keep them happy were intent on maintaining the South's low-wage advantage. Workers were often complacent, not only because they faced intense repression by employers and local authorities but also because they were afraid of losing some of the best jobs they had ever had if they unionized.[103]

The failure to make organizing gains in the South posed a tremendous barrier to labor's goal of achieving a more egalitarian and progressive society. In their struggles with unions, employers could move—or threaten to move—to the low-wage, low-unionization South, or they could cite their competitive disadvantage with firms that were already there. Southern politicians also used their political power in Congress to fight organized labor's efforts to level the playing field through public policies to promote national labor markets and standards, and they constantly challenged labor's position within the Democratic coalition. The disparity between union power in and outside the South as well as labor's growing liberal political agenda—including civil rights, the most explosive issue of all—ensured that the clash between the two wings of the Democratic Party would extend beyond labor legislation like Taft-Hartley. This irreconcilable tension was epitomized in the 1948 presidential election.

The 1948 Elections: Labor, Civil Rights, and the Future of the Democratic Party

By 1948, cracks in the New Deal Democratic coalition had grown into a full-scale schism. As Truman aide Clark Clifford's famous memo outlining strategy for the 1948 presidential elections noted, "The basic premise of this memorandum—that the Democratic Party is an unhappy alliance of Southern conservatives, Western progressives and Big City labor—is very trite, but it is also very true."[104] These wings often shared a common orientation on foreign policy, which helped both Roosevelt and Truman downplay growing divisions in the party during the war. But with the return of domestic policy to center stage, Truman was forced to confront the realities of a crumbling party. As with the Taft-Hartley veto, Truman had to decide whether he wanted to placate Southern conservatives and risk alienating liberals and labor or whether he wanted to side with the liberals and labor and risk losing the solid South. His decision to veto Taft-Hartley was an early indication that he would take the latter route.

Over the course of 1947 and 1948, Truman worked to solidify the labor-liberal coalition with little consideration for Southern opposition. As the Clifford memo noted, "It is inconceivable that any policies initiated by the Truman Administration no matter how 'liberal' could so alienate the South in the next year that it would revolt. As always, the South can be considered safely Democratic. And in formulating national policy, it can be safely ignored."[105] In pursuing this strategy, the Truman administration benefited from Republican control of Congress. Clifford argued, "The only pragmatic reason for conciliating the South in normal times is because of its tremendous strength in the Congress. Since the Congress is Republican and the Democratic President has, therefore, no real chance to get his own program approved by it, particularly in an election year, he has no real necessity for 'getting along' with the Southern conservatives. He must, however, get along with the Westerners and with labor if he is to be reelected."[106] Thus with few negative consequences, Truman could rail against the "do-nothing Congress" while reminding voters of his opposition to Taft-Hartley and, in a first for a Democratic presidential candidate, his support for civil rights.

The passage and veto of Taft-Hartley pushed the labor movement closer to the national Democratic Party and, as Truman intended, dampened labor's enthusiasm for third-party politics, which had grown during the reconversion period.[107] Labor's alliance with the Democrats did not reflect a rejection of class-based politics or the political centrism of labor leaders but rather a strategic adaptation to the realities of the political system. Taft-Hartley taught labor leaders how important it was to have an ally, if not a best friend, in the White House, and it encouraged them to pursue a safe political strategy.[108] When Henry Wallace announced his presidential candidacy under the Progressive Party of America, CIO unions controlled or significantly influenced by Communists again pushed for labor to break away from the Democratic Party, as they had for years.[109] But in a three-way race most of the union leadership, including Walter Reuther, who had long been interested in forming a third party, concluded that labor's best strategy was to maintain an alliance with the Democrats.[110] The AFL and CIO each spent more than a million dollars on the election and launched unprecedented efforts to mobilize voters and assist Truman's campaign.[111] Taft-Hartley was a blow to labor, but without Democratic friends in the White House and Congress, the Republican-controlled Congress might have passed an even more damaging bill gutting the NLRA in 1947. If labor had thrown its support behind a third-party candidate and Dewey had won the presidency, conservatives might have built on Taft-Hartley to launch additional attacks on organized labor following the 1948 elections. Instead, labor helped elect a president pledged to Taft-Hartley's repeal.

Moreover, labor had close Democratic allies in Congress. In the face of widespread public hostility to labor, non-Southern Democrats overall had remained quite supportive. Labor concluded that trying to pull the Democratic Party to the left was more likely to pay off than fighting an uphill battle to build a third party that would have as much difficulty controlling Congress as liberal Democrats—or possibly more. There was never much serious talk of third-party labor politics after 1948 at the national level. Organized labor continued to participate in a coalition of progressive forces often referred to as the "labor-liberal alliance" that endeavored over the next few decades to realign the Democratic Party away from Southern conservatives and toward its more social democratic wing. Advocating civil rights, the other major issue dividing the Democratic Party, became an important part of this strategy.

The cleavage between non-Southern and Southern Democrats on labor issues increasingly overlapped with the cleavage on civil rights issues. FDR brought African Americans into his electoral coalition with economic appeals but generally made only symbolic overtures on civil rights. An exception was FDR's creation by executive order in 1941 of a Fair Employment Practices Committee (FEPC), which targeted discrimination in defense industries. Roosevelt made this decision in order to fend off a proposed march on Washington organized by A. Philip Randolph, the president of the almost all-black Brotherhood of Sleeping Car Porters. As elaborated in Chapter 4, the CIO and other activists in the labor-liberal alliance worked to expand New Deal liberalism to include civil rights. Thus, despite the absence of presidential leadership, the civil rights issue percolated in Congress with the support of many New Deal liberals.

As with labor bills, civil rights legislation was often the victim of congressional institutions. The Rules Committee was the major obstacle to civil rights in the House because most Republicans on the committee cooperated with Southern Democrats to block civil rights bills. But the conservative coalition did not always operate against civil rights bills on the floor. By the 1940s, non-Southern Democrats were the biggest supporters of labor and civil rights bills, and Southerners were the biggest opponents. But the support of Republicans made the difference on civil rights bills. Because bills often had to be discharged from Rules through the petition process, Republican support had to be active, and it was not always forthcoming. There appeared to be quid pro quo agreements between Southern Democrats and amenable Republicans on some bills whereby

Republicans failed to support civil rights bills in exchange for Southerners' opposition to labor bills. A number of Republicans also opposed enforceable employment antidiscrimination bills because of employer resistance, which undermined Truman's efforts to create a permanent FEPC.[112] Even though they would be killed by Southerners in the Senate, bills to abolish the poll tax passed in the House in 1942, 1943, 1945, and 1947 with high levels of support from Republicans and non-Southern Democrats. Both were in competition for blacks' votes, which were crucial to Truman's 1948 election strategy.

Truman took a number of actions to appeal to black voters and liberal advocates of civil rights such as labor. Early in 1948, he requested congressional action on a ten-point legislative program addressing civil rights issues such as lynching, voting rights, and discrimination in interstate transportation facilities and employment. He expected that Southerners would be successful in obstructing his program in Congress. However, Southerners were not successful in obstructing the effort of liberals, led by Minnesota Senate candidate Hubert Humphrey and Wisconsin House candidate (and future AFL-CIO lobbyist) Andrew Biemiller, at the 1948 Democratic convention to get a strong civil rights plank in the party's platform for the first time in the party's history. The inclusion of the plank reflected the determination of liberal groups like the CIO, Americans for Democratic Action, and the NAACP to force a confrontation over civil rights that national party leaders would have preferred to avoid. The Mississippi delegation and part of the Alabama delegation walked out. Later that month, Truman issued two momentous executive orders, one mandating the desegregation of the military and the other creating a Fair Employment Board to fight discrimination in federal employment. Southern segregationists could not tolerate the shift in the national Democratic Party, and many defected to support the States' Rights Democratic Party, dubbed the Dixiecrats, and its nominee, South Carolina governor Strom Thurmond.

The Electoral Outcome

The solid South crumbled in 1948, but Truman's strategy worked. The electoral college votes of Alabama, Louisiana, Mississippi, and South Carolina went to Thurmond. But the remainder of the Southern states and the border states stayed in the Democratic column. All of the electoral votes of the Northeastern states, except Massachusetts and Rhode Island, went to Republican Dewey. But many urban areas remained heavily Democratic, and several of the Northeastern states only narrowly went to Dewey, including Dewey's home state of New

York, because liberal forces were split between Truman and Wallace's third-party candidacy. Truman also won in industrial Midwestern states like Ohio and Illinois, where union members' votes were pivotal.[113] Although Truman lost most of the Northern states and needed the votes of some of the Southern states to win (unlike Roosevelt), the strategy for the 1948 presidential election in many ways presaged the future of the Democratic Party after Southern conservatives left for the Republican fold. Liberal constituencies were central to Truman's surprising and truly remarkable victory. After the election, Truman exclaimed to the press, "Labor did it!"[114]

The 1948 election was a pivotal moment in which the labor movement committed to an alliance with the Democratic Party and the national party staked its future on maintaining the support of liberal constituencies with a socially progressive platform. While the outcome of the 1948 election is viewed as the continuation of the New Deal coalition, the prominence of the civil rights issue and the defection of a handful of Southern states signaled the beginning of a partisan realignment of the South.[115] The migration of Southern voters continued in the 1952 and 1956 elections, in which several Southern states went Republican in Dwight Eisenhower's landslides, as well as in the 1960 election. By 1964, five of the only six states that went for Republican nominee Barry Goldwater were in the deep South. At the same time labor moved into an even closer alliance with the national Democratic Party, with both the AFL and the CIO formally endorsing the Democratic presidential nominee for the first time in 1952. The merged AFL-CIO would endorse every subsequent Democratic presidential nominee, with the exception of George McGovern in 1972, and labor would become the most important organized player in the national Democratic Party.[116] Despite the dominance of labor and its liberal allies in the national Democratic Party, Southern Democrats remained very powerful in Congress through the 1970s, feeding a constant struggle between the two wings of the party.

In 1948, the labor-liberal components of the New Deal coalition managed to prevail in a national election without FDR on the ticket. But the constituencies that reelected Truman did not have the same leverage in congressional elections. The national electorate backed a president who ran as a liberal, campaigning on civil rights, pro-labor policies, and an expansive welfare state; meanwhile, the electorates of the various congressional districts and states produced a Congress that was very resistant to these policies. R. Alton Lee argues that this outcome reflected the existence of a "dual constituency" in American politics that was largely a result of the one-party system and limited voter participation in the South.[117] Yet it is also important to acknowledge Republican strength. Outside the South, Republicans won a larger share of the popular vote than Democrats in all the House elections from 1938 to 1952.[118] Moreover, malapportionment of congressional districts produced a Republican edge worth about twenty seats from 1946 to 1960.[119] At this point in history, labor-oriented Democrats simply were not strong enough in the rest of the country to counter the influence of conservative Southern Democrats. Thus Truman's successful electoral strategy was not a successful legislative strategy, as is detailed in the next chapter. Unlike many Southern voters, Southern Democratic members of Congress had shown and would continue to show a willingness—even an eagerness—to take on the administration.

Conclusion

The American labor movement made unprecedented gains in the 1930s and 1940s as a result of favorable public policies and aggressive organizing. While unionization rates increased throughout the country, gains were not equal across states and regions. More than half of the union members added from 1939 to 1953 were located in just six states, New York, California, Pennsylvania, Michigan, Illinois, and Ohio.[120] The organizing surge, particularly of the CIO, had the greatest impact in previously unorganized sectors of the economy in the Midwest, which became a highly unionized region like the Northeast and the West Coast.[121] By the early 1950s, unionization rates in many industrialized states were comparable to those in the more highly unionized areas of Europe, but they lagged behind in the politically crucial region of the South.[122] The regional concentration of organized labor was the movement's greatest weakness, and legislative institutions like the Rules Committee magnified its impact.

In their analysis of congressional roll call votes, Poole and Rosenthal argue, "The period from the late New Deal until the mid-1970s saw the development of the only genuine three-political-party system in American history."[123] These three parties formed different legislative coalitions depending on the issue. Southern Democrats joined Republicans in the conservative coalition to oppose pro-labor and many welfare state policies, as elaborated in the next chapter. In contrast, non-Southern Democrats joined many Northeastern Republicans in support of civil rights.[124] The two wings of the Democratic Party hung together on most other policies. Although a number of observers argue that labor would have been better off rejecting the Democratic Party and pursuing its own party in the 1940s,[125] it is not at all clear that a labor party would have changed this informal three-party dynamic. Even if a labor party could have overcome the barriers to third parties in the electoral system, it would have likely been strongest in areas where pro-labor, pro–civil rights Democrats fared well. This rarely represented a majority of congressional seats. A labor party could have put together an uncompromised pro-labor platform, but like the liberal Democrats, it would have probably had trouble delivering on it.[126]

In choosing to continue to work within the national Democratic Party in the 1940s, labor set off a slow-moving chain reaction that would shape the course of American politics over the next six decades. In the 1944 debate on an anti–poll tax bill supported by organized labor, Senator Josiah W. Bailey (D-NC) asserted on the Senate floor, "I make no threats, but I will simply say that when Sidney Hillman (chairman of the political action committee) and the Communist crew in the name of the CIO come in the doors and the windows of the party in which my father and I lived and served, I will go out."[127] The Southern losses for the Democrats in the 1948 election provided a glimpse of the future. Both the CIO and the AFL came into the Democratic Party, and eventually Southern conservatives like Bailey left. Organized labor became a powerful progressive force within the Democratic Party in the postwar period, allying with other liberal constituencies to push the party to endorse civil rights legislation, welfare state programs, and congressional reforms to undermine the dominance of conservative Southern Democrats in the legislative process. After substantial progress on these goals was finally made in the 1960s and 1970s, Southern conservatives began to leave the Democratic Party to find a new and more comfortable home in the Republican fold. This allowed the Democratic Party to gradually move to the left. But whether working with Republicans in the conservative coalition or *as* Republicans in later decades, Southern conservatives continued to effectively oppose much of labor's policy agenda, as explored in the following chapters.

Labor, the Conservative Coalition, and the Welfare State

Following the unprecedented growth of union membership and political activism during the war years, the leaders of the labor movement expected to use their newfound power to help liberal forces build a comprehensive welfare state. Labor supported policies to ensure full employment and high wages as well as generous national government programs for retirement, disability, unemployment, and health care. But the same political forces that united in a backlash against organized labor and New Deal labor policies in the late thirties and forties were largely opposed to this agenda. During the first decades of the postwar period, the influence of the conservative coalition of Southern Democrats and Republicans extended beyond labor issues to many of the public policies that labor endorsed. At a pivotal moment in history when welfare states were expanding across the Western world with recovery from the war, when ideas for reform proliferated, and when labor represented a third of the workforce and appeared to still be growing, labor's ambitious policy goals collided with an inhospitable postwar political reality.

The conservative coalition dominated congressional policy making from the 1940s through the early 1960s and remained influential into the 1970s. During this period, the coalition exerted power in both Democrat- and Republican-controlled Congresses, challenging the agenda of Democratic presidents Harry S. Truman and John F. Kennedy. Labor accused the conservative coalition of working with Republican president Dwight Eisenhower to pass "veto-proof" legislation, but even some of Eisenhower's proposals were rebuffed. As a UAW staff member noted, "Whichever Party is nominally in power, the Southern Democrats manage to get along fairly well in serving the immediate interests of the economically and politically powerful minorities in their Districts and States."[1] At times the conservative coalition controlled legislative outcomes because of its unambiguous numerical superiority in the House, the Senate, or both as it did during the passage of the Taft-Hartley Act. At other times, under larger Democratic majorities, liberals' impact on legislative outcomes was undercut by the conservative coalition's use of various institutions in the legislative process. While the conservative coalition initiated the legislation to restrain organized labor discussed in the previous chapter, it played its most prominent role in shaping public policy by watering down, stalling, and obstructing liberal proposals, particularly when the Democrats controlled the presidency.

This chapter explores the efforts of labor-liberals to build on New Deal welfare state programs and to restore New Deal labor law at the height of the conservative coalition's power in the 1940s and 1950s. It looks at efforts in four policy areas: to establish Keynesian-style coordinated economic planning for full employment in the Employment Act of 1946; to improve and standardize workers' income security programs in fights over the minimum wage, unemployment compensation, and disability insurance; to provide universal access to health care in a single-payer, government-funded national health insurance program; and to repeal Taft-Hartley and fight further Taft-Hartley amendments in the union anticorruption bill known as Landrum-Griffin. This period produced a pattern of incremental growth in economic planning and income security programs, within boundaries acceptable to the conservative coalition. But liberal and conservative forces were largely drawn to a stalemate on national health care and restoring New Deal labor law because compromises could not be reached that could attract support from some members of the conservative coalition while retaining support from labor-liberals. The more steadfast labor and other advocates of reform were in their preferred policy approach, the less likely there was to be action. The comprehensive, universal, and national policies and programs that dominated labor's postwar agenda were seemingly impossible.

The Postwar Agenda to Expand the Welfare State

One of the most significant changes for organized labor during the New Deal was its growing support for welfare state programs, government management of the economy, and government intervention in industrial relations and working conditions. Previously, the AFL emphasized what its long-serving president Samuel Gompers termed "pure and simple unionism," or business unionism, which focused on collective bargaining over political action and social reform. Labor had been very suspicious of government because its actions had so often been hostile, from courts issuing injunctions against strikes and other collective union activity to the president ordering troops to disband strikes. From the late 1800s through the early years of the New Deal, the courts also routinely invalidated legislation pushed by unions to improve working conditions, such as minimum wage laws. A number of scholars argue that court doctrines discouraged labor from wasting resources on seemingly futile political activity.[2] But the severity of the Great Depression led many labor leaders to call for government policies to address the economic crisis. This interest in government action was reinforced by Roosevelt's overtures to labor as well as growing court deference to the elected branches on social and economic legislation as signaled in the famous 1937 Supreme Court case *National Labor Relations Board vs. Jones & Laughlin Steel Co.*, which ruled the NLRA constitutional. Initially the CIO was more committed than the AFL to improving the quality of life for workers through legislation and government programs because CIO unions did not have the resources of more established unions to provide their members with benefits for health care, unemployment, or retirement and the unskilled workers targeted by the CIO were in a weaker position to demand these benefits from their employers.[3] But gradually the positions of the two federations converged.

While the foundation of the modern welfare state was laid during the New Deal, the agenda for its expansion was developed during World War II and the reconversion period. Almost all the welfare state initiatives of the Roosevelt years were passed by 1938, including the Social Security old-age assistance and insurance programs, a joint federal-state program of assistance to the poor, a joint federal-state program of unemployment compensation, and the FLSA. As discussed in the previous chapter, the FLSA reflected the death knell of the New Deal as the pro–welfare state coalition shrank in Congress and Roosevelt's focus shifted to the crisis in Europe. But during the war, the administration continued to develop a domestic agenda that was outlined in FDR's 1944 State of the Union address, in which he called for an "Economic Bill of Rights." These rights included a job, food, clothing, recreation, housing, education, medical care, and economic security in old age, sickness, disability, and unemployment. Roosevelt concluded his address by noting, "All these rights spell security. And after this war is won, we must move forward in the implementation of these rights to new goals of human happiness and well being."[4] The CIO made Roosevelt's Bill of Rights the preamble to its proposals for the 1948 party conventions, and the AFL proposals reflected the same priorities.[5] Roosevelt did not live to see these plans through, but Truman picked up his agenda.

Shortly after the conclusion of the war, Truman sent a special message to Congress containing a twenty-one-point legislative program based on Roosevelt's postwar agenda.[6] In what would become Truman's "Fair Deal," he called for expanded unemployment compensation, a higher minimum wage, housing legislation, public works projects, full-employment planning, and a permanent Fair Employment Practices Committee to fight racial discrimination, among other proposals to deal with reconversion and defense. Two months later, Truman called for congressional action on a five-point health program including national health insurance. Had these proposals become law in the postwar period, social welfare policies in the United States would have become quite comparable to those in other Western countries with influential labor and social democratic parties. But Truman and organized labor pushed this agenda at the height of the conservative coalition's power in Congress, during the 1940s and 1950s.

The Heyday of the Conservative Coalition

Divisions over labor issues led to the emergence of the conservative coalition, but the issues associated with World War II and reconversion made the coalition a consistent force in Congress that would play an influential policy-making role into the 1970s.[7] As table 2.1 indicates, the conservative coalition began to appear more frequently on roll call votes in the 1940s in both the House and the Senate, and it began to prevail in a higher percentage of those votes. This pattern remained fairly consistent through the 1950s. Although the conservative coalition continued to appear on a sizable percentage of roll call votes, its success rate started to fall in the early sixties, reaching a low point

Table 2.1.   Appearance and Success of Conservative Coalition

	House		Senate	
Period	Average Annual Appearances as Percentage of Nonunanimous Votes	Success Rate When It Appeared (%)	Average Annual Appearances as Percentage of Nonunanimous Votes	Success Rate When It Appeared (%)
1933–39	4	62	6	67
1940–49	23	91	15	86
1950–59	20	88	19	92
1960–64	20	58	24	54
1965–66	31	28	32	46
1967–69	36	68	31	68
1970–74	35	72	35	64
1975–79	37	60	31	59

Source: Based on calculations from data on conservative coalition roll calls in Shelley, *Permanent Majority*, 24–25, 30–31. A conservative coalition vote is one in which half or more of Southern Democrats and Republicans vote on one side of an issue and half or more of non-Southern Democrats vote on the other side.

during the height of the Great Society in the 89th Congress, only to rebound in the late sixties.

Partisan patterns diverged among the Southern and non-Southern wings of the Democratic Party over time. Many of the non-Southern Democrats who frequently voted with Republicans in the 1930s were gradually replaced in Congress by Republicans. Thus Julius Turner finds that the Democratic contingent of the conservative coalition became increasingly Southern from 1937 to 1944.[8] The prominence of Southern Democrats in the conservative coalition was due to one-party dominance in the South. The conservative districts and states that produced the most faithful Southern members of the conservative coalition would have likely elected Republicans had those districts and states been in areas with a competitive two-party system. As conservative Democrats from regions outside the South were pushed out of Congress, non-Southern Democrats became more unified on conservative coalition roll call votes, as indicated in table 2.2.[9] Most non-Southern Democrats were increasingly tied to the labor-liberal constituencies of the party, which fostered greater cohesion on conservative coalition votes, peaking at the height of the Great Society. But while Southerners, even liberal Southerners, voted as a solid block in opposition to civil rights policies and were fairly unified in their opposition to pro-

Table 2.2. Cohesion on Conservative Coalition Votes of
Southern versus Non-Southern Democrats

Period	House		Senate	
	Average Annual Cohesion of Southern Democrats	Average Annual Cohesion of Non-Southern Democrats	Average Annual Cohesion of Southern Democrats	Average Annual Cohesion of Non-Southern Democrats
1933–39	76	69	63	62
1940–49	77	76	72	72
1950–59	75	84	71	73
1960–64	69	87	76	79
1965–66	69	88	73	82
1967–69	77	83	76	74
1970–74	74	77	77	79
1975–79	69	75	75	76

Source: Based on calculations from data on conservative coalition roll calls provided by Shelley, *Permanent Majority.* Cohesion is the average percentage of representatives in each category who voted together on conservative coalition votes.

labor policies, they were more divided on most other policies favored by liberal Democrats. The cohesion among Southern Democrats was typically lower than among non-Southern Democrats, particularly among House members, after 1950. Many Southern Democrats were torn between party loyalty and constituency pressures, which varied between Southerners and non-Southerners. While middle-class voters turned out at roughly equal rates across the country, working-class voters turned out at considerably lower rates in the South, producing more conservative districts.[10] As a result, the Southerners were often a "swing" group that determined whether a policy would succeed or fail based on the percentage that decided to side with the rest of the party.[11]

Analyses of congressional roll call votes to determine which areas of public policy were subject to the conservative coalition's influence have produced varied findings depending on the time period examined and the breakdown of issue areas. V. O. Key found that the conservative coalition did not appear on most policies in the selected Congresses he examined from 1933 to 1945.[12] In contrast, looking at selected congressional sessions from 1921 through 1964, Turner found the conservative coalition to be active on a range of issues including labor, immigration, internal security, housing, monetary and fiscal policy, and states' rights.[13] Looking at all congressional sessions from 1933 to 1980,

Mark C. Shelley also found the conservative coalition active on a number of categories of issues from international involvement to social welfare, with the greatest impact on government management of the economy, regulation of labor unions, federal budgets, and federalism.[14] Looking at 150 roll call votes from 1933 to 1950 and using a more refined division of issue categories, Katznelson, Kim Geiger, and Daniel Kryder found the conservative coalition to be influential only in the area of labor policy, with the two wings of the Democratic Party surprisingly cooperative on welfare state, fiscal, regulatory, and planning issues during this period.[15] A major limitation of roll call analysis, acknowledged by most of these scholars, is that it misses the substantial influence of the conservative coalition exerted in other stages of the legislative process. The case studies in this chapter suggest that roll call analysis significantly underestimates the coalition's influence on labor's agenda.

In addition to the Rules Committee discussed in the previous chapter, the conservative coalition benefited from several institutions in the legislative process that often hurt labor's interests. The heyday of the power of the conservative coalition and that of congressional committees overlapped in the "era of committee government," in which the committees did most of the work of legislating. Which committee a bill was referred to and the ideology of its membership as well as its chair could determine whether the bill was reported out and in what form. Some committees defended labor, while others were very hostile. Further hurting labor's position, seniority governed the selection of committee chairs during this period, a system that evolved in part to suppress factional conflicts in the parties.[16] Southern Democrats faced less electoral competition in the one-party region until the 1970s and thus served more terms and built up greater seniority. As a result, the seniority system often gave some of labor's most ardent foes a privileged position in the legislative process. As a New York City labor leader declared in calling for congressional reform in the mid-sixties, these Southern chairs were "elected by a handful of lilywhite Southern votes." Yet each could "bottle up legislation—even legislation proposed by a President—and keep it from coming to a vote of the Congress."[17] Even when legislation opposed by the conservative coalition managed to make it to the floor, the coalition often prevailed because its experienced leaders had a better understanding of how to manipulate parliamentary procedures to their advantage. As Speaker Sam Rayburn (TX) noted to freshman congressman and future AFL-CIO lobbyist Andy Biemiller when he arrived in Washington in 1944, "We have virtually nobody from the North or West that knows the rules. Only the southerners know the rules, and I'm having troubles."[18] Conference committees, required to resolve differences in legislation between the House and the Senate, were another veto point in the legislative process whereby a victory in one chamber could be undermined by the intransigence of the other chamber's conferees. The conservative coalition was so successful in these realms in the House that its members in the Senate rarely needed to resort to filibusters before the mid-1960s.[19]

In order to give a more comprehensive picture of the impact of both legislative institutions and the conservative coalition on labor's policy agenda, the remainder of this chapter traces major policies from the time they were proposed through each stage of the legislative process. The conservative coalition did not always exert its influence through the institutions discussed above. Sometimes it controlled floor majorities and shaped bills such as the minimum wage through the regular amendment process on the floor. In contrast, legislation like health care never got a roll call vote because it died in committee. But in other cases, such as the full-employment bill, the committee the bill was referred to in the House, the Rules Committee, and the conference committee all worked to undermine labor's goals even though the bill reflected overwhelming support from all quarters on final passage. Sometimes welfare state measures failed and sometimes they passed. But the fingerprints of the conservative coalition were always left on the policies that made it into law. Careful analysis shows that the conservative coalition successfully fought a range of policies that might increase the power of the executive branch relative to Congress, increase the power of the federal government over the states or the local labor force, or increase the power of organized labor. All these factors were reflected in the full-employment bill, which was one of the first major domestic proposals taken up by Congress in the postwar period.

The Full-Employment Struggle

Interest in government planning to avert unemployment rose with the end of the war, the cancellation of defense contracts, and the return of soldiers to the civilian workforce in 1945. The first proposal for full employment through Keynesian-style national investments was produced by the National Farmers' Union with the assistance of Alvin Hansen, the premier American economist associated with Keynes's theories and a former economist for the National Resources Planning Board (NRPB). The NRPB developed plans for an "American

Beveridge Plan" in the Roosevelt administration comparable to Great Britain's postwar blueprint for an expanded welfare state.[20] In January 1945, Senate War Contracts Subcommittee chairman Senator James Murray (D-MT) introduced a more comprehensive full-employment proposal cosponsored by a bipartisan coalition of liberals. The bill's opening statement echoed Roosevelt's language in the Economic Bill of Rights: "All Americans able to work and seeking work have the *right* to a useful and remunerative job in the industries, or shops, or offices, or farms, or mines of the nation."[21] To ensure this right, the president would develop a "National Production and Employment Budget" to achieve full employment by adjusting government spending and programs in accordance with economic forecasts. Building on the corporatist model of economic mobilization for the two world wars, the executive branch would consult major stakeholders such as business, agriculture, and labor in the planning process. Anticipating the concerns of conservatives who feared the growth of the executive branch at the expense of Congress, the bill provided for a Joint Committee on the Budget in Congress to study and report on the president's proposals.

Organized labor emerged as the major supporter of full-employment legislation. Initially the support was qualified and lukewarm. In contrast to the AFL's old business unionism approach, leaders of the AFL now expressed the belief that the government bore a responsibility to ensure full employment, while the left wing of the CIO favored planning by industry councils composed of representatives of labor and management. However, the AFL was suspicious that the full-employment legislation was the brainchild of its rival the CIO and thus had some reservations.[22] Some labor leaders also questioned whether an effective full-employment policy could pass Congress and feared the legislation might crowd out more pressing and feasible proposals such as a national system of unemployment insurance.[23] Labor support for the bill grew as it appeared more politically viable, as rank-and-file support for full employment became apparent, and as the employment picture turned bleaker with the end of the war. Moreover, the rivalry between the federations encouraged both to support the full-employment bill out of fear that the other would gain prestige by pushing it. Representatives of the CIO and the AFL, as well as the independent UMW and the various railway unions, testified in favor of the bill and worked for passage. In the first major legislative battle in which the AFL and CIO coordinated their activities, both labor federations joined the Continuations Group, a coalition of dozens of organizations operating to pass the legislation that included the National Farmers' Union, the NAACP, and the American Veterans Committee.

Murray's proposal moved fairly easily through the Senate. The bill was referred to a hospitable committee, the Banking and Currency Committee, chaired by Senator Wagner, the author of the NLRA, and reported favorably with few substantive changes. On the Senate floor a series of amendments softened the language of the bill and reduced the rhetorical commitment of the federal government to do everything in its power to ensure full employment. But the technical and administrative provisions of the bill were barely touched.[24] It was approved on the Senate floor by the large margin of 71–10 in September 1945, three weeks after Truman submitted his twenty-one-point program.

The interest group opposition to full-employment legislation was caught off guard by Senate action and moved quickly to undermine the bill in the House. Major opponents were the National Association of Manufacturers; local Chambers of Commerce (although the national president supported the bill and essentially recused himself from lobbying on it); the American Farm Bureau, which represented large farmers; and the conservative ideological organization the Committee for Constitutional Government. The opposition argued that the bill made unrealistic promises, reflected unsound economic theories, restricted free enterprise, encouraged totalitarianism, and was thus un-American.

The opposition also tried to associate full-employment legislation with what it depicted as the growing and dangerous power of organized labor. A bulletin by the Ohio Chamber of Commerce distributed to its members and placed in the congressional record of the hearings in the House reflects this sentiment. It noted that the CIO-PAC was creating "fake" "unemployment crisis propaganda" and asserted:

The Communist-sparked C.I.O.-P.A.C. aided by its political fellow travelers, is now making the drive which has been in preparation for years. Everything that has happened up to now has been but a preliminary.

This is the hour, almost the moment, of historic decision. The basic goal of C.I.O.-P.A.C. is to overturn our system of competitive, private enterprise and substitute for it complete government control over capital and labor alike. . . .

Keystone of the new group of "crisis" legislative enactments, devised by the same cunning brains that have guided this boasted bloodless revolution, is the full employment bill, now being seriously considered in Washington.

Labeled in fraud and deception as a bill designed to preserve private enterprise, if enacted, it would be the scaffold on which private enterprise could be dropped to its death.

The alarmist bulletin concluded, "If the C.I.O.-P.A.C. Federal legislative program succeeds, the Government moves in as the new management of your company."[25] This attack was especially effective in building support among small and medium-size companies that were least likely to be organized and perhaps feared unions most of all. The opposition of the Farm Bureau was rooted in the fear that full employment would make it impossible to recruit cheap farm labor, especially if the government was willing to fund decent-paying public works projects to keep employment high.

The bill faced more challenges in the House than in the Senate. The first obstacle emerged in committee. Instead of being referred to the House Banking and Currency Committee or the House Labor Committee, the full-employment bill was referred to the House Committee on Expenditures in the Executive Departments, which had jurisdiction over the Budget Bureau. As a UAW staffer would later note, "The history of the bill and its final form would have been substantially better if it had been handled by the more liberal Banking and Currency Committee."[26] The Committee on Expenditures was weighted with conservatives, and its chairman, Carter Manasco of Alabama, was very conservative and antilabor. The CIO's evaluation of Manasco's voting record in 1946 found that on twelve issues of interest to the CIO Manasco voted in favor of the CIO's position only once.[27] The Truman administration realized that the full-employment bill faced trouble in committee and tried to secure the support of Southern Democrats Manasco, William Whittington of Mississippi, and Joseph Mansfield of Texas. While Mansfield appeared open to an appeal to party loyalty, Manasco and Whittington demanded considerable concessions from the administration. The two finally promised they would report some form of a full-employment bill out of committee but it would not be the Senate bill or the House bill as introduced and might not even include the phrase "full employment."[28] The Truman administration conceded, realizing this might be the only way to move the bill to the House floor. Once a bill made it through the House, the administration would have another shot at pushing a stronger bill in conference committee. As Manasco presided over committee hearings in October, Truman went on the air and publicly reprimanded the committee for delaying the bill, and he put pressure on the House leadership to pass it by Thanksgiving. At the completion of the hearings in early November, the full committee rejected the House bill as introduced and appointed a subcommittee—consisting of Manasco, Whittington, conservative Republican Clare Hoffman, liberal Republican George Bender, and liberal Democrat John Cochran—to write a substitute version.

The subcommittee transformed the bill. The language recognizing the *right* to employment and the obligation of the government to ensure full employment by commanding all necessary federal resources was eliminated. Instead, the new bill recognized that the government should aim for a "high" level of employment, production, and purchasing power and avoid economic fluctuations through spending on public works and loans. But it also mandated that the government avoid competition with private enterprise. To minimize the role of the executive branch, the president's National Production and Employment Budget was eliminated and its purposes scaled back. Instead, a report on general economic activity was to be prepared by a three-member Council of Economic Advisors (CEA) subject to Senate confirmation. The emasculation of the bill's provisions under the conservative committee chairman became known as the "Manasco-lation" of full-employment legislation.[29] Although a number of more liberal committee members were disappointed by the attenuated bill, only four diehard conservatives voted against it, and the substitute was reported favorably.

The full House took up the measure, now named the Employment Act of 1946 rather than the *Full* Employment Act, in mid-December. The Rules Committee shaped the final outcome by granting Manasco's request to put two of the members most hostile to a strong full-employment bill in control of floor debate and to bar a roll call vote on the Senate bill or the House bill as originally introduced. Liberals would have to vote for the gutted bill or have no bill at all. The Truman administration supported the substitute again, hoping to strengthen it in conference. Ultimately it passed 255–126 and headed to conference with the Senate. It had the support of 90% of Democrats and 36% of Republicans. The real strength of the conservative coalition is not apparent in this roll call because its members scaled the bill back to something they could accept before it ever reached the floor.

The conference committee was roughly split between liberals and conservatives, with the Senate delegation biased in favor of a stronger bill and the House delegation (the same members of the House subcommittee who formulated the House substitute bill) biased in favor of a weak bill. Because the conservative members, particularly Manasco and Hoffman, preferred no bill to a strong bill, the liberals, who were eager to see a bill passed, bore the burden of compromise.

Thus the final product resembled the weaker House bill more than the stronger Senate bill. The original proposal's declarations of a right to a job and the federal government's obligation and ability to ensure that one was available were considerably scaled back. In votes that again did not reveal the power of the conservative coalition in shaping the outcome, the bill passed the House 320–84 and the Senate without opposition. It was signed by Truman in February 1946.

The failure to pass a strong full-employment bill and the watered-down version that finally did pass suggested that the national government would never develop the capacity to plan and implement full-employment policy. Instead, taxing and spending policies would be coordinated haphazardly, and oftentimes ineffectively, through periodic negotiation between the president and Congress. Improvements in workers' income security programs were handled in much the same way.

Incrementalism in Workers' Income Security Programs

In his twenty-one-point program, Truman proposed building on the protections for workers' incomes established during the New Deal. He called for creating federal standards for the joint federal-state unemployment compensation system, improving the minimum wage, and expanding the Social Security program to cover disability. These were three of the highest priorities for the labor movement. Over the course of the Truman and Eisenhower administrations, there were incremental improvements in each of these programs. As had been true even at the height of the New Deal, the key to successful compromises was state discretion in the administration of programs or limitations on the categories of workers covered or a combination of both. These compromises attracted enough members of the conservative coalition to pass, but in doing so, they often fell short of labor's goals.

Improving the Unemployment Compensation System

Organized labor has consistently advocated a strong federal role in and federal standards for the unemployment compensation system, whereas conservatives have supported maximum control by the states. Established as part of the 1935 Social Security Act, the unemployment insurance program is based on a payroll tax collected by the federal government and distributed to the states to run their own programs. States have wide discretion in determining which employees are covered and the duration and amount of benefits. Southern and poorer states tend to have less generous systems than those in the Northeast and industrial West, where labor is strongest. In the mid-1940s, liberals saw nationalization of the unemployment system as central to a comprehensive welfare state that would provide security to all workers regardless of their region or occupation. Reflecting this goal, three congressmen—NLRA author Senator Wagner, full-employment-bill sponsor Senator Murray, and Representative John Dingell (D-MI)—introduced a legislative package that included a national unemployment system, a disability insurance program, and national health care, which went nowhere in Congress. In 1945, Truman called for emergency action to expand the unemployment program's coverage and to improve benefits in anticipation of high unemployment during the reconversion period. But the conservative coalition on the House Ways and Means Committee killed a weakened bill extending the duration of benefits passed by the Senate.[30] The only action Congress took on the issue during the Truman administration actually made it harder for the federal government to enforce the limited federal standards in place.[31]

Although Congress continued to reject federal standards, additional workers were covered under the unemployment program during the Eisenhower administration, and a pattern developed of repeated short-term extensions in benefits to deal with cyclical surges in unemployment. In 1954, in the first major change to the program since it was created twenty years earlier, Congress rejected Eisenhower's call to modernize the program through a significant expansion in coverage but incorporated federal government employees and more small businesses.[32] In 1958, in the midst of a recession, the AFL-CIO and Senator John F. Kennedy (D-MA) made a major push for federal standards to extend the duration of benefits and coverage.[33] As a result of the conservative coalition's actions on the floor of both the House and the Senate, the final bill authorized federal loans to states that *chose* to extend the duration of benefit payments, thus preserving the states' autonomy in administering the program. Echoing the criticisms of the Employment Act of 1946, Senator Kennedy observed, "As a solution to the economic problems caused by widespread unemployment [the bill] is completely ineffective. It offers the illusion of assistance . . . without the substance of effective help."[34] The following year, Kennedy again led an effort to create federal standards for the system, and the AFL-CIO held a high-profile conference in Washington to call attention to the plight of the unemployed, but congressional action was limited to a three-month extension of the temporary provisions of the 1958 legislation. This pattern of emergency extensions and limited expansions of coverage continued into the twenty-first century as the unemployment compensation system became too outdated in most states to protect a changing workforce.

Expanding the Fair Labor Standards Act

While Southerners could fend off uniform national standards in the unemployment compensation system, they had already lost the battle for regional wage differentials in the passage of the original FLSA. So they concentrated on keeping the minimum wage low and restricting the number of workers covered by it. Minimum wage legislation ultimately became law during the Truman administration with overwhelming support. But the scope of the final bill was considerably scaled back from what the president, liberals, and organized labor advocated, and it took four years to pass. Truman's first effort was killed by the House Rules Committee, and the second effort succeeded only under threat of a discharge petition.[35] The bill finally passed 361–35, following a series of procedural maneuvers that amended the bill to *reduce*—rather than expand—minimum wage coverage from what it was in the existing law but kept the administration's proposed wage increase intact. Under pressure from Senate conferees, the final bill scaled back the number of workers who would lose coverage. A reduction in coverage was the price supporters had to pay to get a substantial increase in the minimum wage. Labor leaders praised the limited accomplishments in the bill but vowed to return to fight another day.[36] As with the Employment Act of 1946, the final bill received overwhelming support in the roll call, but only after the conservative coalition had shaped the bill in committee, on Rules, and in conference.

Similar struggles over the minimum wage occurred in the Eisenhower administration. In the pattern of incremental expansion that became the norm for minimum wage legislation, the wage was increased again, but despite Eisenhower's support, coverage was not expanded. By 1959, still only one-third of the labor force was covered by the FLSA.[37] Senator Kennedy, who had become a leading advocate of labor's causes, introduced a minimum wage bill based on the AFL-CIO's recommendations in 1960, but it died in conference committee. The chairman of the Rules Committee refused to send the bill to conference until he was assured that the conferees would insist on the watered-down House version. Senate conferees—under pressure from the AFL-CIO—refused to sacrifice extended coverage.[38] This time labor and its congressional allies figured they would have a better shot at a good bill after the 1960 elections.

Social Security Disability

The one policy area in which labor was relatively, if belatedly, satisfied was Social Security, which gradually grew into a comprehensive social insurance program protecting almost all workers from poverty in old age and disability. Both the Truman administration and organized labor tried but failed to expand Social Security coverage and benefits in the 1940s. However, during the 1950s, the Social Security program grew with every Congress, embodying the incrementalism that has been so characteristic of policy development in the United States. Support for the popular old-age program became more bipartisan and widespread among business, the states, and the insurance industry.[39] Amendments to the Social Security Act in 1950 produced the most significant expansion of coverage in the program's history, and benefits were substantially increased.[40] Benefits were increased again in 1952, and coverage was made almost universal in 1954.[41]

Expanding coverage to disability proved more daunting. While organized labor was the most powerful advocate of expanding the program, the American Medical Association (AMA) was the most powerful opponent.[42] Doctors feared that government involvement in the determination of disability was a slippery slope toward government intervention in the field of medicine. Despite the AMA's influence, the House included a disability provision in its version of the 1950 amendments. Indicating the influence of institutions, the measure likely survived because the Rules Committee, under pressure from the Speaker of the House, reported the bill under a closed rule, which prohibited amendments on the House floor. The Speaker was able to use the threat of the recently adopted twenty-one-day rule (discussed in Chapter 4), which allowed the House to bypass a committee if it bottled up the bill for twenty-one days.[43] But the disability provision was dropped at the insistence of Senate members of the conference committee.[44] However, as a compromise the bill established federal grants to the states to provide assistance to the needy disabled, which was agreeable to Southerners because it preserved state control over the distribution of benefits. This proved to be an opening wedge. The 1954 amendments preserved old-age insurance rights for covered workers who became permanently disabled, reflecting one of the first defeats for the AMA.[45] The conservative coalition was once again divided because the bill left the determination of disability up to the states. In 1956, the newly merged AFL-CIO made disability coverage its top priority because lobbyists were convinced it was politically feasible.[46] A compromise that covered workers over age fifty and left the determination of eligibility to the states passed the House.[47] The Senate Finance Committee refused to accept the measure, but AFL-CIO president George Meany convinced the chairman, Walter George (D-GA), a stalwart of the conservative coalition, to sponsor an amendment on the floor to add the disability provision.[48] Historian Edward Berkowitz suggests that George was open to Meany's appeal because local craft workers stood by him when he was targeted by Roosevelt's 1938 purge. Majority Leader Lyndon Johnson (TX) closely coordinated the floor vote with Nelson Cruikshank, then the director of the AFL-CIO Social Security Department, giving him an hour to round up 6 necessary votes.[49] The bill narrowly passed (47–45) over the Eisenhower administration's opposition because the conservative coalition was once again split. While only 14% of Republicans voted for the amendment, 76% of Southern Democrats did.[50] All but one non-Southern Democrat voted for it. It was not the fully federal, universal disability program that Roosevelt, Truman, and labor once favored but rather, as Berkowitz observes, "an amalgam of New Deal aspirations and postwar realities."[51] Four years later, disability coverage was extended to workers under age fifty without much debate, finally filling a major hole in the social safety net long targeted by organized labor. The successes in the incremental expansion of Social Security contrasted with the deadlock on national health insurance during the same time period.

The Push for National Health Insurance

Perhaps no policy better illustrates the disconnect between the policy goals of organized labor and the political reality it confronted in the postwar period than the pursuit of health care reform in the late 1940s. Conservatives were fundamentally opposed to a universal government-financed health care system, whereas labor-liberals were unwilling at this point to accept a system based on private insurance. In the first battle over universal health care, one of many that would take place over the next sixty years, legislative institutions like the Rules Committee did not kill any particular bill. Instead, the advocates of a national health insurance system did not have enough votes in committee—and in all likelihood on the floor—for their plan, and no other compromise could attract a viable legislative coalition. Not enough players, including organized labor, were willing to make concessions, and legislation failed to clear the first hurdle in the legislative process because of the unity of the conservative coalition's opposition.

The First Legislative Battles

Organized labor has been one of the most influential and enduring advocates of universal health care. Although the AFL initially opposed government-sponsored health insurance as part of Gompers's "pure and simple unionism," it later changed its position. In 1938, AFL president William Green announced the federation would work in the states to amend existing accident compensation programs to include health insurance. In the 1940s, as with unemployment compensation, organized labor endorsed the nationalization of social insurance programs to avoid regional and state variation. The AFL was joined by the CIO in its call for a national health insurance program. Both Green and representatives of the CIO participated in the development of the national health insurance provisions of a series of Wagner-Murray-Dingell bills. Supporters of the first version, referred to House and Senate committees controlled by the conservative coalition, knew it had no realistic chance of passage in the 78th Congress (1943–44) but hoped to use it to build momentum for a postwar domestic program.[52]

In an effort to win the loyalty of labor-liberals and make his own mark on social policy, Truman called for congressional action in 1945 on a plan of federally funded hospital construction, expanded public health programs, medical research, and medical education along with two social insurance programs: one for replacement of lost wages due to sickness or disability, and the other to provide a program of national health insurance funded through Social Security taxes.[53] Introduced in another Wagner-Murray-Dingell bill, the national health insurance plan's financing provisions were written so that it could be referred to the Education and Labor Committee, chaired by Senator Murray, rather than the more conservative Finance Committee. But even this committee failed to report a bill before the Republicans took over Congress in the 1946 elections. National health insurance became a major issue in the 1948 campaign when Truman railed against the "do nothing" Congress and accused Republicans of allying with the AMA—which had been highly critical of Truman's proposal—to obstruct health care reform. Even though Democrats picked up seats, the conservative coalition still held the balance of power, and Truman's plan fared no better. Once again, health care reform died in committee. Although Truman never abandoned his proposal for national health insurance, the Democrats lost seats in the 1950 elections, and the conservative coalition emerged even stronger.

In a pattern that would continue to characterize battles over health reform for the rest of the century, there were deep divisions over how to approach the issue. These divisions appeared on the first day of hearings on the Wagner-Murray-Dingell bill when Senator Taft interrupted Murray's opening remarks to assert that Murray's health care bill, like his full-employment bill, came straight out of the Soviet constitution. Taft later sponsored a bill providing grants to the states to offer health coverage for those who could not afford it. Other proposals built on the developing system of private health insurance. Democratic senator Lister Hill of Alabama joined Republican senator George Aiken in introducing a bill to provide federal assistance to the states to subsidize private insurance premiums for low-income people. A pair of Republicans senators, Ralph Flanders (R-VT) and Irving Ives (R-NY), introduced a bill to set up locally managed private insurance systems with premiums scaled to participants' incomes. Organized labor and most liberal advocates of national health insurance were adamantly opposed to such private-sector plans. The most promising effort at compromise, which even gained the support of organized labor, occurred in late 1947 when advocates of national health insurance, hoping to go into the 1948 elections with a unified Democratic position, entered into negotiations with Southern Democrats on a plan to set up compulsory health insurance for lower-income groups under Social Security and allow upper-income groups to obtain private insurance.[54] These negotiations broke down the following spring after Truman made it clear he planned to pursue the issue of civil rights. Although the public appeared open to both government and private-sector approaches, no reform proposal had enough support in Congress to make it out of committee.[55] Without a compromise that could draw some support from the conservative coalition while retaining the backing of labor-liberals, health care reform had no chance of passing.

The same dynamic on health care was also apparent in the Eisenhower administration. Hoping to induce private insurers to offer coverage of vulnerable populations, Eisenhower proposed a reinsurance plan in which the government would pick up catastrophic health care costs.[56] The AMA denounced the bill as a step in the direction of socialized medicine, while the AFL, the CIO, and other liberal groups criticized the bill as wholly inadequate. When the reinsurance proposal reached the House floor in 1954, the overwhelming majority of Democrats and more than a third of Republicans voted to recommit it.[57] Diehard conservatives in both parties voted against the bill because they did not want the government interfering with private insurance, while liberal Democrats voted against it because they favored a more comprehensive approach. However, labor and most Democrats did support an Eisenhower proposal to codify the exemption of employer-provided health insurance from taxes, which ultimately encouraged the growth of private health insurance.[58] Successful legislative coalitions were also built behind bills in both the Truman and Eisenhower administrations to expand government-subsidized hospital construction and medical research. But a compromise on health care coverage proved elusive.[59]

Lessons from the Health Care Fight

The strength of interest group opposition to national health care and the weakness of interest group support—primarily organized labor—are often cited as major factors in the failure of health reform during the Truman years.[60] The powerful AMA, with locally prominent and politically active doctors in every congressional district, fought national health insurance tooth and nail. The AMA was joined by other organizations that had a stake in fending off national health insurance, such as the nonprofit and commercial health insurance providers that proliferated in the early to mid-forties including the American Hospital Association, which provided Blue Cross / Blue Shield plans. Influential business groups such as the Chamber of Commerce also opposed the bill on general principles as anti–free enterprise and un-American. Interest group opponents of national health insurance were particularly effective in tapping into the rising red scare by identifying the proposal with socialist and Communist influence. To counter these groups, supporters of national health insurance formed the Committee for the Nation's Health (CNH), a coalition of labor, farm, minority, and consumer organizations plus a liberal, splinter group of doctors that supported greater government involvement in health care. The AFL and the CIO were two of the more active members, and they made extensive efforts to build the support of their memberships and the general public for national health insurance. But the spending of the AMA to fight the proposal dwarfed that of the CNH and other national health insurance supporters.

However, as several scholars have pointed out, the interest group opposition alone was not determinative of the outcome on national health insurance.[61] Groups like the AMA were influential because their interests coincided with those of pivotal players in Congress and other interest groups such as business.[62] Republicans were vociferously opposed to Truman's domestic agenda, and conservative rural and Southern Democrats were unwilling to go along with what they saw as legislation geared to Truman's urban and labor constituencies. Southern Democrats were also concerned about the attention to equality of access to health care in Truman's proposals and supported his hospital construction bill only after securing provisions protecting segregated facilities.[63] Thus, committees with majorities hostile to national health insurance were quite receptive to the arguments of interest group opponents. In other fights, such as the struggle over disability policy, the AMA's opposition was overcome because the proponents of reform made concessions that broke the unity of the conservative coalition. But this did not happen in the struggle over national health insurance.

Labor responded to the lack of movement on national health insurance in two ways. As detailed in the next chapter, organized labor increasingly sought to negotiate private health insurance benefits through collective bargaining, and it shifted to a focus on more incremental reforms, recognizing the need to accommodate to political reality. In a fight within the CNH in early 1950 over the coalition's strategy, the AFL and CIO tipped the balance in favor of continued focus on lobbying for national health insurance instead of shifting to more obtainable but less comprehensive goals as advocated by some groups. However, after the 1950 elections and particularly after the 1952 election of Eisenhower, attention within the labor movement and other reform circles turned to incremental proposals. This shift in attention would later result in the push for Medicare, which picked up momentum in the late fifties and early sixties. As Jacob Hacker has emphasized, institutions are central to the evolution of policy, but so are the timing and sequence of events.[64] The failure of national health insurance in the 1940s largely foreclosed the chance of ever adopting universal, comprehensive, government-funded single-payer health care because the subsequent growth of private insurance in the absence of a government program shut off that option. Universal health care might still be possible, but it was likely to build on, rather than replace, the existing system. However, it would be decades before labor would fully back away from its support of a single-payer system.

Continuing Influence of the Conservative Coalition on Labor Law

As with health care reform, liberals and conservatives were drawn to a stalemate on labor law reform for a little over a decade. Liberals could not repeal Taft-Hartley, and conservatives could not pass greater restrictions on organized labor. But in contrast to the stalemate on health care, that on labor law was briefly and unexpectedly broken in 1959 when Congress passed the Landrum-Griffin bill—which was targeted at union corruption—in a form opposed by organized labor. But the stalemate resumed after the passage of this legislation and has held for the past fifty years.

The Effort to Repeal Taft-Hartley

Just as Republicans had viewed their election in 1946 as a mandate to curb union power, organized labor viewed the 1948 results as a mandate for repeal of Taft-Hartley.[65] But the American electoral and party systems rarely produce clear voter mandates on public policy. A congressional majority of those who had voted for Taft-Hartley in the first place returned to Congress in 1948.[66] The entire state Democratic delegations of Alabama, Arkansas, Georgia, Mississippi, North Carolina, South Carolina, Texas, and Virginia were opposed to repeal.

If the conservative coalition remained unified, there was little chance of repealing Taft-Hartley, but the Truman administration and congressional allies made an effort to reward their labor supporters. After initial disputes on strategy, the Truman administration and organized labor put together a bill to repeal Taft-Hartley while incorporating several provisions to take care of widespread concerns about particular labor abuses that had been addressed in Taft-Hartley. Unlike most of the other legislation discussed in this chapter, the House Labor and Education Committee's action on the repeal of Taft-Hartley was favorable to labor because of the composition of the committee and because it was chaired by the sponsor of the bill, Representative John Lesinksi (D-MI). However, the Rules Committee refused to grant Lesinksi's request for a closed rule, which prohibited floor amendments. The conservative coalition favored a substitute bill sponsored by Representative John S. Wood (D-GA) that would have preserved most of Taft-Hartley's provisions. House Speaker Sam Rayburn's efforts to whittle away support for the Wood bill in favor of another compromise were undermined when, in a hasty answer to a reporter's question at a press conference that angered Southern Democrats, Truman publicly claimed he would use a vote on repeal to award patronage.[67] The Wood substitute was narrowly adopted (217–203), with 66% of Southern Democrats joining 87% of Republicans in support of the bill. Only 7% of non-Southern Democrats supported the substitute. Labor and administration forces successfully maneuvered to have the substitute recommitted instead of allowing it to pass on the floor. Labor fared no better in the Senate. Senator Taft, assisted by yet another miners' strike and the support of the conservative coalition, narrowly succeeded in pushing amendments to the administration bill that would have preserved most of Taft-Hartley's provisions. The amended bill passed the Senate but died along with the Wood bill in the House Committee on Education and Labor under labor pressure. AFL president William Green argued that the failure to achieve repeal was due to the "obstructionists" in Congress and added that the "leaders of Toryism welded the surviving remnants of the Republican forces into a tight coalition with the Southern Democrats" to check the mandate of the 1948 elections.[68] Repeal of the full Taft-Hartley Act was never considered again in Congress.

Stalemate on labor law reform continued into the Eisenhower years. The administration initially indicated it was open to repeal of some Taft-Hartley provisions.[69] However, when information leaked that the administration was considering the repeal of 14(b), which permitted states to pass right-to-work laws, there was an immediate backlash among business interests. The flap ultimately led to the resignation of Eisenhower's labor secretary, and the president dropped his support for repeal. The Republican Party as a whole was far too closely allied with business interests to make it a viable vehicle for pro-labor law reform, and labor's partisan political activities minimized its influence with the administration.

The multiple veto points in the legislative process that so often benefited labor's opponents by allowing them to kill a bill could also help organized labor when it was under attack, and party loyalty occasionally worked to labor's advantage. Although liberal forces were not strong enough to push pro-labor changes to Taft-Hartley, they were strong enough to fend off pro-business changes. As they did in the aftermath of the 1946 elections, business and conservatives viewed unified Republican control of the government produced by the 1952 elections as an opportunity to further scale back the legal protections for organized labor. Conservatives on the House Committee on Education and Labor drew up proposals to expand Taft-Hartley to prohibit all union security arrangements by national law and to cede a great deal of authority over labor relations to state governments. Weak labor states could ensure they remained that way, and businesses could try to curtail labor power in another arena. Liberals on the committee rallied to labor's side, and a bill was never reported. A similar effort to grant power to the states was led in the Senate by Senator Barry Goldwater (R-AZ) in 1954. When the bill came up for a floor vote, labor lobbyists in a frenetic effort supported by then minority leader Johnson managed to muster enough votes, including those of a number of Southern Democrats, to recommit the bill and avert a floor vote.[70]

The Path to Landrum-Griffin

In the late fifties the issue of labor law reform picked up steam again. Public interest was fed by the 1954 release of the Academy Award–winning *On the Waterfront*, which focused on the corruption of the longshoremen's union. Conservatives, having been unsuccessful in passing legislation to curb labor's power, hoped to take advantage of the corruption issue.[71] In 1957 the Senate authorized a special committee to investigate union corruption headed by conservative Southern Democrat John McClellan (D-AR). The highly publicized investigations focused on the misappropriation of funds, extortion, and ties to organized crime of the Teamsters under the infamous Jimmy Hoffa and a handful of other unions. They largely ignored employers' role, instead portraying complicit employers as victims of power-hungry union leaders.[72] The growing backlash led the AFL-CIO to expel the Teamsters. The hearings also called attention to unions like the United Mine Workers, which developed under the autocratic leadership of John L. Lewis into a union with no protections or voice for the rank and file or insurgent leaders. Three-quarters of the public claimed to have heard about union corruption and racketeering in the news in 1958, and by 1959, 67% felt "the government should do a lot more to regulate the activities of labor unions."[73]

Afraid the issue of union corruption would become a problem for the Democratic Party, which conservatives portrayed as captive to labor,[74] and fearing that failure to act might lead to draconian antiunion legislation, Senator John F. Kennedy took the lead in proposing legislation to deal with the problem in both the 85th and 86th Congresses. Kennedy's legislation required unions and their officers to file public reports regarding their finances and promoted democratic procedures in the administration of unions. The main issue in terms of legislative strategy was whether a clean anticorruption bill could pass or whether conservatives and administration forces would succeed in attaching amendments closing loopholes in the Taft-Hartley Act's prohibition of secondary boycotts and banning organizational picketing, whereby unions picketed plants to try to get the workers to join. Kennedy was successful in shepherding his first bill, cosponsored with Senator Ives (R-NY), through committee and floor consideration without substantial changes. Labor grudgingly accepted the bill in the Senate but found an opportunity to stop it in the House Education and Labor Committee, where labor had successfully lobbied for the appointment of pro-labor members to vacant seats, gradually shifting the committee to the left. Pro-labor members and conservative members deadlocked and could not report a bill.[75] An effort to pass a bill on the floor under suspension of the rules, a rarely used procedure that allows a vote on a bill that has not been reported by a committee but requires a two-thirds majority to pass, was unsuccessful. Labor would not be so lucky in the 86th Congress.

A wave of liberals were elected in 1958, and organized labor had high hopes that the conservative coalition might be destabilized on a range of issues including labor law reform. The newly merged AFL-CIO planned a campaign to repeal some of the most hated Taft-Hartley provisions, including Section 14(b), in the 86th Congress. However, an unexpected turn of events in 1959 resulted not in the repeal of unfavorable provisions but in the passage of a handful of amendments to Taft-Hartley—in a bill targeting union corruption—that labor opposed. As in the previous Congress, the conservative coalition did not pose significant problems in committee on the corruption bill. Instead, trouble emerged on the House floor, where labor and liberal forces were simply outmaneuvered by the seasoned old hands of the conservative coalition.

Now clearly an aspiring presidential candidate, Kennedy joined with Senator Sam Ervin (D-NC) to introduce a new anticorruption measure in 1959 that incorporated many of the measures of Kennedy's earlier bill but added a few "sweeteners" to make it more palatable to labor. Conservatives were again determined to attach antilabor Taft-Hartley amendments to the anticorruption bill, while labor resisted compromise because it overestimated its power to stop the bill in the new Congress. After all, labor had managed to defeat the anticorruption legislation in the House in 1958, and numerous liberals had been added in the 1958 elections. Acting as labor's advocate, Kennedy preserved the sweeteners and fended off most of the proposed antilabor Taft-Hartley provisions in committee and on the Senate floor. But labor again tried to get the House to drop the bill altogether or at least reduce its scope. By the time the bill was taken up in the House, labor union leaders and lobbyists were described by Representative Richard Bolling (D-MO) as "bullish" about their legislative prospects.[76] However, as the McClellan investigations continued into the summer, picking up more newspaper headlines, Speaker Rayburn made it clear that Democrats had to get a bill.[77] Democratic leaders were concerned about the party's prospects in a presidential election year if it looked responsible for obstructing an anti-corruption bill. Labor allies in the House warned lobbyists to confront the reality that a bill was going to pass, probably with provisions that labor opposed, and they had better get into the negotiations or risk losing influence on the bill.

After extensive negotiations and debate, the House Education and Labor Committee finally reported a bill similar to the modified Senate bill on a narrow vote. Shortly thereafter, two conservative representatives, Phil Landrum (D-GA) and Robert Griffin (R-MI), introduced another bill favored by conservatives that contained the provisions dealing with secondary boycotts and organizational picketing. Dissatisfied with the committee bill, the AFL-CIO had Representative John Shelley (D-CA), a former leader of the California AFL-CIO, introduce yet another anticorruption measure. When the issue came to the floor, things moved very quickly, and neither labor lobbyists nor their allies in the House were able to keep up. With the disarray caused by a division of liberal forces between the committee bill and the AFL-CIO bill, enhanced by a lack of communication and time for building consensus, the Landrum-Griffin language was substituted for the committee bill on the House floor by a vote of 229–201. It was a tremendous victory for the conservative coalition and a big defeat for the ascendant liberal Democrats: only 6% of non-Southern Democrats voted for the substitute, compared with 78% of Southern Democrats and 89% of Republicans.[78] George Meany blamed the large numbers of Southern Democrats defecting from the party leadership's position on a deal between the Southerners and Republicans to produce the antilabor legislation in exchange for help fighting civil rights legislation.[79] After several procedural maneuvers, the bill finally passed the House by a large margin because even liberals felt they had to have a union corruption bill and this was the only option left. In conference, Kennedy struggled to soften the provisions that were most objectionable to labor and even to include new sweeteners. But the House conferees knew that Kennedy, as an aspiring presidential candidate, had to have a bill, and they barely budged. The final bill was much closer to the House version. It was through this convoluted series of events that the most liberal Congress since the mid-thirties managed to pass a labor bill staunchly opposed by organized labor.

Several lessons came out of labor's defeat on Landrum-Griffin. Liberals realized they needed to strengthen their procedural skills and information networks if they were going to successfully take on the conservative coalition. As discussed in Chapter 4, passage of Landrum-Griffin spurred the creation of the Democratic Study Group, a coalition dedicated to countering the influence of the conservative coalition by more effectively leveraging the power of House liberals in the Democratic Caucus and the legislative process. It also became clear that given labor's limited influence in the South, it was necessary to win big elsewhere in order to be able to overcome the conservative coalition on contentious labor issues. As a 1960 report from the merged AFL-CIO's electoral arm, the Committee on Political Education (COPE), noted, "Using the vote on the Landrum-Griffin substitute as a criterion, it will be necessary to reelect all incumbent liberals and gain at least 14 to obtain a liberal majority in the House."[80] But labor leaders felt that their ability to build a liberal majority was undermined by the South's role in the Democratic Party and its prominence in a series of interlocking institutions in the electoral system and the legislative process.

Labor's Increasing Frustration

The failure of Congress to act on much of the Fair Deal agenda or to repeal Taft-Hartley in Truman's second term, after labor had worked so hard to elect him and a Democratic Congress, led to growing calls for reform. Near the conclusion of the Truman administration, a report prepared by CIO president Philip Murray before his unexpected death, which was to have been presented to the CIO's convention, summed up labor's position:

> The control over the 82nd Congress by the "Dixiegop Coalition" reemphasizes the urgent need for reforms in election procedures and revision of the methods by which Congress conducts its legislative business.
>
> Anti-democratic conditions that persist in the selection of Senators and Representatives in parts of our nation, coupled with the Congressional committee tenure system, continue to concentrate power over legislation in the hands of a comparatively small number of reactionary members.

Gerrymandered Congressional Districts and widespread failure of states to re-apportion districts in accordance with population shifts are denying millions of Americans the full value of their vote. These factors, in combination with the poll tax, permit a minority of the population to control Congress and open the door to overwhelming influence on legislation by reactionary vested interests.

Labor has been made especially aware of this shortcoming through the fantas-tic make-up of the House Labor Committee, which has been dominated by mem-bers from agricultural districts who possess practically no understanding at all of the complexities of industrial relations.[81]

Labor called for civil rights legislation and reforms of the electoral process as well as reforms of congressional procedures, including the filibuster in the Sen-ate, the role of seniority in selecting members for powerful committees and committee chairs in the House, and the power of the House Rules Commit-tee. As Richard Bensel has noted, Democratic congressional leaders and non-Southern committee chairs defended the congressional committee system and seniority as a way to preserve what he terms the "bipolar coalition" of Southern and non-Southern Democrats by keeping divisive battles off the floor and be-hind closed doors.[82] While these institutions had developed in part to minimize intraparty struggles, by the 1950s, as liberals became increasingly frustrated with conservatives' use of the committee system to undermine their policy goals, these institutions became an independent source of conflict in the party.

A lengthy 1950 letter from UAW president Walter Reuther to Democratic National Committee chair William Boyle railed against House Speaker Sam Rayburn's leadership and the Senate Democratic leaders who had struggled to hold the disparate segments of the party together. The letter noted, "At some point in our political life this question of re-alignment of power within the Democratic Party must be faced up to by both labor supporters of the Fair Deal and by the Fair Deal segments within the Democratic Party."[83] Labor leaders stressed to party leaders that reforms were key to building an effective liberal coalition. Without them, labor argued, the electoral fortunes of the Democratic Party would be compromised because the party could not deliver on its prom-ises. Reuther's letter threatened, "We just cannot keep on getting out the vote for 2 and 4 years more of defeat by persons and groups who, while technically Democratic, are actually working with reactionary Republicans to defeat the program for which we seek to enlist our members' support through PAC, regis-tration and voting."[84] Reuther and others stressed that Southern obstruction on civil rights and the Fair Deal agenda was undermining the appeal of the party outside the South. Although there were many other factors involved, the 1952 elections reinforced these observations. The only states that the Democratic nominee, Adlai Stevenson, carried were in the South or the border states, and control of Congress was returned to the Republicans.

Throughout the Eisenhower administration, labor and its liberal allies argued that the cooperation of Southern Democrats with the administration undermined the Democrats' electoral appeal. Democrats debated the future of the party in the wake of the 1952 election with the Southern wing arguing that the party had moved too far to the left and the urban labor-liberal wing arguing that the party was tarnished by the power exerted by Southern conservatives. Donald Montgomery, chief lobbyist of the UAW, noted that the continued appeasement of Southern conservatives "would mean decline of the Democratic Party to a sectional status" and the triumph of the Republicans and their policies "for years to come." He implored his boss, Walter Reuther, "A determined fight must be made NOW to save the Democratic Party, not for its own sake, but for the welfare and security of the Nation and the cause of freedom everywhere."[85] Frustration among labor leaders reached a new level in the late fifties and early sixties.[86] In 1960 labor leaders, angered by inaction on their legislative program and the passage of Landrum-Griffin, again threatened Democratic officials with boycotting the 1960 elections unless the Democratic Party seriously pursued congressional reform to weaken the power of the conservative coalition.[87]

Following Kennedy's election, a 1961 AFL-CIO pamphlet entitled "Labor's Goals for a Better America" noted, "The new Administration and the new Congress have much to do in the days ahead, and much of it must be done quickly. A wide range of progressive measures has already been subjected to exhaustive hearings and thorough debate; what they need now is enactment, not further investigation. . . . Freed from the threat of Presidential veto, guided by leadership that looks forward instead of back, Congress can now enact with confidence what it knows is best for the nation."[88] The pamphlet proceeded to tick off a list of labor's legislative priorities that were stalled at some point in the legislative process. Aid to depressed areas had been vetoed twice, and a veto threat held back health benefits for the aged. Public housing and urban renewal bills had passed the Senate only to be stymied by the House Rules Committee. Eisenhower had thrice requested another labor priority, legislation to reverse a court decision that forbade certain forms of picketing on construction sites, but it died in the Rules Committee in the House and was filibustered in the Senate Labor Committee.[89] The Rules Committee also effectively killed a bill on federal aid to education when it refused to send the House-passed bill to conference with the Senate. A minimum wage bill died in conference between the House and Senate. The pamphlet also noted that "effective civil rights legislation" could never be "realistically expected" unless the filibuster rule in the Senate was altered to allow cloture to be invoked by a simple majority rather than two-thirds vote. The labor movement hoped that the Kennedy administration might finally bring about the destabilization of the conservative coalition and its hold on Congress. This did not happen. But as the next chapter explains, after Kennedy's tragic assassination, Lyndon Johnson's administration did enjoy a brief period during which the conservative coalition was temporarily overwhelmed.

Conclusion

While union membership reached its peak of 35% of the nonagricultural labor force in 1954, union density was not translated into commensurate political accomplishments.[90] After decades of concentrating on improving workers' status through collective bargaining rather than public policy, organized labor became the most powerful advocate of expansion of the welfare state in the postwar period. But the political coalition favoring a comprehensive, national, universal welfare state and pro-labor policies was not strong enough to overcome the opposition of the conservative coalition. The only measures that were successful were those that could peel off support from the conservative coalition. This typically meant incremental or targeted programs that preserved the autonomy of the states or limited coverage. In fact, this did not mark much of a break with the New Deal. The social insurance and public assistance programs in the Social Security Act, the NLRA, the FLSA, and many of the other major accomplishments of the 1930s were similarly compromised to gain Southern support. Although some scholars suggest that the liberal postwar agenda was a move to the right of the New Deal,[91] a program like universal, national health insurance moved beyond the political consensus behind most New Deal programs. Many New Deal reformers may have envisioned more far-reaching proposals, but it is not clear they ever had a chance of passing in Congress. A number of scholars mourn labor's "depoliticization" and acceptance of "consensus politics" in the forties, suggesting that if labor had been less willing to settle, it would have had a better chance of securing social democratic–style policies.[92] But given the political context, it is hard to see how this was possible. In fact, as David Plotke has suggested, "the main alternatives" were not social democracy but "well to the right" of the direction policy actually took.[93] Moreover, as indicated by labor's position on national health insurance, labor did not always move to the center in the 1940s. But lowered expectations shaped the legislative agenda going into the Great Society years.

3

Possibilities and Limits in the Great Society

After the many disappointments from the 1940s through the early 1960s, the unprecedented legislative victories of the Great Society years finally rewarded organized labor's efforts to expand the welfare state. Labor leaders attended one Rose Garden signing ceremony after another in which they watched President Lyndon Johnson sign into law legislation labor had worked on for years.[1] Many of the programs of America's unique, targeted welfare state were passed during this brief period of time. The Great Society years illustrate the pattern of American welfare state development in which the United States tends to develop programs in waves, or "big bangs."[2] The first big bang was during the New Deal as government struggled to deal with the Great Depression. The second was during the Great Society, in which Johnson built on respect for a slain President Kennedy's legacy. Large Democratic congressional majorities produced by unusual circumstances facilitated both periods of frenetic legislative action. In the mid-sixties the liberal majorities were temporarily large enough to overcome the resistance of the conservative coalition on a range of issues.

Although many of the successes of the mid-sixties were made possible by the extraordinary political environment, they also reflected the role of a more politically sophisticated labor movement. Labor is often perceived as a collection of inflexible bureaucracies incapable of adapting to political circumstances; however, organized labor did respond to the political failures of the 1940s and 1950s. Politics and political institutions, in fact, had a profound impact on the structure of the labor movement and its political agenda. In the 1940s the labor movement aspired to become an economic and political force comparable to its peers in other Western industrialized nations. But it became clear during the Truman administration that the labor movement's aspirations could not be realized unless something changed. While continuing to press for congressional reform and civil rights legislation, labor also adapted in several ways: the AFL and CIO reunited into one stronger federation that made great strides in developing its electoral, lobbying, and public policy research operations; unions pursued a range of benefits from employers that were provided by government programs in other countries; and the new AFL-CIO pushed more incremental policies compared with its agenda in the forties. The turn to collective bargaining and incrementalism in public policy was not a reflection of the exceptional, conservative nature of the American labor movement but rather a reasonable response to the difficulty of getting comprehensive welfare state policies through the legislative process.

In comparison with its ambitious agenda of a comprehensive welfare state in the 1940s, organized labor entered the 1960s with more modest immediate goals. In the area of full-employment policy, the AFL-CIO continued to call for "a rational national economic planning process" involving the "democratic participation" of key groups along with the government and the creation of a National Planning Agency.[3] Affiliated unions like the UAW continued to stress this approach.[4] But in lieu of planning, the AFL-CIO accepted a myriad of government jobs programs, public works spending, and stimulation of private-sector demand to keep the labor market tight, as well as job training for those at the bottom of the labor market.[5] Learning from the failure of national health insurance in the Truman years, labor focused on more limited but politically obtainable legislation to provide health coverage to the elderly through Medicare. In the area of labor law reform, organized labor shifted from repeal of the entire Taft-Hartley Act to repeal of its most odious provision, Section 14(b). In the AFL-CIO's approach to worker income security programs, it continued to call for the incremental improvement of the minimum wage and federal standards for the unemployment compensation system.

Despite the surge of legislation in the Johnson years, there were still limits on labor's achievements. Given the size of the liberal majorities, the role of institutions in undermining labor's position was more definitive. Legislative institutions restricted liberals' power in the forties and fifties, but there were many instances in which labor lost because its position was not supported by congressional majorities, at least not in both chambers. During the 1960s, obstruction by a reformed Rules Committee declined considerably, but the influence of other powerful House committees, like Ways and Means, became more apparent, particularly in slowing down the passage of Medicare and opposing federal standards for unemployment compensation. While the filibuster was finally overcome on civil rights legislation (discussed in Chapter 4), it emerged as a powerful obstacle to labor law reform. Minimum wage is the only policy considered here that moved through the legislative process relatively unscathed. In short, a unified conservative coalition could still effectively challenge labor's goals through several institutions in the legislative process even during the heyday of the Great Society.

This chapter demonstrates both the possibilities and the enduring constraints on labor's influence in the policy-making process. It first explores the factors that led to the destabilization of the conservative coalition's influence over policy making. It then looks at the ways the labor movement responded to the political failures of the 1940s and 1950s and how it became a more effective political actor on the national stage. Finally, the chapter looks at labor's efforts to pass Medicare, repeal 14(b) of the Taft-Hartley Act, and improve the minimum wage and unemployment compensation systems.

Destabilization of the Conservative Coalition

After dominating domestic policy making over two decades, the conservative coalition began to lose influence in the 1960s as the labor-liberal wing of the Democratic Party grew in Congress. The non-Southern contingent of the Democratic Caucus in the House surged in the 1958 elections, contracted slightly during the Kennedy years, and surged again in the 1964 elections (table 3.1). The percentage of non-Southern Democrats would never again fall below 60%. The conservative coalition's success on roll call votes fell considerably during the Kennedy years and reached a low in the 89th Congress (1965–66) of 28% on the House floor and 46% on the Senate floor (see table 2.1).

Despite the declining success of the conservative coalition on the floor in

Table 3.1.   Rise of Non-Southern Democrats within the House Democratic Caucus

Year	Total Number of Democrats	Non-Southern Percentage
1945	242	52
1947	188	39
1949	263	55
1951	234	50
1953	213	48
1955	232	53
1957	234	53
1959	283	61
1961	263	58
1963	250	59
1965	294	66
1967	247	63
1969	246	64
1971	255	65
1973	243	65
1975	290	69
1977	292	69
1979	276	69

Source: Based on calculations from data in Shelley, *Permanent Majority*, table 8-1.

the early sixties, the Kennedy years remained a period of intense frustration for organized labor.[6] Kennedy's election raised labor's expectations, but as a report by the Textile Workers Union noted, "The election did not change the archaic rules under which Congress operates or fails to operate—rules which make it comparatively easy for the conservative coalition to block progress."[7] While many Southerners cooperated with the administration on controversial legislation dealing with taxes, farm subsidies, trade, and the national debt, they continued to buck the party line on labor and minimum wage bills.[8] Although the coalition was less successful on roll calls, it continued to obstruct and shape legislation and the legislative agenda in the committee process. Even in the committee process, change was starting to take place. Under pressure from liberal House members and groups like organized labor, the House Rules Committee was expanded in 1961 to allow the appointment of additional liberals. Loyal Democrats were also placed in vacant seats on Ways and Means and Appropriations, two of the most important committees.[9] But key bills of interest to labor in Kennedy's legislative program still stalled.

After working so hard to mobilize union members in the 1960 election, labor leaders feared that lower-level activists would become disillusioned with the political process. The AFL-CIO distributed a pamphlet to local union leaders to encourage them to explain to union members the numerous obstacles to progressive legislation with the goal of invigorating grassroots political participation. The pamphlet opened with the question: "Why can't a popular President with a Congressional majority carry through his legislative program? This question is being asked by many union members. If the answers they get do not create an understanding of the political problems involved in the legislative process, the result may be apathy and disillusionment. If, on the other hand, we understand WHY legislation we support is bogged down, we can work effectively to eliminate the roadblocks."[10] The pamphlet explained the legislative process and detailed seven "Roadblocks to Liberal Legislation." These roadblocks are virtually the same as those identified in this book: the conservative coalition in Congress, overrepresentation of rural areas, seniority control of committees, the power of committee chairs, the power of the House Rules Committee, the Senate filibuster, and, finally, lack of public concern. The AFL-CIO's 1963 evaluation of Congress noted, "Too often Congress fails to meet urgent public needs because these antiquated, outdated rules and procedures give unwarranted, unjustifiable veto power to a conservative minority."[11] These roadblocks would be temporarily overcome in several policy areas during the early Johnson years.

Although the labor movement was initially skeptical of Lyndon Johnson when he assumed the presidency following Kennedy's assassination in 1963, he emerged as one of the strongest presidential allies of organized labor in American history, perhaps the strongest. The Democratic surge in the 1964 elections put both labor and Johnson in an advantageous position. After the election, George Meany observed that "to a greater degree than ever before in the history of this country, the stated goals of the administration and of Congress, on one hand, and of the labor movement, on the other, are identical."[12]

Although Johnson's legislative skills no doubt played a role in the administration's victories, his greater legislative success compared with Kennedy's was primarily a result of the larger Democratic majority—and the larger percentage of non-Southerners in this majority—in the 89th Congress. The party unity of non-Southern Democrats remained roughly the same over the Kennedy-Johnson years, while the party unity of Southern Democrats actually declined.[13] Not only did the number of loyal Democrats make floor majorities possible, but the size of the Democratic majority changed the committee ratios, enabling the appointment of new members, which broke the lock of the conservative coalition on a number of important committees. The sustained efforts of the labor movement over the previous two decades helped make this changed political environment possible, and organized labor was prepared for the opportunities that opened up in the Johnson years.

Labor's Response to Political Failures

The Merger

The legislative setbacks of the 1940s and 1950s convinced many labor leaders that the movement's influence in the political process had to be strengthened. The AFL and the CIO worked together on issues like full-employment legislation, national health insurance, and the repeal of Taft-Hartley. They also increasingly cooperated in elections. By the 1950 elections, the CIO-PAC and the AFL's Labor's League for Political Education (LLPE) were coordinating political activities in more than a dozen states.[14] Although jurisdictional struggles and organizing rivalries continued between the affiliates of the two federations, there was growing talk of a merger to build labor's political clout.

The two federations came together as the AFL-CIO in 1955 out of perceived political necessity. In addition to the stalemate on social welfare legislation and Taft-Hartley repeal, Eisenhower's appointees to the NLRB weighted the board toward employers' interests. There was also a growing backlash at the state level, largely in the form of right-to-work laws. Even though George Meany, president of the AFL and newly merged AFL-CIO, came from the more traditional and conservative building trades wing of the labor movement, he was an experienced political operator and fully committed to political action. Meany argued the merger was the "key" to greater electoral influence and "the passage of liberal legislation."[15] Walter Reuther, the president of the CIO and the UAW, hoped the merger would end wasteful jurisdictional battles and spur new organizing drives in the South and other antiunion strongholds. He optimistically speculated that two to four million new workers would be organized within two years.[16] Although the two leaders would become bitter rivals with different visions for the labor movement over the next decade, at the time of the merger both Meany and Reuther shared the goal of expanding labor's political influence and social commitments.

The merger did not produce substantial organizing gains, but it did result in a much more powerful political operation by the 1960s. As Robert Zieger notes,

COPE, the AFL-CIO's electoral arm, "soon combined the efficiency and idealism of CIO-PAC and the broad grass-roots coverage of its AFL counterpart, Labor's League for Political Education."[17] While roughly one in three workers belonged to a union in the mid-fifties, COPE staff estimated that only 30% of union members were even registered to vote.[18] So COPE focused on registering union members and their families and getting them to the polls. One of the most useful innovations was the card file method, which allowed union activists to track the political participation of individual members and set up lists for phone banks and precinct walks. The overall registration rate of union members rose to 52% by 1961, even though many areas still did not use the system.[19] To encourage state- and local-level leaders to become politically active, which was often the key to electoral success, the AFL-CIO set up a program in which national COPE would match two dollars for every dollar raised by state and local central bodies or local unions for political activities such as voter registration or voter turnout drives.

COPE became increasingly well organized and better funded with each election cycle, and organized labor became a more respected, if not omnipotent, electoral force. Coming off a number of congressional victories in 1958, the AFL-CIO played an unprecedented role in the 1960 and especially the 1964 elections.[20] Scholars such as Michael Harrington and J. David Greenstone argue that the AFL-CIO assumed a role within the Democratic Party very similar to that of many European labor movements in their allied labor and social democratic parties. In the industrialized states where labor was strongest, the AFL-CIO's political organization resembled a party.[21] Union leaders could not convince all their members to vote for labor-endorsed candidates, but sizable majorities typically did, and so the key was to get as many union members to the polls as possible. In addition, the AFL-CIO tried to maximize the turnout of other Democratic constituencies such as minorities and increasingly senior citizens.[22]

The AFL-CIO's lobbying operation also developed a reputation for skill and influence in the late fifties and sixties. The Washington office of the AFL-CIO worked in cooperation with the politically active internationals and the state and local AFL-CIO central bodies to build organized labor's power in the legislative process. Andrew Biemiller, a former congressman who was a strong advocate of civil rights, national health care, and other liberal causes, served as the chief lobbyist for the federation, becoming one of the most knowledgeable and effective legislative representatives in Washington over his twenty years of service. The federation also set up a sophisticated public policy research infrastructure that was responsible for developing a number of prominent policy proposals including Medicare. Harrington suggests that labor was "the strongest single force for progressive social legislation in Washington" in the sixties, becoming an "invisible mass movement" for "social democracy."[23]

Pursuit of Private-Sector Benefits

Labor's strength in the economy, which peaked in the 1950s and 1960s, expanded the fruits of collective bargaining, permanently altering the context for public policy innovation. The policy failures of the 1940s and 1950s encouraged unions to turn to collective bargaining to obtain the benefits labor could not achieve through legislation. As Walter Reuther observed in 1946, "There is no evidence to encourage the belief that we may look to Congress for relief. In the immediate future, security will be won for our people only to the extent that the union succeeds in obtaining such security through collective bargaining."[24] Some labor leaders also believed growing private-sector benefits would encourage employers to support the expansion of public programs to assume the costs.[25] While the labor movement was unsuccessful in significantly expanding the welfare state in the early postwar years, organized labor was quite successful in collective bargaining, developing what Marie Gottschalk has termed a "shadow welfare state" of private benefits provided by employers.[26]

Government policies during the war and reconversion promoted employee benefits. A windfall profits tax was imposed on corporations, and employers' expenditures on benefits were made tax-exempt. This tax treatment, in combination with a government-imposed wage freeze and tight labor markets, encouraged employers to attract and retain employees through fringe benefits. But when corporations tried to pull back on these benefits after the war, pensions, health insurance, and employer contributions to health and welfare funds became major sources of conflict in collective bargaining.

Truman hoped to avoid this conflict through his welfare state agenda. Workers would gain a large measure of their economic security from government programs rather than collective bargaining, which would foster industrial peace. He noted in his veto message of the Case bill in 1946:

> It must always be remembered that industrial strife is a symptom of basic underlying maladjustments. A solution to labor-management difficulties is to be found not only in well considered legislation dealing directly with industrial relations, but, also, in the comprehensive legislative program which I have submitted to the

Congress designed to deal with the immediate dangers of inflation and prevent ultimate economic collapse. For example, legislation which would really make possible price controls and protect labor's standard of living, legislation which would bolster market demand when it sags, and basic legislation which would extend social security benefits, provide health and medical insurance, and adequate minimum wages would contribute more to the solution of labor-management strife than punitive legislation of this type.[27]

However, the conservative coalition in Congress did not share Truman's vision. Without adequate government insurance programs, benefit-related strikes proliferated. One of the bitterest strikes of the coal miners was over Lewis's demand in 1946 that the mine operators contribute to a health and welfare fund that would have been unnecessary if Truman's national health insurance proposal had been adopted.[28] The mine operators wanted to restrict the scope of collective bargaining and argued that the health and welfare fund "would establish by contract a new social and economic philosophy which is properly the field of social legislation."[29] However, the miners ultimately got their fund, and other unions sought to include similar benefits in their contracts. The NLRB ruled that pensions and insurance were valid subjects of collective bargaining in two cases in 1948, and the next year Truman's steel mediation board recommended steel operators' acceptance of the Steelworkers' demands for pension and social insurance.[30] The floodgates opened. Fifty-five percent of strikes in 1949 and 70% in the first half of 1950 were over health and welfare issues.[31]

Most employers eventually gave ground, and benefits such as pensions and group health insurance became standard features of union contracts. By 1954 three-quarters of union members were covered by a health or pension plan.[32] Although contested in the reconversion period by many employers, collective bargaining became routine behavior accepted by much of American industry in the 1950s. The strong postwar economy underwrote unprecedented gains for organized labor at the bargaining table in wages, vacation time, and benefits. Collective bargaining helped produce the burgeoning middle class and American standard of living associated with the fifties in American popular culture. In order to fend off unionization and remain competitive in recruiting workers, many nonunionized firms offered union wage rates and the benefit packages that unions obtained through collective bargaining.

The rise of private-sector benefits had a number of consequences for the workforce, organized labor, and public policy. Dependence on employer-sponsored benefits made American workers more vulnerable to economic downturns, job loss, and competitive downward pressures on compensation than workers in other countries with more extensive welfare states. A two-tiered labor force also emerged, with white-collar and unionized workers enjoying good wages and benefits and low-skilled workers in largely nonunionized industries often going without.[33] This made unionized workforces more expensive, which contributed to the contentiousness of collective bargaining and increased the resistance of some employers to unionization. Yet the prevalence of private insurance also gave the majority of workers a stake in the existing system and has further complicated health care reform efforts.[34] Noting the impact of employer-provided health insurance on the history of health care reform, Hacker argues, "Each intermediate step in favor of privatized social welfare approaches increases the probability that future steps will occur in the same direction."[35] Policies encouraging the proliferation of private health benefits created "policy feedbacks" that made a national health care system less likely in the future.

Some observers suggest that unions' success in collective bargaining for benefits led organized labor to pull back from its support for expansion of the welfare state, but the evidence is clear that the AFL-CIO and many of the internationals continued to push for programs like universal health care.[36] However, the proliferation of employer-sponsored benefits took the urgency out of the pursuit of government programs, and it certainly affected the level of concern of the secondary labor leadership and the rank and file.[37] Generous employer-provided benefits also made compromise on health care reform more difficult because organized labor—and most insured Americans in general—have wanted government programs to be just as comprehensive or more so, which drives up their cost. The insured fear reform will make them worse off. These concerns about destabilizing existing employer-provided benefits made Medicare an attractive, incremental expansion of the welfare state because targeting government programs to the retired would complement the existing system of employer benefits rather than replace it.

Medicare: The Fight for Incremental National Health Insurance

The failure of Truman's national health insurance proposal to make any progress by 1950 convinced many health care reform advocates that plans would have to be scaled back to attract more support in Congress. As Theodore Marmor notes, the inability of Truman to "extract" social legislation from "powerful, independent committees" served as a lesson for reformers. "The strategy of the incrementalists after 1952 was consensus-mongering: the identification of less disputed problems and the advocacy of modest solutions which ideological conservatives would have difficulty in attacking."[38] In pursuing an incremental approach to national health insurance, reformers saw advantages in terms of public policy and politics in targeting the elderly first. Of all demographic categories, this group faced the highest average health costs, had the lowest average incomes, was unlikely to have employer-provided benefits in retirement, and found it difficult and often prohibitively expensive to obtain private insurance. The elderly were also a sympathetic population, and health benefits could be sold politically as a logical extension of the Social Security program. The administrator in charge of the Social Security program, Oscar Ewing, eventually endorsed a proposal to provide coverage for hospital costs for the elderly, which was at this time the most expensive and potentially economically devastating medical expense for senior citizens.[39]

The push for medical assistance for the aged gained momentum in the late fifties in part because the newly merged AFL-CIO made it a top legislative priority. It was clear to labor leaders that an incremental approach had a better chance of prevailing in Congress, and they hoped that coverage for the aged would be the first step toward a universal system of national health insurance. The newly merged AFL-CIO created its own in-house public policy research division, which worked with old public policy hands from the Roosevelt and Truman administrations to prepare a plan to cover hospital, surgical, and nursing home benefits for the elderly as an extension of Social Security. The plan was introduced in Congress by Representative Aime Forand (D-NJ) in 1957. In 1961 the AFL-CIO joined the Democratic National Committee to fund the National Council of Senior Citizens (NCSC), dedicated to developing grassroots support for Medicare and mobilizing the elderly in politics.[40] The AFL-CIO also launched a major effort to educate union members about the need for health care assistance for the elderly and ran persistent letter-writing campaigns to build support in Congress in the late fifties and early sixties.

Even such a radically scaled-back government health care program faced considerable obstacles to passage. The threat of Eisenhower's veto and the absence of presidential leadership discouraged action in the fifties. The opposition of Wilbur Mills (D-AR), who became the chair of the powerful House Ways and Means Committee in 1957, also hurt Medicare's prospects. Mills argued that the program would be fiscally unsound given the growing costs of medical care and that the level of taxation necessary to support the program might undermine support for Social Security.[41] His opposition was hard to overcome because the majority on the committee remained hostile to Medicare until the 1964 election. Much like the Rules Committee, Ways and Means was a prestigious committee dominated by senior members with low levels of turnover. Appointments to Ways and Means were by custom controlled by regional party caucuses, giving the leadership and the Democratic Caucus as a whole less say in the committee's composition. The geographic distribution of seats was also frozen in a pattern that favored Southerners over the rising population of urban, pro-labor Democratic House members.[42] For years, liberal congressional gains in elections were not reflected in commensurate liberal gains on Ways and Means. In 1960, in the first vote taken on the Forand bill, the House Ways and Means Committee voted 17–8 to table the proposal. The ten Republicans on the committee were joined by Mills and six other Southern Democrats in voting to kill the bill.

The approach of the 1960 elections kept the issue of medical care for the elderly alive. In an effort to forestall more significant reform, Eisenhower proposed his own plan early in the year to offer matching grants to interested states to provide medical benefits for the low-income elderly. A Senate version was endorsed by Republican presidential candidate Richard Nixon, and Chairman Mills supported a version in the House. A scaled-down proposal for grants to the states, known as the Kerr-Mills or the "charity" approach, passed Congress as part of the 1960 Social Security amendments. But because of the lack of interest in the states, the program never covered very many elderly.[43]

Democratic presidential nominee John F. Kennedy was a sponsor of a Senate version of the Forand bill, and he and the AFL-CIO made medical care for the elderly a major campaign issue. Kennedy's election sent liberal hopes for passage of a Forand-type bill soaring. Soon the more liberal, social insurance approach gained the title "Medicare." Eager to exploit the political opening, the AFL-CIO stepped up its lobbying campaign. Retired from Congress, Representative Forand assumed the top position at the NCSC to push for Medicare. A Medicare bill, introduced in the 87th Congress by Representative Cecil King (D-CA) and Senator Clinton Anderson (D-NM), embodied Kennedy's proposal and replaced Forand's bill as the focus of reformers.

Despite growing public support for greater health care assistance to the elderly, Ways and Means remained an obstacle.[44] In the first year of Kennedy's administration, the AFL-CIO created a new labor task force to secure support for the King-Anderson bill. The task force recruited staff and volunteers from the affiliates to work with AFL-CIO staffers to mobilize grassroots support in the districts of resistant Ways and Means members including Mills's.[45] Mills reportedly promised a United Steelworkers leader that he would allow discussion of the proposal if the unions would stop "stirring up grass roots complaints in his district."[46] The committee held hearings in 1961 but did not take a vote.

The administration and liberal groups including the AFL-CIO mounted a sustained campaign to try to ensure that only Medicare supporters were appointed to vacancies on Ways and Means. As Nelson Polsby notes of this period, "The advocacy of a liberal agenda in the House required prudent management as of a slow-growing garden, the preparation of soil, the nurturing of tender shoots, patient cultivation, and waiting for an eventual, occasional harvest. This is what committee packing was all about: the clearing of channels through which—later on—proposals could move without excessive hindrance."[47] Anti-Medicare Southern Democrats were gradually replaced with Southern supporters of the King-Anderson bill. When two Democratic seats came open on Ways and Means in the wake of the 1962 election, John W. Edelman of the Textile Workers argued that the Speaker and the White House could influence the selection of replacements and that "from this very moment till the decision is made those of us who want to be sure to get this aid-for-the-aging bill this time had better get busy doing at least a dozen different things and keep at it day after day" to ensure the seats were filled with Medicare supporters.[48] A "liberal revolt" in the Democratic Caucus under pressure from labor defeated an attempt to put Representative Landrum (D-GA), the conservative sponsor of the hated Landrum-Griffin bill, into one of these seats.[49] As a result of these efforts, the margin of opposition on Ways and Means shrunk from 17–8 in 1960 to 15–10 in 1962 and 13–12 in 1964.[50]

Supporters were also getting closer to victory in the Senate. In 1962 Senator Anderson's effort to add his proposal to a House-passed welfare bill narrowly lost by a vote of 52–48 in favor of tabling the amendment.[51] There was likely more support for the Medicare proposal, but some senators opposed circumventing the committee process while others feared the House would never accede to the Medicare proposal in conference and the passage of the underlying bill might be delayed or jeopardized. But the vote on the tabling motion once again reflected the opposition of the conservative coalition of Southern Democrats and Republicans to expansion of the welfare state and the near unanimity of support among non-Southern Democrats. Ninety-five percent of non-Southern Democrats opposed the tabling motion, compared with 17% of Southern Democrats and 14% of Republicans.

After Kennedy's assassination and Lyndon Johnson's assumption of power, a flood of legislation began to move in Congress. The most dramatic victory occurred in the passage of the far-reaching Civil Rights Act of 1964, which passed the House and finally the Senate after cloture was invoked, ending a fifty-seven-day filibuster. The logjam in the Senate on Medicare was also finally broken. A modified form of King-Anderson was introduced at the beginning of the 88th Congress that expanded health coverage to all elderly, not just Social Security recipients. The proposal failed to make it out of committee in the Senate. But late in the congressional session just before the 1964 elections, Senator Albert Gore (D-TN) proposed an amendment to a House-passed Social Security bill that encompassed the King-Anderson proposal. The amendment passed 49–44 in the Senate with the support of 98% of non-Southern Democrats but only 21% of Southern Democrats and 15% of Republicans. Chairman Mills appeared to search in earnest for a compromise proposal he thought would fare well on the House floor.[52] But Ways and Means once again failed to report a bill when a pair of Southerners made it clear they would oppose a pending compromise and several other committee members expressed reservation about taking the vote before the election.[53] The administration's count in the House showed sixty Democrats against Medicare, all from the South or the border states of Kentucky and Oklahoma, and all but fifteen Republicans opposed.[54] The administration considered trying to put members on the record in the House by forcing a floor vote to instruct the conference committee to accept the Senate version of the bill over Mill's objection but decided against it.[55] Mills appointed a narrow majority of House conferees opposed to the Medicare proposal, whereas the balance of Senate conferees supported it. The conference ended in deadlock, and the underlying Social Security increase died along with the Medicare proposal. The *New York Times* labeled Mills the "One-Man Veto on Medicare."[56] However, the conference outcome masked a breakthrough for Medicare supporters. Mills promised the liberals on his committee that Medicare would be the top legislative priority in the next session.

The outcome of the 1964 elections made passage of some form of Medicare inevitable. The AFL-CIO, President Johnson, and numerous congressional candidates made Medicare a central campaign issue. The AFL-CIO made a special effort to mobilize senior citizens. Johnson won a landslide, and the Democrats gained fifty-eight seats in the House, giving them a majority of two to one over Republicans. The Democrats had the most sizable majority and the largest percentage of non-Southern Democrats (see table 3.1) since the 1930s. The conservative coalition could finally be reined in because it lost its institutional lock on power. Because of the size of the Democratic victory, the party ratios on committees changed and liberals in the House, their labor allies, and the Johnson administration pressed for the additional seats to go to loyal Democrats.[57] Ways and Means picked up two Democrats committed to Medicare and lost two Republicans, producing a pro-Medicare majority. But the drama over Medicare was not over yet.

Confronting the likelihood of defeat, Medicare opponents introduced alternative proposals in early 1965. One of the criticisms of the King-Anderson approach was that it covered only hospital and nursing home care and it would not open access of poor elderly to services such as doctor visits and medical tests. The AMA tried to exploit this weakness by offering an "eldercare" proposal to provide a comprehensive package of medical benefits to the indigent elderly. Another proposal dubbed "bettercare" offered Social Security recipients federally subsidized private insurance for a complete package of benefits with a graduated premium based on income. The introduction of these proposals produced unexpected consequences for the anti-Medicare forces.[58]

Members of Congress including Chairman Mills had grown worried that the public perceived the Medicare proposal to be far more comprehensive than it actually was and that there might be a backlash when the bill went into effect. Leading Democrats worried that seniors would become fully aware of the limits on the coverage in the two years preceding the 1968 election and Republicans would be able to argue that they had defended a more comprehensive plan, even if it covered very few people.[59] Facing political realities and finally convinced that the program could be made financially solvent, Mills maneuvered successfully to add a package of more comprehensive benefits to the Medicare proposal reported out of Ways and Means.[60] Liberals and the AFL-CIO were pleased with the move and eventually built on the momentum to lobby for even more generous benefits in the Senate.

The final Medicare bill significantly expanded the government safety net. It included two parts addressed to senior citizens. The first part embodied the King-Anderson proposal for compulsory hospital and nursing home insurance for all elderly to be funded through a payroll tax. The second part provided a voluntary comprehensive program of benefits including doctor visits, nursing care, and lab tests (though not prescription drugs) in which the elderly could enroll upon turning sixty-five with the payment of a subsidized monthly premium. The bill also strengthened the Kerr-Mills program in what became known as Medicaid, a joint federal-state program to cover medical care for the indigent of all ages and the disabled. A role for the states was preserved in the welfare program, but the Medicare program, like Social Security, would be open to all elderly citizens and administered by the federal government.

Mills's new and improved version of the Medicare bill moved fairly quickly through the legislative process. The conservative coalition's opposition was destabilized. With its pro-Medicare contingency strengthened by the election, years of lobbying to put only pro-Medicare members into open Democratic committee slots, and the change of heart of its chair, House Ways and Means finally reported the bill on a strict party-line vote in March 1965. The Rules Committee, which also reflected a new ideological balance because of the election, quickly reported the bill with a favorable rule, with all but one Republican voting against the rule and all but one Democrat (Representative Colmer of Mississippi) voting in favor. The AMA's opposition was diffused by the payment system adopted, and it could not break the congressional momentum. The Medicare bill passed the House by a vote of 313–115 with the support of all but two non-Southern Democrats, more than a majority of Southern Democrats, and just slightly less than a majority of Republicans. A version passed the Senate in early July by a vote of 68–21 with all non-Southern Democrats and roughly two-thirds of Southern Democrats supporting the bill and Republicans almost evenly split. The conference committee was uneventful.

The legislative struggle that began twenty years earlier with Truman's national health insurance proposal culminated in a dramatic presidential bill-signing ceremony at the Truman Library in Missouri with Truman in attendance. The final passage of Medicare was made possible by a number of factors, which reveal both the potential and the constraints for broad-based social welfare legislation in the United States. Central to the bill's success was the incremental approach of targeting the elderly rather than the working-age population, which after the passage of two prosperous decades showed much higher rates of coverage by private insurance. The growing political savvy and legislative influence of organized labor also played a role. Mobilization of grassroots support, particularly among the elderly, in addition to the persistent and strategic push of the lobbyists and leaders of the AFL-CIO and many of the international unions year after year, built momentum—and a numerical majority in the case of the Ways and Means Committee—behind the bill. Most important was the large Democratic congressional majority, with many Democrats elected from outside the South. The 1964 elections might be interpreted as a mandate for social reform given Johnson's record and the Democratic Party platform. However, the size of the Democratic majority was made possible by anomalies in the political environment in 1964, including public reverence for the slain Kennedy and the Republican nomination of a presidential candidate considered by mainstream America to be too far to the right. Almost a historical accident, the 1964 election results produced a liberal majority that was strong enough to overcome temporarily the institutional obstacles that had impeded Medicare's passage before. But it is also important to recognize the role of labor in laying the groundwork.

The size of the victories on the final Medicare bill in the House and Senate votes meant little as a direct measure of representatives' support because once legislation gains the air of inevitability, the dynamic changes, and many legislators pile on. The most important goal for reformers seeking popular legislation in the American public policy process at this point was to break the institutional obstacles early in the process—typically at the stage of committee action—that prevented full consideration of bills many legislators were just as happy not to have to cast a vote on and risk angering powerful interest groups like the AMA. This is a major reason that the discharge petition process is rarely successful.[61] When legislation was stymied by committee action, rank-and-file members could defend themselves to advocates of the legislation like the AFL-CIO by claiming they never had the opportunity to vote on the bill. The remaking of the membership of the Ways and Means Committee over time and the size of the Democrats' majority in 1965 broke this dynamic. Liberals gained ground in the Democratic Caucus, and they wanted—and in fact felt they needed—a vote on the bill to keep their constituents happy.

The AFL-CIO hoped that the success of Medicare would build support for extending government health insurance to the larger population. In 1967, a year after Medicare benefits went into effect, the AFL-CIO again publicized its support for a program of national health insurance. The next year organized labor supported the creation of a new organization, the Committee for National Health Insurance. However, the legislative window opened by the unusual confluence of events in 1965 quickly closed, and the more typical pattern of gridlock in American politics returned in the area of health care. In the area of labor law reform, the gridlock never ended.

The Effort to Repeal 14(b)

The passage of Medicare, Social Security improvements, the Voting Rights Act, aid to education, a major public works program, an improved housing program, and various War on Poverty measures in 1965 led the AFL-CIO to sum up the year as "the most productive congressional session ever held."[62] However, organized labor's legislative record in 1965 was marked by one bitter defeat— failure to obtain favorable changes in the Taft-Hartley Act. Despite legislative success on labor's social welfare priorities, efforts to repeal 14(b) demonstrated that political institutions designed to protect the minority were a major obstacle to labor legislation.

Just as organized labor narrowed its focus from national health insurance to medical assistance to the elderly, it shifted from total repeal of Taft-Hartley to repeal of the most burdensome provisions. The most hated provision was Section 14(b), which allowed states to pass right-to-work laws prohibiting union security agreements such as the union shop (where employees must join a union or pay union dues) from being negotiated in collective bargaining agreements. Most of the Southern states and many nonindustrial states in the West passed right-to-work laws shortly after the passage of Taft-Hartley.

Section 14(b) posed several problems for labor. Union leaders argued it was difficult to organize in states with right-to-work laws because it was harder to establish fledgling unions without security arrangements. Moreover, the National Right to Work Committee, formed in 1955 to exploit 14(b), pushed right-to-work referenda or legislation not only to fight unionization but also to divert labor's attention and resources. To some degree the strategy backfired.[63] The state right-to-work battles brought the state and local AFL and CIO affiliates into closer cooperation in their political activities. When right-to-work referenda were put on state ballots, they resulted in massive voter registration and education campaigns of union members and allies. These fights generally produced a coattails effect in the election of more liberals to state governments and Congress. Yet labor leaders recognized that these fights were diverting resources from the national labor organizations and that, once a state right-to-work law passed, it was extremely hard to repeal. The provision held symbolic importance for the labor movement as a continuing reminder of labor's geographic vulnerability. In pursuing right-to-work laws, labor's foes could shift the political battle away from areas where labor was stronger, at the national level and in industrial states, to areas where it was weaker. Thus, repeal of 14(b) became the top legislative priority by the late fifties. Eisenhower ultimately came out against 14(b) repeal, and there was not enough support in Congress during either his or Kennedy's presidency to pass repeal. However, the 1964 election results gave labor new hope, and AFL-CIO leaders immediately began to explore the chances for repeal.[64]

Johnson promised organized labor that repealing 14(b) would be a priority for his administration. But he convinced AFL-CIO president Meany of the need to hold off until after passage of major Great Society programs—such as Medicare, federal aid to education, and public works—that were also on labor's legislative agenda. The House finally took up 14(b) in the summer of 1965 after the Medicare bill went to the Senate. Labor lobbyists had already spent six months laying the groundwork.

An internal AFL-CIO memo summing up the day-by-day chronology of action in the fifteen-month battle over repeal of 14(b) in the 89th Congress reads like a textbook case study of the obstacle path that is the American legislative process. Labor leaders first consulted with President Johnson and various congressional leaders on how to proceed. Representative Frank Thompson Jr. (D-NJ), the chairman of the Special Subcommittee on Labor of the House Committee on Education and Labor, agreed to sponsor the bill and urged AFL-CIO lobbyist Andy Biemiller to make sure the bill was referred to his subcommittee because a competing subcommittee would not be as favorable. Meany and Biemiller then met with the chairman of the House Education and Labor Committee, Representative Adam Clayton Powell (D-NY), and got his commitment to refer the bill to Thompson's subcommittee. Meany and Biemiller also met with Speaker John McCormack (D-MA) in late December to discuss the AFL-CIO's legislative program in general and 14(b) in particular. The Speaker agreed that 14(b) repeal was feasible and assured them of his support.

The Speaker emphasized that the fate of 14(b) would probably be linked to reinstatement of a procedural rule in the House known as the "twenty-one-day rule" that was adopted in 1949 but repealed again in 1951. It allowed a chair to call a bill favorably reported out of his or her committee to the floor if Rules did not report it within twenty-one days. As discussed in the next chapter, the twenty-one-day rule was pushed by the liberal majority within the Democratic Party to break the power of the conservatives on Rules. Within a week of the meeting, the twenty-one-day rule passed 224–201 after the labor movement secured the votes of numerous Republicans endorsed by COPE in the 1964 elections. Without the procedural change, 14(b) would have likely died in the Rules Committee.

Labor and administration lobbyists estimated that roughly 222 representatives supported repeal in the House, which meant labor needed to work to maintain the slim majority of support. The AFL-CIO spearheaded a major lobbying effort up and down the ranks of the labor movement in which every angle was pursued. Biemiller met with the secretary of agriculture to get help securing the farm-state vote.[65] He also firmed up the support of the small contingency of Republicans considered to be labor allies. Labor lobbyists got pledges of assistance from civil rights and various liberal religious organizations. Labor lobbyists felt confident things were moving smoothly in the House. The Thompson subcommittee reported the bill on June 9.

The first kink in the legislative process came when Chairman Powell threatened to hold up the bill until the House passed amendments to Title 7 of the Civil Rights Act dealing with the Fair Employment Practices Commission (FEPC). Hearings on the amendments were held on June 15. The next day Meany and Biemiller met with Speaker McCormack, who agreed to do "everything to stop Powell's move, including help in taking Committee from Powell, if necessary."[66] Biemiller then made sure there were enough votes to "take the Committee from Powell." Under pressure, Powell agreed to file the necessary resolution to take up the bill under the twenty-one-day rule. After another round of lobbying, including a final push for support from Republicans and feasible Southern Democrats, the bill passed 221–203 on July 28. The vote was a defeat for the conservative coalition, with 96% of non-Southern Democrats voting for the bill compared with 19% of Southern Democrats and 15% of Republicans.

President Johnson called Meany on the House floor to urge immediate action on 14(b) in the Senate, which was to prove impossible. For months Senate minority leader Everett Dirksen (R-IL) suggested he might launch a filibuster against 14(b) repeal. In an early August meeting with Meany and Biemiller, Dirksen suggested he would try to attach an amendment to 14(b) repeal to pass a constitutional amendment invalidating the Supreme Court's 1964 "one man, one vote" ruling requiring both houses of bicameral state legislatures to be apportioned based on population. Dirksen had become the champion of rural and conservative interests who stood to lose if the state—and later national congressional districts—were reapportioned to reflect equal populations as ordered by the Court. The labor movement greeted the reapportionment decisions with great relief because political power would finally be redistributed to the metropolitan majority. The AFL-CIO identified the overrepresentation of rural interests at the expense of urban interests as a major impediment to progressive legislation.[67] Dirksen offered to drop the filibuster threat if the AFL-CIO would drop its opposition to the constitutional amendment. Meany rejected the offer. Dirksen warned he would "use every weapon at his command in the fight ahead," but Democratic leaders downplayed the threat.[68] Amid these negotiations, the Labor Subcommittee approved 14(b) repeal on August 12.

More trouble emerged as the full Senate Labor and Public Welfare Committee took up the bill. A "baby" filibuster developed in committee, which is an effort by opponents to stall a bill through endless committee debate and amendments.[69] At the same time Democratic leaders were losing confidence that a filibuster could be avoided. The bill was finally reported on September 9, and Senator Dirksen announced his intention to filibuster, stating that if 14(b) was brought up, the Congress would be in session until "the snow falls." Senate majority leader Mike Mansfield (MT) was very skeptical that cloture could be invoked, although out of the Democratic Party's obligation to labor, he eventually called up the bill.[70] However, he put off scheduling it until other priority legislation had been taken up, and he repeatedly rejected labor leaders' requests for round-the-clock sessions to make the filibuster more burdensome on its supporters.

At no point did cloture seem within reach. Labor lobbyists counted 54 votes in support of repeal and 40 against with 6 undecided.[71] Unless some of the declared opponents could be convinced to allow a vote on the bill, there was no way to get the two-thirds majority necessary to end the filibuster. Labor leaders throughout the movement worked the Hill but made little progress. Mansfield called a cloture vote on October 11 that failed 47–45 with a 50–50 tie possible if all senators' commitments were taken into consideration. The next day Mansfield told Biemiller he would shut off debate in a couple of days and adjourn the Senate.

The labor movement had to decide what step to take next. Biemiller reported to an October meeting of the AFL-CIO Executive Council that his most optimistic count showed sixty senators might support cloture—still well short of the sixty-seven needed. The discussion in the meeting turned to the ire and determination of Dirksen, who Meany noted "was bitter because his constitutional amendment on reapportionment had been defeated."[72] He pointed out "that vested selfish financial interests had great influence, and in many instances, dominated rural representatives in state legislatures" and it was his opinion that Dirksen was "desperately trying to keep this practice in effect by keeping at least one House of each state legislature dominated by rural legislatures [*sic*]." Dirksen was clearly unwilling to drop the filibuster unless his demands were met. There was also discussion of making reform of Rule 22, the Senate rule that governs cloture, the top legislative priority, but the AFL-CIO also did not have the votes to change the rule. The rules change itself would have inevitably been successfully filibustered.[73] After all the work on the Great Society programs, labor leaders wanted to see a purely "labor" bill pass. Given the intense focus on 14(b), they could hardly drop the bill without making another effort in the next congressional session, but it would be all but impossible to come up with 67 votes for cloture.

The Johnson administration and Senator Mansfield kept their commitment to labor and took up the bill in the next session, but they had little expectation it would pass.[74] As an administration staffer warned Walter Reuther, "Organized labor, with its vast political resources, would have to call its chits sharply and force an impressive, broad uprising of liberal Senators to demand of the leadership immediate consideration and determined floor action to out last the filibuster." He stressed that this was "just not something [the President could] effectively do."[75] In a memo from Biemiller and other AFL-CIO staff to Meany in late October, the lobbyists laid out a strategy for 14(b) repeal in the next congressional session.[76] It stressed a full-scale campaign-style approach focused on grassroots lobbying and a public relations blitz that would among other things stress the right of the Senate in a democracy to cast its vote. The strategy included more targeted appeals such as the loss of jobs from non–right-to-work states to right-to-work states, which was of special interest to Northeastern Republicans. Labor lobbyists and Al Barkan, the director of the COPE campaign operation, met informally with a group of influential and friendly senators to convince them to put pressure on Mansfield to hold round-the-clock sessions. While some senators supported the idea, others stressed it was simply not "realistic" unless the votes for cloture "were in sight," which they were not.[77] Mansfield, who did not even hold round-the-clock sessions in the filibuster of the 1964 Civil Rights Act, continued to refuse but agreed to extended sessions. All these efforts produced only one additional vote for cloture. On February 8, there was a vote of 51–48 in favor of cloture with one pro-repeal senator absent due to illness. Reflecting the enduring power of the conservative coalition, 89%

of non-Southern Democrats voted for cloture, compared with only 23% of Southern Democrats and 19% of Republicans.[78] Another vote was taken two days later in which Senator George McGovern (D-SD), in a vote that would come back to haunt him, switched and voted against cloture. Recognizing the situation as futile, Senator Mansfield adjourned the Senate. The fight for 14(b) repeal was lost. The unusually large liberal majority in the 89th Congress narrowed in the 1966 elections, and the prospects for labor law reform and the rest of the unfinished Great Society initiatives dimmed.[79]

In the wake of the defeat, many labor leaders lashed out at President Johnson and the Democrats in Congress. Criticism was particularly strident at the state and local level among the secondary labor leadership.[80] Although contemporary observers speculated that Johnson was not fully committed to repeal of 14(b) and that he did not work as hard as he could have to ensure its passage, there is considerable evidence that the administration did as much as it reasonably could to demonstrate its commitment to labor. The White House appears to have pressured Senate majority leader Mansfield to take up the bill in October when he expressed interest in pushing it over to the next session. Johnson and administration officials repeatedly met with Meany, Biemiller, and other labor officials to coordinate strategy.[81] Vice President Hubert Humphrey, the former senator from Minnesota, was enlisted to use his ties to rural legislators to maximize their vote.[82] The White House contacted sixty-one senators to urge a vote in favor of cloture.[83] The Democratic National Committee, acting as an arm of the White House, also lobbied for the bill.

It is true that the administration postponed consideration of 14(b) and that Johnson did not personally invest himself in the legislation the way he did with civil rights or Medicare. Not only was this due to the nature of the legislation, which did not carry the moral weight of civil rights and was not as popular or consequential as Medicare, but it was also due to the fact that repeal of 14(b) was never seen by the administration as achievable once Dirksen decided to filibuster. Twenty years after the battle, White House staffer Lawrence O'Brien suggested that if 14(b) repeal had been Johnson's top priority it still would not have succeeded. He noted that the bill was put off because it was "an impossible task." Had the situation been more promising, the administration would have been willing to take up the bill earlier. O'Brien suggested that "if labor had a head count jointly with us that showed a reasonable prospect of success, then obviously we would have moved at an earlier time. But it wasn't there throughout the session and the record shows it wasn't there. . . .We weren't conning labor or trying to avoid our responsibilities. . . . We weren't dragging our feet; it just wasn't there."[84] The administration's most optimistic counts showed 53 votes in support of 14(b) in the Senate.[85] All the arm-twisting in the world was unlikely to produce another 14 votes for cloture, which would have required the support of numerous Southerners and senators from right-to-work states.

Because of the administration's efforts, Johnson himself grew testy with criticism of his handling of the repeal issue. A staff memo advising him that there should be visible White House efforts on common situs picketing, minimum wage, and unemployment compensation to "offset any unfavorable image in the labor movement on 14B" had scribbled in Johnson's handwriting beside it "I am sick of having to offset any image."[86] Johnson felt the administration had done all it could do without wasting political capital on a bill that had no chance of passage.

National AFL-CIO leaders and lobbyists acknowledged Johnson's role. In reference to the fight for repeal, Biemiller later noted that Johnson went out of his way and that "there wasn't any question that our relations with Lyndon were so good as to be almost incredible."[87] Both Meany and Reuther agreed to leave the timing of 14(b) to the administration and were willing to accept postponement until after other priority legislation cleared.[88] Reuther even apparently told Secretary of Labor Willard Wirtz that he thought the AFL-CIO pursuing 14(b) in the second congressional session was a mistake.[89] The main issue in the failure of repeal of 14(b) was not the lack of presidential commitment but the filibuster that allowed a minority of senators to obstruct action.

Organized labor managed to avoid or overcome almost every obstacle that stood in its way before—the opposition of the president, a deadlock in committee, the hostility of committee chairs, and the opposition of the House Rules Committee. However, organized labor could not overcome the filibuster and the bias in the Senate toward the representation of rural areas, making labor's recruitment of the support of sixty-seven senators even more difficult. The votes for cloture came from senators representing 61% of the population.[90] In 1965 organized labor faced the best prospects for labor law reform since the passage of Taft-Hartley, but while the labor movement could muster a majority for repeal, the necessary supermajority was beyond its grasp. This failure may be, and was, attributed to organized labor's weakness, but labor appeared weak in the 14(b) struggle because the bar was so high. It had the support of the Democratic administration, a majority in the House and Senate, and the overwhelming support of non-Southern Democrats.

Perhaps if Meany had been willing to make a deal with Dirksen on the reapportionment issue, repeal of 14(b) could have made it through. However, in making a deal to get around minority obstruction on this one bill, labor would have had to jeopardize the enduring reform of another feature in the American political system that had long privileged rural minorities at the expense of urban, labor-oriented majorities. In a speech to the 1965 AFL-CIO convention Meany railed against Dirksen:

> The issue of 14(b) repeal and the issue of reapportionment in particular and progress in general are solidly and inescapably intertwined. There is no illusion about that either in our minds or the mind of the Senate Minority Leader. The filibuster is a punitive and coercive tactic. It is a cynical invitation to a "deal." It is crafty politician's way of saying: "Come around to the back door. Give up your opposition to the reapportionment amendment and you can have 14(b) repeal."
>
> Well, as badly as I want 14(b) repealed, I do not want it that badly. And the Senate Minority Leader and all his anti-labor stooges can filibuster until hell freezes over before I will agree to sell the people short for that kind of a deal.[91]

More than any other legislative battle, the 1965–66 fight over 14(b) vividly demonstrates the institutional conundrum faced by organized labor. The failure to gain favorable labor law changes makes it more difficult for the labor movement to organize outside its geographic base, which in turn makes it seemingly impossible for organized labor to muster the supermajority support in the Senate necessary to change labor laws. While the filibuster had predominantly been used on civil rights legislation in the postwar period, its use on repeal of 14(b) was an early indication that the filibuster would become a common tactic as conservatives' control over other institutions like congressional committees declined over the next two decades.

Common Situs

After the failure on 14(b), some labor leaders still hoped to get a consolation provision passed dealing with the common situs picketing issue. It would have eased stringent limits placed on picketing in the construction industry by a Supreme Court decision that prohibited employees in a dispute with one contractor on a construction site from picketing the entire site. However, some liberals in the House were not very enthusiastic about the measure because of the poor record of the construction unions on civil rights and the greater support among construction unions for Republicans. Other House members wanted to wait for the Senate to act first after sticking their neck out for 14(b) repeal only to see it killed by a filibuster. Chairman Powell of the House Education and Labor Committee refused to call it up for a floor vote until a controversial measure dealing with employment discrimination was passed, and it never reached the floor.[92] The AFL-CIO also backed off in the Senate for fear the legislation would attract unfavorable Taft-Hartley amendments and it would likely be filibustered with the same outcome as 14(b) repeal.[93]

Efforts to Improve Workers' Income Security Programs

While the outcomes were divergent in the areas of health care and labor law reform, both the prospects and limits for policy change backed by organized labor could be seen in the workers' income security programs. The protections of the Fair Labor Standards Act were again significantly improved, but proposals for national standards for unemployment compensation again failed to make it into law—this time because of differences between the House and Senate.

Minimum Wage

The pattern of incrementalism—and extended wrangling across several congressional sessions—on the minimum wage that developed in the postwar decades continued through the height of the Great Society. After his minimum wage bill died in conference committee with the House while he was running for president, Kennedy resumed the fight from the White House. A Senate proposal largely embodied the recommendations of the president and the AFL-CIO, but the House passed a much weaker bill. This time the conference committee was pulled in the Senate's direction, and the final bill resulted in the first significant expansion of coverage since the passage of the original FLSA in 1938 and a 25% increase in the minimum wage. Johnson resumed the enduring battle over the FLSA in 1964 when he called for further expanding coverage and increasing overtime pay from time and a half to double time as a measure to address unemployment. The legislation did not move beyond committee consideration for two years, and in fact the administration behind the scenes opposed the bill eventually reported by the House Education and Labor Committee as providing too inflationary an increase in the minimum wage, one that even exceeded labor's demands.[94] But in the only notable legislative victory for the labor movement in 1966, a major minimum wage bill finally passed that increased the wage, expanded coverage to an estimated nine million workers, and lowered the threshold for overtime pay from forty-four to forty hours.[95] The conservative coalition appeared but lost on votes to remove coverage of agricultural workers from the bill. Once again the Senate's more generous bill largely prevailed in conference. The AFL-CIO termed the bill "the most important and best minimum wage law that has ever been passed."[96] Even in this instance, labor had called for much more, including a thirty-five-hour work-week. But various labor leaders closely negotiated the details with the administration to get an acceptable—and politically feasible—bill.[97]

Unemployment Insurance

Another agenda item carried over from the Truman years into the Great Society was federal standards to improve the unemployment insurance program. But as with the stalemate on labor law reform in both periods, Congress also failed to act on unemployment compensation. Like Truman, both Kennedy and Johnson proposed minimum federal standards for the amount and duration of benefit payments to minimize the variation among states. Kennedy's proposals went nowhere, and Johnson's proposals were not acted on until 1966. Even though Chairman Mills sponsored the administration's bill and promised he would "get out a good bill," the same House Ways and Means Committee that supported the Medicare bill stripped the federal standards from the unemployment bill.[98] Labor lobbyists had been optimistic, but when the Ways and Means legislation passed overwhelmingly on the House floor, AFL-CIO president George Meany termed it "a mere token measure."[99] As was typically true of Ways and Means bills, it was considered under a closed rule, so amendments adding the federal standards back in could not be considered. In narrow votes both in the Senate Finance Committee and on the Senate floor, federal standards were added back into the bill over the opposition of the conservative coalition. The House delayed sending the bill to conference, where it ultimately died with the end of the session. The House conferees refused to accept the federal standards, and the Senate conferees refused to concede them. Labor, too, was unwilling to accept a bill without federal benefit standards and preferred to resume the battle in another Congress. As with the nationalization of the labor law reflected in 14(b) repeal, there was still significant opposition to federal standards for unemployment benefits, and the conservative coalition succeeded in killing the proposal in conference.

The Window Closes

After the explosion of legislative activity in the 89th Congress, the power of the conservative coalition rebounded in the 90th (see table 2.1). Many factors played a role—fatigue with the rapid legislative pace, rising concern about the Vietnam War, and growing disillusionment with Johnson's leadership. But probably the most consequential factor was the loss of liberal Democrats in the 1966 elections. In the wake of the elections even George Meany indicated that he was going to try to dissuade the AFL-CIO's Executive Council from urging legislation.[100] By summer of 1967, after a surprisingly large defeat on a small but symbolic bill dealing with federal funding for rat extermination in urban areas, House Speaker Carl Albert referred to a "rebellious mood" in the House and recommended that no "new programs" be sent to the House floor for the "remainder" of the session.[101] Johnson's need to make serious concessions to get anything accomplished in Congress led to increased sparring between labor and the administration. Labor leaders were particularly upset by the administration's acquiescence in substantial budget cuts in order to get congressional support for a tax surcharge necessary to fund the Vietnam War.[102] Even prior to the elections, there were signs of growing dissatisfaction within the lower ranks of the labor movement over the failure of repeal of 14(b), administration efforts to control inflation through wage-price guidelines, and Vietnam.[103] Although national labor leaders remained one of Johnson's closest allies, sticking with him even on the war, the heady days of the Great Society were over. Congress would give labor very few victories in the last session of Johnson's presidency.

Conclusion

Observations by political scientist J. David Greenstone and others that labor has often been more successful on welfare state initiatives than labor legislation are well illustrated by organized labor's track record in the sixties.[104] In the purest test of labor's influence, organized labor could not obtain repeal of 14(b) because of the filibuster. But labor did succeed on a range of broader issues such as civil rights legislation, minimum wage improvements, public works spending, federal aid to education, and medical assistance to the elderly. These achievements should be neither underestimated nor overvalued.

The legislative successes represented a high level of influence in the political process for organized labor, but they also show the limitations in the American political system on broad welfare state measures. Most of the successful initiatives involved significant compromises necessary to overcome legislative veto points, even during a period with sizable liberal majorities in both houses of Congress. The civil rights bills did not bring an end to discrimination. The minimum wage increases were not adequate to eliminate poverty among all working families. Federal aid to elementary and secondary education targeted at disadvantaged schools was not adequate to overcome the disparities in education. The Medicare bill was national health insurance targeted to the elderly rather than the entire population. Yet even these compromised pieces of legislation taken as a whole reflect a significant expansion in the size and reach of the American welfare state that has benefited millions of Americans within and outside the labor movement.

Labor was a much stronger political force in the mid-sixties than it had been in the mid-fifties. There was greater unity in the political efforts of the labor movement under the merged AFL-CIO. The AFL-CIO's political operation also became one of the—if not *the*—most sophisticated and respected forces in Washington. Despite these strengths, labor's power was obviously limited by institutions like the filibuster, even with unusually large liberal majorities in Congress and a supportive president. It was clear there would have to be changes in the political system for organized labor to achieve more. As discussed in the next chapter, labor responded to the failures of the mid-sixties by redoubling its commitment to transforming the Democratic Party and congressional institutions.

4

Changing the Rules of the Game

From the 1940s through the 1970s, labor dedicated considerable effort to real-igning the Democratic Party toward its urban, liberal, labor-oriented wing and empowering this wing of the party in the policy-making process. To reach these goals labor pursued two main strategies: first, advocating civil rights and mobi-lizing African Americans in the electorate in order to transform Southern poli-tics and, second, pushing congressional reforms to minimize the role of power-ful conservative Southern Democrats in the legislative process.

Organized labor was by no means the only force pushing for these changes. The labor-liberal alliance produced a dynamic reform coalition in the 1940s dedicated to furthering the cause of postwar liberalism, especially within the Democratic Party. The members of the coalition included the CIO, eventually the AFL-CIO, unions like the UAW, liberal reform organizations like Americans for Democratic Action (ADA) and the National Committee for an Effective Congress (NCEC), left-leaning religious groups including Catholic and Jew-ish organizations, and civil rights groups such as the NAACP.[1] All the groups brought different resources to the battle, but labor was one of the best organized and best funded, as well as one of the few participants with significant grassroots reach. Many of the constituencies advocating reform were concentrated in a few cities, but labor was organized across a broad range of communities outside the South.[2]

Civil rights was one of the top priorities for the labor-liberal coalition, which broadened the New Deal's focus on economic justice to include equal rights before the law. The cause of civil rights was both a moral issue and a way to reorient the political system by challenging Southern conservatives' power. But because Southern conservatives were able to obstruct civil rights legislation, congressional reform became the labor-liberal coalition's most immediate goal. Procedural reform and civil rights were almost synonymous in the forties and fifties before the issues started to diverge after 1964. In the wake of Kennedy's assassination and amid the growing momentum of the civil rights movement, the labor-liberal coalition helped piece together a temporary bipartisan supermajority on civil rights that finally overwhelmed minority obstruction. But congressional reform remained a priority for organized labor and other constituencies on the left, and the greatest progress came after the breakthrough on civil rights.

Throughout the sixties and into the early seventies, labor and its liberal allies, including a number of reformers in Congress, pushed a series of congressional changes that finally chipped away at the institutional bases of the conservative coalition's power. Diverse interests, both in and outside Congress, pursued reforms not only to open up the system to liberal policies but also to make the legislative process more transparent and to build the capacity of Congress relative to the president.[3] The labor-liberal coalition had long expected civil rights legislation to shift politics to the left. But the immediate fallout of the civil rights issue in combination with Vietnam destabilized the labor-liberal alliance and the old Democratic electoral coalition, contributing to the election of Republican president Richard Nixon. Nixon's challenges to liberals in Congress and the Watergate scandal broadened the coalition behind congressional reform and ultimately contributed to the election of enough non-Southern Democrats to make it possible.

This chapter is divided into three sections that tie together these multiple developments. The first section looks at labor's efforts to pass civil rights legislation and mobilize African American voters. The second looks at the impact that civil rights and other issues had in widening rifts in the labor-liberal alliance, destabilizing the Democratic presidential electoral coalition, and electing

Nixon. The final section discusses roughly three decades of congressional reform that coincided with the rise and fall of the conservative coalition.

Restructuring Politics Part I: Civil Rights

Organized labor endorsed civil rights legislation not only out of a sense of social justice but in order to enfranchise a natural political ally. Labor unions and African Americans were both held back by the Southern political economy, which depended on low wages, a pliable workforce, a racial caste system, and the veto power of Southern politicians in the national government. The politicians who fought civil rights also fought organized labor, often railing against the NAACP, the CIO, and later the AFL-CIO in the same speech. Prominent leaders in the White Citizens Councils were also leaders in the fight for state right-to-work laws.[4] The same police forces used to fight Operation Dixie were used to fight the civil rights movement. Civil rights advocates and trade unionists thus shared a common interest in destabilizing the political and economic power structure in the South. Labor failed to build its own strength in the South to counter Southern conservatives, but political rights for Southern blacks could achieve the same end.[5]

The two groups also shared public policy goals. African Americans were disproportionately poor and working class and therefore stood to benefit from the expansion of the welfare state organized labor advocated. In an address to the AFL-CIO's 1961 convention, Martin Luther King Jr. noted of black people, "Our needs are identical with labor's needs, decent wages, fair working-conditions, livable housing, old age security, health and welfare measures, conditions in which families can grow, have education for their children and respect in the community." King added that the labor movement should "tap the vast reservoir of Negro political power. Negroes given the vote, will vote liberal and labor because they need the same liberal legislation labor needs."[6] The help the civil rights movement had offered to labor forces in fighting the various state right-to-work referenda that cropped up in the late fifties suggested the benefits of cooperation.[7] First the CIO, and later the AFL-CIO along with progressive member unions, tried to build the political strength of their potential allies by pushing the Democratic Party to engage the civil rights issue, lobbying for civil rights legislation, and conducting and assisting voter registration and turnout drives of minority voters.

Pushing the Democratic Party on Civil Rights

Organized labor, particularly the CIO, played a leading role in bringing the fight over civil rights to a head within the Democratic Party by creating a political environment that made it impossible to continue to avoid the issue as party leaders had done for years to appease Southerners. Labor leaders such as Walter Reuther were important power brokers at national Democratic conventions, pushing the party to take a more progressive stance on civil rights. As discussed in Chapter 1, CIO activists worked with other civil rights advocates to get a strong civil rights plank included in the 1948 Democratic platform. National leaders wanting to pull back in the 1952 platform faced the opposition of these liberal activists. When told that the Southerners threatened to walk out of the convention if a strong civil rights plank was adopted, Reuther quipped, "If it so chooses, let this happen; let the realignment of the parties proceed."[8] At the next convention in 1956, Reuther joined Senator Herbert Lehman (D-NY), and Roy Wilkins, executive secretary of the NAACP, to lead three hundred delegates in plans for a floor challenge to the moderate civil rights plank that was abandoned only after an appeal for party unity by Eleanor Roosevelt.[9]

CIO actions at the state and local level helped shift the position of the Democratic Party's base on civil rights. Brian Feinstein and Schickler find that union activists pushed state Democratic Party organizations outside the South to adopt civil rights planks that made the Democrats more progressive on the issue than Republicans, the chief advocates of civil rights since the Civil War, in most states by the mid-1940s and early 1950s.[10] Local CIO activists also provided the ground troops for efforts such as collecting signatures to place a fair employment practices initiative on the ballot in California in the mid-1940s.[11] Even among voters, public opinion polls indicate that economic liberalism, racial liberalism, and Democratic vote choice were increasingly associated outside the South, and to a more limited degree within the South, by the late 1930s and into the 1940s.[12] These factors combined with the migration of African Americans to cities outside the South to create a new political coalition for civil rights in the Democratic Party.

Although the CIO was out in front, the AFL eventually became more progressive on civil rights. Both the AFL and the CIO advocated legislation in the 1940s against lynching, poll taxes, and employment discrimination. The AFL's William Green joined the CIO's Philip Murray on the Leadership Conference for Civil Rights, founded in 1950 to coordinate the efforts of civil rights, labor, civic, and religious groups in the fight for civil rights legislation in Congress. On the eve of the reunification of the AFL and the CIO, George Meany announced his belief that "the merger would mean more effective means to attain a fair employment practices bill on a national scale, and in attempts to assure civil rights in other fields."[13]

Amid these changes, a number of non-Southern congressional Democrats became key leaders in the legislative fight for civil rights. Schickler and his colleagues find that non-Southern Democrats were more willing than Republicans to sign discharge petitions to force civil rights legislation to the floor of the House by the mid-forties.[14] They further find that union density in a Congress member's state was associated with the likelihood that Democratic members of Congress would sign these petitions.[15] The vehemence of Southern congressional members' opposition to the CIO stemmed from their conviction that it was responsible for pushing reluctant Democratic leaders to take up various civil rights measures in Congress in the 1940s.[16] In contrast to an influential assessment by Edward Carmines and James Stimson that the parties realigned on civil rights in the mid-1960s largely because of the strategic decisions of the 1964 presidential nominees, the parties had been realigning for some two decades because of pressure up and down the ranks of the Democratic Party.[17] When the civil rights movement took actions that forced the issue to the top of the political agenda in the late fifties and early sixties, the groundwork for Democratic leadership on the issue had already been laid.

The Road to the Civil Rights Act of 1964

Like much of the rest of labor's agenda, progress on civil rights legislation was hampered by the institutional position of Southern conservatives. Southerners used the committee system and the filibuster to thwart civil rights bills, including poll tax and fair employment practices legislation, throughout the 1940s. The Civil Rights Acts of 1957 and 1960, the first significant bills to pass, were watered down in order to appease Southerners. Some observers argue that Southern senators acquiesced in the passage of these bills only because they feared their continued obstruction might lead to filibuster reform, but they demanded significant concessions in return.[18] However, the political environment soon shifted.

The reaction to Kennedy's assassination, President Johnson's commitment, and the mounting pressure placed on Congress by the civil rights movement and public opinion outside the South all built momentum behind passing a comprehensive and effective civil rights act in 1964. Sensing victory was possible on a long-standing goal of the labor movement, Meany demanded that the law include a strong fair employment practices section targeting union discrimination, which he insisted the AFL-CIO was not empowered to stop. In 1963 testimony before the House Judiciary Committee Meany argued, "Primarily because the labor movement is not what its enemies say it is—a monolithic, dictatorial, centralized body that imposes its will on the helpless dues payers . . . we need a federal law to help us do what we want to do: mop up those areas of discrimination which still persist in our own ranks."[19] Kennedy's civil rights bill had not contained a fair employment practices section because the administration was afraid it would make the bill impossible to pass. But the AFL-CIO was instrumental in getting Title VII, the Equal Employment Opportunity section, passed in the 1964 legislation.[20] Opponents of civil rights tried to exacerbate tensions within the labor movement between the leadership and the rank and file by distributing information to union members warning that the fair employment practices section would require racial quotas in hiring, displace union members in skilled jobs, and end union seniority and job referral systems, but such ploys failed to change the AFL-CIO's position.[21]

Despite organized labor's role in getting the provision into the legislation in the first place, opponents circulated the rumor that labor was not committed to retaining the employment provision as the legislation neared a vote in the House. The AFL-CIO sent a letter to every representative warning that "reports that the AFL-CIO is not seriously concerned about retaining Title VII in the bill are not true," with Meany's testimony and AFL-CIO convention resolutions attached to make the point. The letter urged support for the entire bill and rejection of any amendments that might weaken it.[22] As the bill moved to the Senate, Biemiller wrote senators to implore them to break a marathon filibuster. Calling the civil rights issue the "most crucial moral issue of our lifetimes," Biemiller stated, "The AFL-CIO, speaking for most of its many millions of members, believes the issue should be decided in favor of the strongest possible civil rights guarantees for all Americans" and stressed that senators should "do everything in their power" to "be present and to assure that the Senate will not want for a quorum until the bill has been passed."[23] Labor lobbyists, working through the Leadership Conference on Civil Rights, did everything they could to sustain momentum behind the bill throughout a fifty-seven-day filibuster. The Senate finally invoked cloture, and the Civil Rights Act of 1964 was passed without crippling amendments.

Like labor legislation, civil rights legislation was particularly vulnerable to filibusters. However, civil rights measures were more likely to have a level of bipartisan support that destabilized the conservative coalition. Although concessions were made to hold the votes of many Republicans, particularly in the areas of public accommodations and employment discrimination, the Civil Rights Act of 1964 passed with the support of 80% of Republicans voting in the House and 82% in the Senate.[24] In contrast, 97% of non-Southern Democrats in the House and Senate voted for the bill. Only 11% of Southern Democrats in the House and 13% in the Senate supported it.

Tensions in the Labor-Liberal Coalition

Despite labor leaders' commitment to civil rights legislation, the larger labor movement was not always a progressive force on civil rights. Labor leaders had to straddle their political goals and the racism and resistance to change among many of the rank and file and secondary union leadership. Thus, labor faced criticism from its political allies in the civil rights and liberal community for not going far enough to address racial discrimination, while it faced criticism from union members and lower-level union leaders, particularly but not exclusively in the South, for going too far in support of civil rights. Although cooperation in passing civil rights legislation eventually helped smooth over these differences between the mainstream labor and civil rights leadership, the emerging New Left and many labor union members were increasingly estranged from the labor movement. The unavoidable tension over race complicated labor's efforts to build a larger liberal coalition.

Racial tension surged in the South in the wake of the *Brown v. Board of Education* decision in 1954 ordering school desegregation, setting the labor movement even further back in this region.[25] A UAW report on the rise of White Citizens Councils and their antilabor and antiblack activities in the mid-fifties noted that "organizers . . . assigned to work in the South know that they must be extremely careful in what they say on the segregation issue at all times. It is becoming much more difficult to organize Negro and white workers employed on the same jobs, especially in areas where the neo-Klan movement has gained a foothold." The report further noted, "The labor movement which has some political and economic power in the larger industrial areas of the South also appears to be immobilized."[26] When progressive forces in the Chattanooga central labor body passed a resolution commending the local school boards' efforts to comply with *Brown v. Board of Education,* nine locals publicly disavowed the declaration and several withdrew from the central body, resulting in a rescinding of the resolution.[27] In other areas unionists attempted to form alternative Klan-oriented labor organizations and to raid existing AFL-CIO unions. Although they were not very successful, the threat sent a message to national union leaders to stay out of local affairs. COPE contributions dried up, and many local labor leaders resigned.[28] Even progressive local leaders were torn between the pressure to support civil rights and the fear of losing their members in the right-to-work states of the South where there were no union security arrangements.[29]

Although some Southern labor leaders were diehard racists, others were committed to building an alliance between labor and the black community. But racial progressives faced enormous challenges and constantly found themselves on the defensive. In 1961, after local papers reported a $5,000 contribution by the AFL-CIO's Industrial Union Department (IUD) to the Congress for Racial Equality (CORE), Claude Ramsey, the progressive president of the Mississippi Labor Council, wrote to George Meany, "A great majority of the leadership of the movement in this state recognize the fact that the AFL-CIO can take only one position, and that is against racial discrimination. . . . We can overcome everything but the contribution of union funds."[30] Ramsey received so many death threats that he carried a firearm at all times.[31] Even in this context, a number of AFL-CIO state councils in the South maintained their support for civil rights, tried to build local labor-black networks around common causes, and launched education efforts to convince white members of the need to ally with black workers.[32] However, as Alan Draper notes of progressive labor leaders in the South, "They tried to build bridges to blacks but to their dismay discovered that their members were unwilling to cross them."[33] In this atmosphere, it was very hard to overturn discriminatory practices of local unions or expand union membership in the South.

Racial tension and union discrimination, however, were not confined to the South. The main complaint of the black community was that white-dominated unions conspired with employers to deny black workers apprenticeship training, job upgrading, and even employment in some firms or industries. Even in

the UAW, long considered a leader on civil rights, black workers found it difficult to break into higher-status jobs in the plants and leadership positions in
the national union into the 1960s.[34] Black members of the United Steelworkers
—not only in Alabama but in Homestead, Pennsylvania—also complained that
they were confined to the lowest wage positions.[35] Discrimination was particularly pervasive in the construction trades. In one of many racial incidents in
the North, union construction workers struck the Bronx Terminal Market construction site when the contractor hired a black and three Puerto Rican workers
who were not union members in an effort to comply with the state's fair employment law.[36]

In the late fifties, the labor movement faced increasing criticism for failing to
eliminate discriminatory practices and a growing rift with civil rights organizations. The NAACP, which had kept its public criticism of the AFL-CIO to a
minimum, became increasingly vocal. It issued a report in 1960 that "argued
that all too often there is a significant disparity between the declared public
policy of the national AFL-CIO and the day-to-day reality as experienced by the
Negro wage-earner in the North as well as in the South."[37] Delegates to the
NAACP's 1960 convention voted to resort to NLRB decertification procedures
and court action, if necessary, to fight union discrimination. Black unionists
joined together in 1960 to form the Negro American Labor Council (NALC) to
push the labor movement to act. A. Philip Randolph, the renowned civil rights
leader, AFL-CIO Executive Council member, and president of the nearly all-
black Brotherhood of Sleeping Car Porters, was elected president. Randolph's
public criticism and his pressure on the AFL-CIO leadership to take immediate
action against discrimination and to make greater efforts to organize black
workers led to his censure by the Executive Council.[38] The rift had widened further by 1962 when the NALC threatened to picket the AFL-CIO convention if
the federation did not deliver on its commitment to end union discrimination.

The AFL-CIO was also criticized for its failure to get involved in early on-the-
ground civil rights struggles such as the Montgomery bus boycott, although
many of the affiliates participated. Most controversial was Meany's opposition
to official participation in the 1963 March on Washington because he argued
that the protest could get out of hand and compromise pending civil rights
legislation.[39] Although his critics suggest this was a pretense, it was a fear other
civil rights advocates shared. Led by Reuther, many members of the Executive
Council fought hard for official sponsorship, but Meany pressed the council to
limit the AFL-CIO's commitment to announcing its support of the goals of the

march and to encouraging affiliates to participate. An estimated 40,000 of the 200,000 marchers were union members.[40]

However, even at the height of the friction between civil rights organizations and the labor movement over union discrimination, there was close cooperation between civil rights groups and the AFL-CIO and many affiliates in the legislative arena. After the passage of the Civil Rights Act of 1964, the previous rifts between labor and civil rights advocates receded.[41] Following the House vote, Clarence Mitchell of the NAACP wrote AFL-CIO legislative director Andrew Biemiller to thank him and noted that passage of the bill "could not have happened without the unstinting and whole hearted manner in which you threw yourself into the fight. . . . There could be no doubt in anyone's mind about the full commitment to support the FEPC after you spoke and acted."[42] Meany announced a civil rights program for the AFL-CIO to bring the affiliates into compliance with the new law. Labor continued to be a key player in the passage of subsequent legislation such as the Voting Rights Act of 1965 and the far more controversial Civil Rights Act of 1968, which addressed discrimination in housing. Randolph dropped his criticism of the AFL-CIO.

The AFL-CIO's role in the civil rights movement outside the legislative arena also expanded. Eventually, the AFL-CIO and a broader cross-section of the affiliates became more willing to participate in the ground battles of the civil rights movement, such as the 1965 Selma-to-Montgomery March.[43] The labor movement also won the praise of the civil rights community by becoming more involved in high-profile struggles of black workers in the late sixties, such as a strike of black sanitation workers in Memphis (the same strike that brought Martin Luther King Jr. to Memphis, where he was assassinated) and a strike of black hospital workers in Charleston, South Carolina.[44] By 1960, African Americans were more likely to be unionized than any other ethnic or racial group, which remains true today.[45]

But the unevenness of the labor movement's commitment to civil rights remained a problem. High-profile struggles over union discrimination, particularly in the construction trades, shaped many young white and black liberals' attitudes toward the labor movement. Whereas labor had been in the vanguard of social justice in the 1930s, it was increasingly viewed as a reactionary force. But these attitudes missed the larger role the labor movement played in the civil rights struggle in the face of bitter internal opposition. Despite growing frictions, organized labor and mainstream civil rights organizations continued to cooperate in both legislative and electoral politics.

Mobilization of Black Voters

Organized labor recognized that in order to destabilize the conservative coalition, African Americans needed more than just equal legal rights—they needed to mobilize in electoral politics. Writing in the 1960s, Greenstone argued that organized labor became an arm of the Democratic Party, maximizing turnout for pro-labor candidates not only by targeting its own members but also by mobilizing other typically Democratic constituencies including blacks.[46] The CIO played this role as early as the 1930s, but the AFL-CIO launched more sophisticated efforts in the late fifties that continue to this day. The union movement began by focusing on registering and turning out black voters in the urban areas where the non-Southern black population was concentrated and then moved to leading or assisting drives to register black voters in the South.

Labor faced an uphill battle, however, in trying to overthrow the power of Southern conservatives through electoral efforts. In a report on the general outlook for the 1960 election, COPE director James McDevitt emphasized the intractability of the conservative coalition and the negative climate in the South as a result of school desegregation and efforts to register black voters. He noted that while Southern liberals tried to slate good candidates, they could not raise enough money, and more conservatives were likely to run unopposed in 1960 than in any recent election. This made a liberal landslide outside the South necessary to break the power of the conservative coalition, demonstrating the difficulty labor had in this period in electing pro-labor congressional majorities. McDevitt stressed the need for long-range efforts in the South, arguing, "The situation cannot be regarded as hopeless. This whole area is becoming more industrial, better educated and less susceptible to demagoguery. While one Representative from Georgia (Landrum) co-authored the Landrum-Griffin substitute, another (Mitchell) braved intensely concentrated pressure to vote against it."[47] Other observers pointed to a successful model in the election of a strong labor-liberal, Ralph Yarborough, to a Texas Senate seat in a special election in 1957 with the support of a coalition of labor, liberal, black, and Latino voters.[48]

COPE began to direct more money toward Southern liberal candidates and to intensify efforts to mobilize black voters in and outside the South. In preparation for the 1960 elections, a year-round COPE program was established in cooperation with fraternal and civic groups to register black voters in Alabama, Florida, Tennessee, Virginia, and Louisiana. The effort to maximize the minority vote in the 1960 election focused on the selection of fifteen states based on "the potential minority group vote and the existence of an effective working relationship between the minority groups and the labor movement."[49] The selected states included old Confederacy states such as Texas, border states such as Kentucky and Maryland, and a range of states with large urban populations including California, Illinois, and New York. Following the 1960 election, McDevitt noted that the heavy Democratic minority vote was "basic" to Kennedy's victory in several crucial industrial states as well as North Carolina, South Carolina, and Texas. He emphasized the prospects for the future, noting that "this great reservoir of liberal votes has still barely been tapped." McDevitt also recognized the need to mobilize other minority voters, noting that only 22% of Puerto Rican voters, who went 88% for Kennedy, voted. The "Latin-American" and Indian vote in Southwestern states had also not been mobilized.[50]

The sophistication of the effort to mobilize minority voters increased over the course of the sixties and seventies as the effectiveness of the overall COPE voter registration and turnout operation improved. Minority turnout for Johnson and the Democratic Party, which had just led the fight for the Civil Rights Act of 1964, reached new highs, helping to produce the liberal electoral triumphs of that year that temporarily destabilized the conservative coalition in Congress. The black vote was viewed as critical to Johnson's victory in a number of Southern states in 1964.[51] After the passage of the Voting Rights Act the next year, Walter Reuther noted, "Instead of . . . Dixiecrats coming out of the deep south and joining forces with the most reactionary Republicans to block social legislation, you are going to have some of the most progressive congressmen coming out of the deep south. This is going to make one tremendous difference in the whole relationship of forces in the political arena of American society."[52]

In 1965 the AFL-CIO made a large contribution to the formation of the A. Philip Randolph Institute, named for the labor and civil rights leader.[53] Bayard Rustin, the prominent civil rights leader hired to coordinate the March on Washington, became the director. The institute was created to strengthen the cooperation between the civil rights and labor movements in pursuit of common legislative objectives dealing with jobs, education, and housing. Labor also hoped the institute would help educate the black community about the labor movement. The mission of the institute reflected the persisting tensions between these two allies. In a letter requesting continued financial support for the Randolph Institute, Don Slaiman, director of the AFL-CIO's Department of Civil Rights, noted, "The present situation, especially in the south, the possibilities of new liberal developments and candidates succeeding because of the increased Negro vote, make all the more important the extension of knowledge of the labor movement's real contributions in the Negro community. At the same time we become increasingly aware that lack of knowledge of labor's program and labor's contributions to civil rights among many in the Negro community permit labor to be made a scapegoat, too often."[54]

Bayard Rustin became a prominent voice in the mainstream wing of the civil rights movement, which, unlike the growing black radical wing, supported coalition with progressive forces and working through the political system. Under Rustin's leadership, the institute mobilized the civil rights community behind particularized trade union goals such as repeal of 14(b). The institute helped launch joint apprenticeship programs with some of the building trades unions to try to recruit more minorities. Within the confines of its tax-exempt status, the institute also came to play a major role in cooperation with the NAACP, the Urban League, and black churches in voter registration and mobilization with financial assistance from the labor movement.

By the 1970s the efforts in the South seemed to be paying off. When liberal Henry Howell just barely lost the governorship of Virginia, COPE director Al Barkan cited the election as "buttressing" his "feeling that more and more, the south is moving into the mainstream of the Democratic party (this, regardless of the fact Howell ran as an independent) and that it will progressively be more fertile ground for liberal governors and national legislators."[55] These hopes were somewhat misplaced, as discussed in greater detail in Chapter 6. Urban districts and districts with large concentrations of black voters in the South did eventually elect liberals, but the South as a whole remained quite conservative. As blacks came into the party, Southern whites left, helping to produce a string of Republican electoral victories first at the presidential level and later in Congress.

Race, Vietnam, and the Election of Nixon

The conflict over race and the war in Vietnam preempted labor's strategy to develop more progressive politics in the late sixties and seventies. The enfranchisement and empowerment of African Americans was necessary to labor's future success and the success of the labor-liberal coalition, but in the aftermath of the major gains of the civil rights movement, race remained a problematic fissure in organized labor and in the Democratic Party. In 1968 and 1972 this fissure contributed to the election of Nixon, who skillfully manipulated the racial issue to destabilize the New Deal electoral coalition.[56] Vietnam produced additional problems for the Democrats and created deep divisions in the labor-liberal coalition.[57] In the party and the labor movement, the issue of Vietnam alienated liberals while the issue of race alienated conservatives, leaving both the party and organized labor sorely disunited.

Emblematic of the disunity in the labor movement in the late sixties was the pullout of the UAW from the AFL-CIO. As a condition of the merger in 1955, Walter Reuther assumed the leadership of the newly created Industrial Union Department. He hoped the department would preserve the CIO's legacy as a social movement within the federation and lead massive organizing drives, particularly in the South. Although the drives in the South were never very large or effective, Reuther's department helped coordinate affiliates' organizing efforts and assisted in the organization of untapped areas such as the service and public sectors. But discontented with his second-rate position and concerned about the stagnating membership base, Reuther became increasingly vocal in his criticism of the leadership and the direction of the federation as the sixties progressed. In an open letter to all UAW locals in December 1966, Reuther asserted that "the AFL-CIO lacks the social vision, the dynamic thrust, the crusading spirit that should characterize the progressive, modern labor movement."[58] He criticized the federation's position on social issues and increasingly its commitment to Vietnam. He also criticized its undemocratic decision-making process.[59] After a series of bizarre actions in 1967 including more open letters, submission and withdrawal of a resolution to the AFL-CIO Executive Council setting up a plan for reform of the labor movement, and a call for a special convention of the federation, the Executive Council suspended the UAW in May 1968 for failure to pay its dues. Several months later the UAW, then the largest union in the AFL-CIO, formally disaffiliated from the federation. Reuther's criticism further reinforced the image held by New Left liberals and activists in the peace, student, and women's movements that the AFL-CIO, along with most of the labor movement, was stale, reactionary, hawkish, and even corrupt.

Continuing internal union problems with racial discrimination further exacerbated the split between the labor movement and other liberals. Particularly in the building trades, union members viewed efforts to ensure minority access and racial diversity as circumventing their hard-won seniority rights and their privilege of sponsoring their children and friends for admittance into apprenticeship programs. Many local unions resisted every effort by government, civic groups, the national union leadership, and the AFL-CIO to cajole or force them into accepting more minority members. As the civil rights movement moved outside the South with controversial policies like open housing initiatives and school busing arrangements, white ethnic communities with a lot of union members revolted.[60] A memo on labor strategy for the 1968 election noted, "In 1966 labor suffered erosion because of the race issue and open occupancy is still political dynamite. The flight of 50% of union members to the suburbs is actually more from GI and FHA financing than from racial tension, but the latter contributed."[61] Many of the rank and file became alienated from the Democratic Party, which they associated with these disruptions to their communities, and the political activities of the AFL-CIO, which continued to support integration. AFL-CIO lobbyist Ken Young noted, "I'm not convinced that our members are bigots or a damn bit different than anyone else. But I'm also sure that the Detroit worker who has finally gotten out of the city damn well doesn't want his kids bused back in. He's scared to death of violence. He knows he now has better schools. And I think he has a case to say who the hell are we to tell him he has to send his kids back in there."[62]

In the South, the revolt of the rank and file continued to present serious management problems for the AFL-CIO. For example, a running feud emerged between the Georgia State AFL-CIO and the regional director assigned to the state by the national federation. The feud finally culminated in a fistfight at the state federation's 1968 convention between the regional director and his allies and the supporters of the state leadership when state officials defied national AFL-CIO policy by working for segregationist George Wallace's presidential candidacy and tried to remove all literature endorsing Democratic presidential nominee Hubert Humphrey from the convention hall.

Despite the splits in the labor movement, organized labor exerted significant influence in the 1968 elections. After Lyndon Johnson, besieged by the Vietnam issue, declined to run again, labor successfully engineered the Democratic nomination of its favored candidate, Vice President Hubert Humphrey, the heir to Johnson's policy in Vietnam.[63] Humphrey had not even participated in the Democratic primaries. Following the convention, labor journalist Victor Riesel noted, "It was, and is, the full coming of age of American labor. The movement has become a party, and this party within a party is on its way to govern, as do its labor brethren in Britain."[64] But Humphrey's nomination infuriated the antiwar contingency within the party. That Humphrey, the crusader for civil rights and the liberal challenger to the status quo in 1948, had become the establishment candidate, whose nomination brought protests in the streets outside the convention, reflected how deep the divisions in the liberal coalition were. Given these divisions, the Wallace candidacy, and the riots in the wake of Martin Luther King Jr.'s assassination, organized labor was fighting an uphill battle to elect Humphrey. COPE documents point out that a particular problem for the Humphrey campaign was "the bankruptcy of the National Democratic Party which made it necessary for the labor movement to supply such basics as buttons, bumper stickers, almost all literature and an important proportion of the funds for routine advance work connected with campaign appearances."[65] Yet Humphrey lost by only 0.7% of the popular vote, or 500,000 votes out of 72 million cast.

Although the media focused a great deal of attention on Wallace's vote counts in early primaries in industrial states, labor's work in the final weeks of the campaign steered union member support from Wallace to Humphrey. Labor-commissioned polls indicated shifts of between 10% and 35% toward Humphrey in certain areas.[66] After initially polling well among union members, Wallace ultimately got only 14% of the union household vote. As a result of the labor effort, the presidential election was much closer than pundits predicted, and the loss of congressional liberals was limited to four senators and two House members. The New Deal coalition largely remained intact in 1968 with the exception of near absolute defection of the South in the presidential election from the party that led the fight for civil rights.

The election of 1972 was a different story. In the wake of the disastrous 1968 Democratic Convention, the party created the McGovern Commission to develop new procedures for the presidential nomination process. The fight over the new rules marked a major rift in the labor-liberal alliance.[67] Most of the reformers pushing for change were openly critical of the role labor and the party establishment played in the selection of Humphrey in 1968 and saw the reforms as a way to open up the nominating process to fresh voices and solidify the ties of the party to the "new politics" social movements. The Democratic Party adopted quotas for delegate slots to the convention for minorities, women, and youth. Delegates also had to be selected by primaries, caucuses, or conventions open to all party members for the first time in 1972. The role of elected politicians and local party regulars in the nominating process was significantly reduced. Many, though not all, labor leaders saw the implementation of the reforms as an effort to undermine labor's deserved power in the party and redistribute it to rivals.[68] George McGovern, the chair of the commission, became the first presidential nominee under the new system in 1972. An embittered Meany convinced the Executive Council to vote against AFL-CIO endorsement of McGovern in an apparent attempt to teach the party a lesson.[69] A significant number of unions, including such large unions as the American Federation of State, County, and Municipal Employees (AFSCME), the Communications Workers (CWA), the International Association of Machinists (IAM), the Oil, Chemical and Atomic Workers (OCAWU), and the Retail Clerks (RCIU), joined two of the major unions outside the AFL-CIO, the UAW and the National Education Association (NEA), in campaigning for McGovern in the general election. But the labor movement was badly fragmented, and a majority of the labor vote and a large victory went to Nixon in 1972, unlike in 1968.

Nixon's appeal to union and other historically Democratic voters was linked to his political strategy to divide the Democratic coalition. In 1969 the Nixon administration initiated the "Philadelphia plan," named after the city where the program was piloted, to require racial quotas for unions working on government contracts. Knowing that the unions would see this as an assault on sacrosanct union seniority and recruiting practices and that organized labor would likely publicly resist the plan, Nixon hoped to split labor and blacks, two of the most important Democratic constituencies. The predicted labor reaction to the plan also exploited the tension between organized labor and other liberal organizations such as Americans for Democratic Action that supported affirmative action. Nixon tapped into what political analysts Richard Scammon and Ben Wattenberg termed the "social issue" in a book that inspired Nixon's 1972 campaign. The "social issue" was the growing frustration of the majority of Americans who were "unyoung, unpoor, and unblack" with "crime, race, values, busing, drugs, disruption, quotas, welfare, pornography, patriotism, draft-dodging, dependency, permissiveness, capital punishment, disparagement of America, and much more."[70] The Nixon campaign effectively tarred the Democratic Party with the economic, cultural, and social disruptions of the sixties and early seventies that frightened middle America and many of the union rank and file.

The Nixon years were rough for organized labor politically, economically, and organizationally. But Nixon's disgraceful exit from office facilitated the election of a wave of liberal Democrats to Congress. Despite the deep divisions within the labor movement and between labor and other liberal groups over Vietnam, labor and the New Left, or "new politics," groups often cooperated in national policy making.[71] These groups expanded the base of the party as well as the reform coalition in Congress. As a result, reformers finally successfully challenged organized labor's nemeses, the conservative coalition, and many of the institutional features of Congress that empowered it.

Restructuring Politics Part II: Congressional Reform

A series of significant congressional reforms was adopted in the early to mid-seventies. Nixon's election reinforced the drive for reform as liberals hoped to exert influence and leadership in Congress to counter the president. But the reform effort was the culmination of more than two decades of endeavors by liberals in Congress to reshape congressional and party institutions to allow liberals and their allies, such as organized labor, greater influence in the legislative process. The AFL-CIO and most of the affiliates were among the most prominent actors outside Congress pushing for congressional reform during this period. Political institutions shaped labor's power, but labor also demonstrated the capacity to exert influence on various political institutions.

Early Skirmishes

The first attempts at congressional reform came in the late 1940s. But instead of favoring the goals of organized labor, early reforms further undermined them. Recognizing that Congress was ineffectively organized and incapable of overseeing or countering the burgeoning executive branch, Congress passed the Legislative Reorganization Act of 1946. Conservatives and liberals deadlocked over reforming seniority provisions and the Rules Committee, and these institutions escaped untouched. But the act cut the number of committees and increased committee staff, making the remaining committee chairs even stronger. Moreover, in the wake of the act, seniority became sacrosanct. The 1946 legislation thus sowed some of the seeds of the liberals' discontent in later decades.

Following the 1948 election, which returned control of Congress to the Democrats, both the House and the Senate opened with a fight over rules reform geared to the passage of civil rights legislation. In the House, the target was the Rules Committee. Over the opposition of many Republicans and Southern Democrats, the House passed the twenty-one-day rule, which allowed the chairs of the committee favorably reporting a bill to call the legislation directly to the floor if the Rules Committee reported unfavorably on it or failed to act within twenty-one calendar days. The rule was used to bring a poll tax repeal bill to the floor in 1949, and the threat of its use led Rules to report a handful of important bills including the 1949 minimum wage increase and 1950 Social Security improvements.[72] But the twenty-one-day rule was repealed with the support of the conservative coalition and its business group allies at the beginning of the next Congress.[73]

The Senate featured a far more contentious fight over cloture reform. Various parliamentary rulings, including one issued in the 1948 fight over a poll tax bill, had made the Senate's cloture rule totally ineffective, allowing unlimited debate on controversial measures. Afraid this might tie the Senate in knots, liberals in Congress, the Truman administration, and the Republican leadership all supported restoring an effective cloture rule. But after the administration came out in favor of the CIO's proposal to allow cloture to be invoked by a simple majority, the congressional coalition for reform began to break down.[74] Republicans felt the administration was being insincere and trying to appease important constituencies with a proposal it knew had no chance of passing. Southerners accused the administration of kowtowing to the CIO and violating the separation of powers by interfering in the legislative branch, with Senator William Fulbright (D-AR) even comparing Truman's cloture proposal to FDR's court-packing plan.[75] The changes that ultimately passed in some ways made cloture even harder to invoke. The rules change did reestablish an effective cloture procedure (except for filibusters against rules changes that were still subject to endless debate), but the cloture threshold was increased from two-thirds of senators present and voting to two-thirds of the entire Senate.

Many labor leaders sensed a conspiracy. While the CIO wanted to take up the cloture issue, AFL leaders warned that it threatened to postpone action on Taft-Hartley repeal until after important spring contract negotiations. One such leader, Communications Workers president J. A. Beirne, argued that the Democratic leadership had fallen victim to an effort by Republicans to derail the administration's legislative agenda in taking up the divisive issue of cloture reform at the beginning of the session.[76] UAW and CIO leaders accused Republicans of backing away from reform in collusion with Southern Democrats based on an agreement that Southerners would oppose repeal of Taft-Hartley in exchange for Republican opposition to meaningful cloture reform.[77]

Spurned in Congress, labor activists tried to make congressional reform a party issue. They joined with other liberal activists to lobby Democratic presidential candidates to endorse reform and to make congressional reform a plank in the party platform.[78] The 1952, 1956, and 1960 Democratic platforms called for improved congressional procedures, but these planks had little effect. As a draft of a UAW memo entitled "Relations with the Democratic Party" noted, "The CIO problem has not been one of counting votes in the national convention. The majority of the delegates are sufficiently friendly and the leading Democrats are sufficiently aware of the importance of the labor vote that they listen to our preferences." The memo argued:

> Our real problem is with the Congress. Here we are not dealing with the Democratic Party as a whole, but only with those who get elected. That is a significant difference. In the party as a whole, the liberals and the friends of labor are in the majority. But when liberal Democrats are defeated by Republicans, and conservative Democrats are elected, the proportion changes. This balance is lowered still farther by a Democratic (and CIO) desire to pick up some Republican votes. Thus, the Democratic position in Congress is not as good as in convention, and what comes of Congress is watered down even more. The question is: How can we tighten up the Democratic Party? How can we make it into an organization? How can we refine its ingredients so as to make them purer liberals? How can we improve its discipline or sense of responsibility so that wandering congressmen can be tied to the party line?

Among the many suggestions were proposals to strengthen the congressional party caucuses and hold committee chairs accountable. The memo suggested a threat should be made "that unless the Democrats in Congress agreed to drop the seniority system and to appoint committee chairmen and members on the basis of ability, loyalty to the program, etc., we would refuse to support the Party and its candidates in 1956. If we really did this, and meant it, it would be a thrilling revolution in American politics. But we won't do it."[79] This last sentence was scratched out in the draft. As much as many labor leaders would have liked to teach the Democrats a lesson by pulling their support, they were afraid to take the risk. The last time labor had largely sat out an election, in 1946, it got a Republican Congress and the Taft-Hartley Act. Thus, labor did not pull its support for Democrats but continued to implore party leaders at every opportunity to take up congressional reform.[80] Many of the changes labor supported were eventually adopted.

Growing Momentum behind Reform

The 1958 elections, which brought many new non-Southern Democrats to Congress, marked a turning point in the reform effort, initiating a period of reform that would extend for two decades. After eight years out of the White House, congressional Democrats wanted to build a platform for the Democratic presidential nominee in the 1960 elections focused on legislation to deal with the problems of urban areas. But this was precisely the type of legislation blocked by the conservative coalition. A growing contingent within the Democratic Party saw the party's future in the liberal, urban, and labor vote and was determined to move the party away from its conservative, rural, Southern past. The reformers wanted to improve Democratic Party discipline and minimize opportunities for minority obstruction in the legislative process. Thus, there were two tracks of reforms—those targeted at the rules and norms of the Democratic caucuses and those targeted at the organization and parliamentary procedures of the Senate and House. Although progress came in fits and starts, the reform movement picked up steam.

Reform in the Senate

In the late fifties and early sixties, a group of liberals led by junior senator Joseph Clark (D-PA) called for party discipline and a clear Democratic agenda. In a speech on the Senate floor in 1959, Clark condemned the strategy of passing "veto-proof" legislation, which was the term conservative Democrats used to describe and defend legislation built on compromises with Republicans and the Eisenhower administration. He added:

> Democrats who come from one-party states do not need a party record on which to run for re-election next year. Their contests are not with Republicans but with other Democrats, and they run on their personal and not their party records.
>
> But those of us who come from states where the two-party competition is rough *do* need a party record. We need a Democratic program—based on the Democratic platform—which will clearly present the Democratic philosophy. . . .
>
> It will not matter which of our Senatorial hopefuls for the Democratic nomination may win the prize, because the record of the Democratic Senate on which he runs will be indistinguishable from the position of the Republican Administration which he is seeking to displace. If the people can detect no difference between the parties, they will hardly vote to make a change.
>
> I hope that those who seek to blur the difference between the parties—who seek to fuse and blend the Democratic and Republican programs, point by point, in the dark recesses of committee and conference action—will ponder the damage they are doing to our party as we prepare for the campaign next year.[81]

These liberals called for strengthening the Democratic Policy Committee, responsible for party policy and strategy in the Senate, and making the Democratic Steering Committee, responsible for committee assignments, more representative and more accountable to the Democratic Caucus. Reformers argued that these committees were far more conservative than the caucus after the 1958 elections. In fact, Clark and another liberal senator, William Proxmire (D-WI), argued that committee assignments in general did not reflect the "industrial base" of the party.[82] In 1965, the Steering Committee was finally enlarged, and Majority Leader Mike Mansfield gradually moved the committee to the left by appointing liberals to vacancies. After Nixon's election, Senate Democrats revived the Democratic Policy Committee, hoping to use it to take on the president, although it never became very influential.[83] Continued liberal attacks on seniority culminated in a caucus decision in 1975 that made it easier to challenge Democratic committee chairs. These changes were not nearly as far reaching as those pursued in the House, and they did not substantially improve party discipline. But they did have an impact on the climate in the Senate, convincing many committee chairs to be more responsive to the rank and file.

The number one goal in reforming Senate rules was modification of Rule 22, which governed cloture. In 1953 and 1957 liberal Senate Democrats and frustrated Republicans attempted to alter Rule 22 because it made passage of civil rights legislation seemingly impossible. Since the 1949 change to require support of two-thirds of the entire Senate to invoke cloture, there had not been a single successful cloture vote. The UAW prepared an influential legal brief in 1951 arguing that Rule 22 was unconstitutional because it permitted "the minority to block the will of the majority," violating founding principles.[84] The brief also suggested a procedural path for reform. It argued that the Senate, like the House, was not a continuing body and that its rules did not carry over from one Congress to the next. Walter Reuther suggested, "This is a convenient piece of folklore invented by those who wish to rule future Senates through the dead hands of past Senates."[85] Instead, new Senate rules could be adopted at the opening of a congressional session with a simple majority vote. Liberals felt this was the only way Rule 22 could be changed because if the existing rules were in effect, efforts to change Rule 22 would inevitably be successfully filibustered. Utilizing this strategy, Senate reformers moved to drop all Senate rules and institute new ones at the beginning of the 1953 and 1957 sessions, but both efforts failed. Testifying before a Senate committee in 1957 in favor of cloture reform, Reuther noted how close the pro-reform coalition was, arguing, "It is inevitable that the foolhardy attempt of March 17, 1949 to 'nail the Senate's feet to the floor for a thousand years' is going to be undone and corrected sooner or later—and not much later. . . . We have 7 Senate votes to go; 7 Senators must be persuaded or elected to support the ending of rule by filibuster and to vote for substitution of majority rule."[86] The founding convention of the AFL-CIO endorsed a change in Rule 22 to permit a majority to invoke cloture, and year in and year out, the federation put the issue high on its agenda.

The influx of liberals arriving in the Senate in 1959 convinced reformers they might finally have the votes to change the cloture rule. As in the Truman years, liberal reformers including organized labor again pushed a proposal to allow cloture to be invoked by a simple majority, but they still did not have enough support. Instead, then majority leader Lyndon Johnson pushed through a compromise to lower the cloture threshold to two-thirds of senators present and voting as it had been before 1949. The change also permitted cloture to be invoked on filibusters of changes to the Senate Rules, improving the prospects for change in the future. Although the change represented a modest improvement in the cloture rule, labor leaders were furious. As UAW leader Roy Reuther suggested in a heated discussion with the secretary to the Senate Majority, "How can we get our people to work for the Democratic Party candidates if this is what happens after we win?"[87]

Cloture reform eluded reformers for another decade and a half. Efforts to reduce the number needed for cloture from two-thirds to three-fifths of the Senate in 1961 and 1963 were both successfully filibustered. As noted in the previous chapter, the AFL-CIO again considered pushing filibuster reform in the midst of the 1965–66 fight over repeal of 14(b), but labor lobbyists counted only 53 votes in support—a majority, but not the supermajority needed to end a filibuster of filibuster reform. Their count was on the mark. In 1967 another effort to invoke cloture to end a filibuster against a reform proposal to reduce the cloture threshold from two-thirds to three-fifths gained exactly 53 votes in support. A successful filibuster of filibuster reform became a biennial ritual in the Senate until 1975, when reformers finally had enough support to invoke cloture. They amended Rule 22 to reduce the majority required to cut off a filibuster to three-fifths of all senators or 60 votes, although a two-thirds majority was still required to invoke cloture on filibusters of Senate rules changes. The gathering momentum behind reform, the increased interest among a broader range of actors, and the liberal gains produced by the fallout from Watergate made the cloture change possible. Over the next several years, additional reforms were passed to make filibusters less disruptive of the Senate calendar and to prevent postcloture dilatory tactics. A minority would still be able to obstruct action in the Senate, but the AFL-CIO hoped it would be much easier to meet a threshold of 60 votes than 67.

Reform in the House

In the House, the first target of reformers was the Rules Committee. A group of liberals pressed Speaker Rayburn at the opening of Congress in 1959 to rein in the power of the Rules Committee, which, under the chairmanship of the famously anti-labor Howard Smith (D-VA) since 1955, remained a graveyard for a number of measures advocated by liberals including most civil rights bills. Like their counterparts in the Senate, liberal House Democrats were concerned about building a Democratic record for the 1960 presidential elections, and Rules was a major obstacle. Not only did Rules refuse to report certain bills, anticipation of Rules Committee opposition affected proposals in other parts of the legislative process, forcing the substantive committees to report out watered-down bills members thought might survive. Liberals on Rules sometimes were even encouraged by the party leadership to make deals with Smith. In such deals, liberals agreed to vote against measures the chairman did not want to release but on which he feared he would not have the cooperation of the Republicans; in exchange, the chairman would vote in favor of other provisions endorsed by the liberals or considered important to the party.[88] Sometimes the chairman would simply not hold committee meetings on a bill he opposed. Rayburn assured the group that Rules would not bottle up legislation in the 86th Congress. But Rayburn could not rein in the committee, and it continued to stymie legislation. However, the obstruction of the Rules Committee was not the only problem for liberals.

Prior to the 1970s explosion in congressional staff, members of the House had rather limited sources of information, which empowered committee chairs and undermined liberals' effectiveness on the floor.[89] Committee chairs were often a conservative force in the legislative process. They controlled the debate, and committee reports on pending bills were not typically made available until just prior to floor consideration, preventing members from evaluating legislation in advance. Political scientists also suggest that the procedure for amendments tended to produce a conservative bias.[90] Prior to a rules change in the early seventies, unrecorded "teller votes" were typically taken on amendments in the Committee of the Whole, where bills are amended. Only a hundred members are required to form a quorum in the Committee of the Whole, a parliamentary device created to allow the House to operate more efficiently. Because these votes were not recorded, fewer than a third of members generally participated, even though amendments could substantially transform legislation. Southern Democrats, typically coming from safe, one-party districts, were far more likely to be on the floor for these teller votes than other Democrats from competitive districts who were busy dealing with constituent affairs.

The smooth passage of Landrum-Griffin in the House reflected many of these problems. The anticorruption bill became an anti-labor bill through the amendment process in the Committee of the Whole, where liberals had not participated in adequate numbers. As a group, the liberals were disorganized with virtually no communications system to alert allies to legislative developments.[91] Complicated amendments to the labor bill were voted on before opponents could mount a defense. The final version of the bill infuriated organized labor, whose active support in elections was deemed crucial to the non-Southern wing of the Democratic Party. The experience with Landrum-Griffin convinced a core group of liberals that something had to be done to strengthen their influence in the party and Congress.

In September 1959, less than a month after the passage of Landrum-Griffin, liberal House members formed the Democratic Study Group (DSG). There were no formal membership lists, but participants in the DSG included a group of eighty members who signed a "liberal manifesto" of legislative goals in 1957 and many of the liberal freshmen elected in 1958. Of a speculative list of DSG founding members put together by Congressional Quarterly, more than two-thirds of all members and four-fifths of the freshmen had received recorded labor union campaign contributions.[92]

The DSG served as an informal liberal caucus within the Democratic Caucus. One of the DSG's most remarkable accomplishments in the sixties was its growing sophistication as an information and whip organization, providing liberals timely information on pending legislation and alerting them to the need to be on the floor for certain votes. The DSG formed task forces to handle special issues, some of which were quite successful in forcing legislation out of committee and preventing crippling amendments on the floor.[93] The Johnson administration utilized the DSG whip system on the Civil Rights Act of 1964 and other Great Society initiatives. The National Committee for an Effective Congress noted of the 1965 Congress, "Whereas in previous years the DSG had to maneuver for the attention of House leaders, not to speak of Presidents, in 1965 it was wooed and consulted almost daily by the White House, the heads of Departments and the House leadership. This difference is reflected in the legislative record."[94] The whip system was tied into the liberal lobbying network to pressure wavering legislators. When new liberals were elected to Congress, the DSG held social events to introduce them to liberal lobbyists and electoral allies in the AFL-CIO and national unions. Over the course of the sixties, the DSG increased turnout for votes in the Committee of the Whole and produced greater cohesion among its members,[95] overall serving labor's goals.

The DSG also mobilized support for congressional reform. The first major accomplishment of the DSG was a successful push to expand the size of the Rules Committee. At the beginning of the 87th Congress, the DSG, labor, and the newly elected Kennedy administration pressured the Democratic congressional leadership to reform the Rules Committee, expected to be a major obstacle to Kennedy's New Frontier agenda. Liberals feared that failure to pass Kennedy's agenda would hurt the Democratic Party's electoral prospects in the populous Northern states. John Blatnik (D-MN) argued on the House floor in January 1961, "My constituents did not cast a free ballot for the office of U.S. Representative to Congress to have the functions of that Office limited by one or two or even six other Members."[96] Rayburn proposed temporarily enlarging the committee from twelve to fifteen, adding one Republican and two Democratic members, which would break the conservative coalition majority.

Because the Rules Committee change made it more likely that liberal proposals would make it into law, numerous interest groups lobbied for and against the enlargement.[97] Smith called on organizations such as the National Association of Manufacturers and the Chamber of Commerce, frequent opponents of labor's agenda, to lobby against the Rules change. Other organizations that opposed Kennedy's legislative priorities, such as the AMA, also lobbied against it. Kennedy called on the labor movement to put as much pressure as possible on Rayburn and the House Democratic leadership to pursue Rules reform, and labor led the lobbying fight to help Rayburn get enough votes to pass it.[98] Labor was joined by many of the affiliates, the National Education Association, the National Farmers Union, the U.S. Conference of Mayors, and civil rights groups.[99]

The House passed the temporary expansion of the Rules Committee 217–212. Only one non-Southern Democrat voted against it, while 57% of Southern Democrats did. The efforts of the AFL-CIO were also crucial in picking up a number of Republican votes, which produced the winning margin and overwhelmingly came from Republicans representing urban, industrialized districts.[100] In 1963 the House voted to make the change permanent. The reform cleared the legislative path for a number of labor-backed measures over the next few years including the groundbreaking Civil Rights Act of 1964, but it did not eliminate obstruction from Rules as various bills of interest to labor continued to face problems. In the next Congress, labor, other organizations within the Leadership Conference on Civil Rights, and the DSG pushed through two more changes.[101] As mentioned in discussion of repeal of 14(b), the twenty-one-day rule was reinstated, allowing committee chairs to call a committee-reported bill to the floor if Rules did not act on the bill within three weeks, and the power of Rules to block bills from going to conference with the Senate was all but eliminated. The Rules Committee's long reign as the institutional stronghold of the conservative coalition was over.

In addition to trying to undermine the power of the conservative coalition through changes in congressional rules, the DSG exerted its power within the Democratic Caucus. The group lobbied for the appointment of liberal members to important committees like Education and Labor, which was stacked with liberals on the Democratic side by the late sixties. The DSG also helped engineer the defeat of the nomination of Phil Landrum (D-GA), the conservative sponsor of the Landrum-Griffin Act, to a prized seat on the Ways and Means Committee (discussed in Chapter 3). The DSG flexed its growing power in 1965 to lead successful efforts in the Democratic Caucus to strip seniority from two Southern Democrats who had supported Barry Goldwater in the election.

The DSG also tried to make rank-and-file Democrats aware of the need for congressional reform. Representative James O'Hara of Michigan, a leading member of the DSG and a strong ally of labor, tried to phone all the DSG members early in 1968 to find out their perceptions and attitudes toward greater congressional reform. He found an "awful lot of ignorance" of the process of how members became chairs.[102] Some members thought the seniority system was provided for in the House rules, federal law, or even the Constitution. The vast majority were unaware that the principle of seniority did not develop until after the revolt against an imperious Speaker at the beginning of the twentieth century and thought it was a sacrosanct parliamentary tradition. Most members had absorbed the philosophy of Speaker Rayburn expressed in the oft repeated phrase "you have to go along to get along," and they were afraid of antagonizing powerful chairs. The complacency of moderate and liberal members was one of the major obstacles to congressional reform, and O'Hara realized "a major education effort" was needed.

The DSG sought the revival of the Democratic Caucus, which had fallen into disuse during the Rayburn years. They called for regular monthly meetings of the caucus at which they hoped informal pressure could be placed on the leadership and committee chairs. The meetings would also allow reformers to educate the rank and file about the rules and procedures of the caucus and the House. The proposal was approved in 1969, more than twenty years after labor leaders first called for strengthening the caucus and making it an instrument to enforce party discipline. The DSG continued to educate the caucus and circulated a number of voting studies revealing the collusion of Democratic committee chairs with Republicans on roll call votes.[103] As a result, rank-and-file Democrats increasingly came to share labor's indignation with the seniority system, which produced chairs who did not serve the national party's goals.

Congressional Reorganization

After the House reformed the Rules Committee, the House and the Senate established a Joint Committee on the Organization of Congress in 1965 to consider other proposals for modernizing the legislative process. But the committee was prohibited from considering contentious issues like filibuster reform and declined to take on seniority. The committee ultimately recommended several proposals, generally endorsed by labor, to curtail the power of committee chairs, open up the committee process to public scrutiny, and strengthen the role of Congress in the budget process. However, organized labor strongly opposed a proposal to split the House Education and Labor Committee and the Senate Committee on Labor and Public Welfare into separate labor and education committees. Labor feared that a labor committee would become ineffective and polarized between staunch liberals and conservatives. The Johnson administration worried that a split would damage "the highly fruitful relationship existing between the lobbying groups" working on health, education, and labor issues. A Johnson staffer noted, "Labor would be isolated in an unpopular committee. Health and education would lose the labor shock troops that help pass bills for them."[104] Legislation based on the committee's recommendations passed the Senate in 1967 but died in the House. However, the growing intensity of the rivalry between Congress and the president kept interest in reorganization alive. Dating from the time of Roosevelt, liberalism had been associated with support for a strong executive branch. Vietnam and Nixon's election ended that association as liberals sought to reassert the power of Congress to counter the executive branch.

Provisions from the 1967 legislation were resuscitated and a compromise Legislative Reorganization Act passed in 1970. Amendments to undercut seniority failed, but a number of provisions reduced committee chairs' influence over legislative outcomes. A committee majority was empowered to call for floor consideration of a bill after it was cleared by Rules.[105] This provision was largely aimed at the House Education and Labor Committee's Chairman Powell, who had refused to call legislation on common situs picketing to the floor for several years. One of the major targets of reformers was the unrecorded teller votes on amendments that allowed members of Congress to escape responsibility for votes on major legislative changes. Rank-and-file representatives were permitted to demand a roll call on amendments. There were several other antisecrecy provisions including public disclosure of roll call votes in committee and the opening of committee meetings to the public. As Burton Sheppard notes, public disclosure "would end the opportunities for 'closet' liberals or conservatives to say one thing and vote another."[106] It also allowed interest groups such as the AFL-CIO to follow congressional members' votes more closely. Not only did this discourage representatives from missing votes, but it also made members more likely to respond to constituent or interest group pressure, rather than pressure from committee chairs. Because of labor opposition, the Joint Committee's original recommendation to split the education and labor committees was not considered. The bill passed both the House and Senate with overwhelming support, including that of a number of Republicans who were also frustrated with the way the House operated.

The Growth of the Reform Coalition

Nixon's election, subsequent political scandals, and the influx of new members into Congress created a hospitable environment for reform that was exploited by a growing reform coalition. In the late sixties and early seventies, a larger range of interest groups mobilized around the reform issue, including new public interest groups such as Common Cause and Public Citizen. Some of the groups had ties to the labor movement. Common Cause, for example, had its origins in the National Urban Coalition, which was formed by various urban interests, liberal unions, and the AFL-CIO to force greater political attention to the needs of urban areas. Although labor cooperated with these groups on a range of shared goals, there was often tension. Many of the leaders and members of these groups were highly critical of the AFL-CIO's support for Vietnam. They also saw labor as a "special interest" that was often a party to backroom deals in smoke-filled rooms. Organized labor, civil rights organizations, and groups like the ADA had been pushing congressional reform since the 1940s in order to make the legislative process more open to the liberal public policies they favored. However, the new public interest groups had a less instrumental view of reform, pushing reform for reform's sake to open up the political system and make it more democratic, rather than to generate a set of public policy outcomes.[107] They opposed the institutions that empowered the conservative coalition because they undermined democratic accountability, not because they blocked labor law or health reform. While there were many areas of agreement, labor ended up in skirmishes with some of the new public interest groups over particular reforms. However, labor's position tended to prevail in these skirmishes.[108] Despite the divisions, these groups helped labor achieve longstanding goals. They brought new assets to the coalition in their effective use of the media and their influence in suburban, middle-class districts, where labor was not very powerful.[109] What had been a trickle of reforms would become a tidal wave in the early seventies.

The Democratic Caucus Takes on Committee Reform

In the early seventies, liberal Democrats returned to the issue of reforming congressional party institutions in addition to House rules. The shift to party reform was reinforced by changes in the composition of the Democratic Caucus. Over the course of the sixties and into the seventies, the two-party system was beginning to creep into the South and into areas of historical Republican dominance in the Northeast. The center of gravity in the Democratic Caucus was pulled to the left.[110] The Democratic Caucus, which met regularly as a result of the reforms of 1969, became the locus of reform efforts. In 1970 the Democratic Caucus chair in the House, Representative Dan Rostenkowski of Illinois, under pressure from the DSG, appointed a committee to recommend caucus reforms that became known as the Hansen Committee after its chairwoman. Its recommendations inspired a series of reforms adopted by the Democratic Caucus in the early seventies.

Reforms continued to chip away at the power of committee chairs. Seniority was the first target. Under pressure from the growing chorus of groups demanding reform, the national Democratic Party also went on record in favor of efforts to strengthen the caucus and weaken seniority. The plank on congressional reform was written with a new level of specificity in 1972, and it railed against seniority as "crippling effective Congressional leadership" and making it "impossible to present and enact a coherent legislative program."[111] As labor leaders had long demanded, the platform called for the election of committee chairs by separate ballots based on their party loyalty. The caucus finally took action to rein in committee chairs in the early seventies, first permitting an open vote on the appointment of individual committee chairs on the request of ten members and then allowing the votes to be secret if 20% of the members requested.[112] Other reforms, such as the so-called Subcommittee Bill of Rights adopted in 1973, weakened the committee chairs by empowering subcommittees. Together these reforms made committee chairs more accountable to the caucus, spread power to more junior members of Congress (who were more likely to be liberal), and constrained the ability of committee chairs to dictate the shape of legislation and to intimidate committee members into voting for the chair's position.

Other proposals were designed to strengthen both the power of the caucus and the party leadership elected by the caucus. In a proposal strongly endorsed by the AFL-CIO and Common Cause, the Rules Committee was required to sit on a bill at least four days when a committee chair requested a closed rule on a bill, which prohibited amendments.[113] During this time, if fifty Democrats wished to submit an amendment to the bill, a caucus would be called to consider whether the amendment could be offered. This proposal was primarily directed at the imperial power of Ways and Means chair Wilbur Mills, who typically got closed rules to keep his work intact on the floor. The AFL-CIO had criticized the conservative bent of legislation emanating from Ways and Means for years. The leadership was given a greater role in committee assignments, and a Democratic Steering and Policy Committee, on which the leadership would serve, was also formed to make recommendations to the caucus regarding party policy.

1974: A Watershed Year for Reform

In addition to the numerous caucus reforms, the whole House took action in 1973 to create a bipartisan Select Committee on Committees under the chairmanship of Representative Richard Bolling (D-MO) to investigate rationalizing committee jurisdictions. Organized labor demonstrated its influence in the reform process by killing a renewed effort to split the House Education and Labor

Committee when the Bolling Committee released its recommendations the next year. The opposition of the AFL-CIO and many of the affiliates to the Bolling plan placed much of the labor movement at odds with some of the good government groups such as Common Cause, which endorsed a dramatic overhaul of the committee system.[114] Ultimately, the far-reaching Bolling plan was rejected in favor of a compromise brokered by the Hansen Committee that made far more modest changes in the committee system backed by organized labor. The AFL-CIO pushed the Hansen proposal, and its lobbyists felt the best provisions of the Bolling plan were retained in the final package of reforms.[115] Other reforms would have a significant impact on the legislative process. One allowed the Speaker to refer bills to multiple committees. Viewed by some as a way to diffuse power on major legislation in the House and by others as a way to empower the Speaker and the majority party,[116] multiple referral made it more likely that a conservative committee's proposal would face competing proposals. Another change tripled the number of professional staff allowed committees, which further enabled Congress to counter administration proposals.

Congress also passed legislation that significantly changed the nation's budgeting process in the Budget and Impoundment Act of 1974. Many of the changes had been called for by the AFL-CIO for years. In part a response to battles with the Nixon administration over spending on social programs, the act was an effort to rationalize the budget process and shift leadership on the budget away from the president and back to Congress. Not only did it alter Congress's role in taxing and spending, but the budget legislation also created a process called reconciliation that would later be used on certain types of bills to circumvent various obstacles in the legislative process including the filibuster. Presidents Ronald Reagan, Bill Clinton, and George W. Bush would later use reconciliation to pass controversial tax legislation. Ultimately, the reconciliation procedure made possible, over unanimous Republican opposition, the passage of the massive health care reform bill worked out between Barack Obama's administration and congressional Democrats.

The 1974 election in the wake of the Watergate scandal produced a large new class of seventy-five Democratic freshmen representatives and the most liberal majority since the 1964 elections, which supported a whole new round of reform. The divisions in the reform coalition were quickly smoothed over as both organized labor and the good government groups recognized the potential for far-reaching reform. The organizational session of the caucus for the 94th Congress held in December passed a wave of additional reforms to strengthen the leadership and the caucus. Most of these reforms came from a package assembled by the DSG in November to quickly take advantage of the outcome of the elections. The power to assign members to the substantive committees was transferred from the Democratic members of Ways and Means, many of whom were more conservative than the average Democrat, to the Democratic Steering and Policy Committee. The power to appoint the chair and the Democratic members of Rules was transferred to the Speaker with caucus approval. There were also limitations on the number of committee chairs a member could hold. Partly in anticipation of an upcoming fight over national health insurance, the Ways and Means Committee was expanded to allow appointment of more junior, and likely more liberal, representatives.[117] Finally, there were several "sunshine" reforms mandating open committee meetings, open conference committee meetings, and release of recorded votes in the Democratic Caucus.

The multiple caucus reforms prior to the 1974 election had marginal impact, but the so-called Watergate babies made use of the reformed procedures to exert a real challenge to seniority and its associated conservatism. In an institution in which deference to seniority had been sacrosanct, the freshmen held their own caucus to drill standing committee chairs about their views.[118] A Common Cause report on the performance of the individual committee chairs that specifically targeted several as unresponsive to party or public sentiment proved quite influential.[119] Many of the freshmen joined with DSG reformers in the Democratic Caucus to replace three sitting chairs, finally launching a successful challenge to seniority.[120] This action put all chairs on notice that they had better pay attention to majority sentiment in the caucus or risk losing their positions. The reforms, combined with the changes in the Southern electorate, eroded the dominance of conservative Southern committee chairs. The era of committee government in Congress had come to an end. Labor alone did not produce this outcome, but it played a very important role in fostering and sustaining the reform coalition that made it possible.

Irritated by the Democratic reforms, Representative John Anderson (IL), then the chair of the GOP Conference (comparable to the Democratic Caucus), provided a cautionary note when he called attention to the fact that a majority of the majority party was still a minority of the House.[121] That would become obvious in labor's legislative failures in the wake of reform. Yet labor and liberals in general stood to benefit from the attacks on the institutional bases of the conservative coalition's power. While reforms did not produce an omnipotent liberal legislative majority, liberals had a better chance of moving legislation that would have died in committee two decades earlier.

Other Reforms

Although organized labor focused on reforming congressional rules and practices, the sixties and seventies were a tumultuous period that produced a range of other reforms that had consequences for organized labor's political position in subsequent decades. Several reforms affected congressional districts. As mentioned in the previous chapter, the Supreme Court took the initiative in addressing the malapportionment of congressional districts and state legislatures in a series of decisions in the mid-sixties that ended the rural domination of state legislatures in many industrial states such as Michigan and reduced the representation of rural interests in the U.S. House. Because of urbanization and redistricting, the number of congressional districts with a rural majority declined from 214 to 130 between the 1964 and 1972 elections, making the House far more representative of metropolitan areas.[122] The court-ordered redistricting also corresponded with the disappearance of a pro-Republican bias in non-Southern congressional districts in which Republicans won a share of seats greater than their share of the vote.[123] This improved the chances of electing pro-labor House members. In the South, the Court's rulings against vote dilution, combined with enforcement of the Voting Rights Act of 1965 and state redistricting efforts, eventually undermined the electoral base of many conservative Southern Democrats.[124] The multiple currents of reform came together in the symbolic defeat of the imperious Rules Committee chairman Howard Smith in the 1966 primary. As a result of court-ordered redistricting, Smith's Virginia district was redrawn to include a sizable black constituency. The AFL-CIO got involved in the election and helped his liberal challenger win.[125] In an ominous sign, however, the seat was won by the Republican candidate in the general election.

Some reforms did not necessarily serve labor's interests even though the AFL-CIO and many of the affiliates played a role in shaping them. The 1971 Federal Election Campaign Act and its 1974 amendments placed limits on campaign contributions but facilitated the precipitous growth of corporate political action committees (PACs). In 1976 Democrats received roughly two-thirds of their PAC contributions from labor; by 1980 the figure had fallen to 43%.[126] A 1978 internal postelection COPE report warned of rising corporate campaign contributions, even to longtime allies of labor. The report suggested that a number of candidates with voting records under 75% in support of labor's position who received significant corporate contributions might "cave to business" on legislation.[127] The diversification of funding for Democratic candidates meant that labor had to step up its lobbying operation in the 1970s and 1980s to ensure the support of non-Southern Democrats it might have previously taken for granted.

Conclusion

Organized labor played a leading role as part of a larger labor-liberal alliance in changing the contours of the American political system in the first three decades of the postwar period. Labor broadened the coalition for civil rights within the Democratic Party, despite tensions within its own ranks, and developed and relentlessly pursued an agenda for congressional reform that was eventually supported by a majority in the party. When organized labor started to advocate civil rights legislation and congressional reform back in the 1940s out of frustration with the conservative coalition's power over public policy, labor strategists hoped the changes would allow labor-liberals to take control of the Democratic Party and the government. When civil rights legislation and congressional reforms were finally adopted in the sixties and seventies, labor did not get the liberal transformation of the political system it expected. The immediate impact was disarray in both the Democratic electoral coalition and the legislative process, resulting in continued stalemate on labor's most ambitious policy goals, as discussed in the next chapter. But the changes during this period set off a slow-moving regional realignment of the parties, with the Republicans eventually becoming strongest in the South and Plains states and the Democrats becoming strongest in the Northeast, industrial Midwest, and Pacific Coast states, where labor—and the broader labor-liberal coalition—was more influential.

5

Postreform Stalemate on Labor's Agenda

The 1970s were tough on organized labor.[1] Manufacturing employment fell as international competition increased and multinational corporations moved production to countries with rock-bottom wages. Employers became quite sophisticated at fighting union organizing, and union membership density entered a period of seemingly endless decline. The economy suffered the twin shocks of soaring inflation and unemployment, which complicated collective bargaining. In the arena of politics, labor appeared to be losing its influence.[2] Two Republican presidents were hostile to labor's agenda, and when a Democrat finally made it into office, he too failed to deliver. Contemporary observers and labor scholars have often suggested that the failure of labor's legislative priorities during Jimmy Carter's presidency was due to his chilly relationship with the labor movement.[3] But enduring institutional constraints in the legislative process also played a very important role in undermining labor's agenda.[4]

As a result of congressional reform, divided government, and the rise of the filibuster, some of labor's proposals took different paths through the legislative process, and labor faced greater uncertainty in devising its legislative strategies. But after three decades of considerable political change, the record of labor's legislative accomplishments during the seventies was quite consistent with the postwar pattern of incrementalism and obstruction. The minimum wage was again increased, but labor law reform again failed. Full-employment legislation in the form of the Humphrey-Hawkins Act passed, but like the employment legislation of 1946, it was largely symbolic and toothless. National health insurance gained a lot of attention but never made much progress toward becoming law. As in the 1940s, labor resisted committing to an incremental approach like Medicare that could attract a viable legislative coalition. Labor leaders hoped the congressional reforms of the late sixties and early seventies would eliminate the institutional roadblocks to their policy priorities. While committee obstruction did decline, the conservative coalition remained a force in floor votes, and other institutional obstacles—the presidential veto during the Nixon and Ford years and the Senate filibuster during the Carter years—prevented many labor-backed proposals from becoming law. Organized labor continued to exert influence in the political system, as reflected in support on roll call votes and Carter's efforts to accommodate labor. But its legislative accomplishments remained far more limited than its goals.

The Nixon-Ford Years

During Nixon's presidency, labor made incremental gains in public policy, despite the mutual hostility between the president and the labor movement. Organized labor was critical of Nixon's handling of the souring economy, particularly his efforts to hold down inflation through wage and price controls and his efforts to reduce spending on social programs. But labor was able to push its legislative agenda in the Democrat-controlled Congress. Several new categories of workers came under the jurisdiction of the NLRB, including postal workers and employees of nonprofit hospitals. The pattern of incremental growth in Social Security continued with substantial increases in benefits in 1969, 1971, and 1972, as well as expansion of the Medicare program to cover the disabled. The business community also suffered several defeats on legislation favored by labor, including one of the most progressive tax bills in history and legislation to shore up employer-provided pensions in the Employee Retirement Income Security Act of 1974 (ERISA).[5] Despite arguments that the labor-liberal coalition was in decline by the late sixties,[6] labor and the emerging public interest movement cooperated on shared areas of concern, and a coalition of old and new liberals helped pass the Coal Mine Health and Safety Act in 1969, the Occupational Safety and Health Act in 1970, a series of landmark environmental bills, and several consumer protection bills.[7] But the New Left encountered the same obstacles in the legislative process as the old Left, and all these bills involved concessions and delays, just as in other policy areas.[8] Organized labor also joined civil and women's rights groups to defeat the Supreme Court nominations of conservative Southerners Clement Haynesworth and Harrold Carswell.

Despite these accomplishments, the presidential veto became a powerful force in policy making, particularly during the Ford years. Nixon's resignation and the resulting election of a wave of Democratic "Watergate babies" in 1974, many of whom were endorsed by organized labor,[9] produced a Congress that was quite supportive of labor-backed legislation.[10] But most of this legislation failed to make it into law. President Ford, politically vulnerable and facing conservative challenger Ronald Reagan for the Republican presidential nomination, vetoed sixty-six bills in his short period in office. Ford vetoed numerous COPE priorities from emergency jobs legislation to legislation on common situs picketing (discussed in more detail below). Congress failed to override most of these vetoes, often coming only a handful of votes short of the two-thirds supermajority needed. Ford killed labor-backed bills, but Congress killed most of Ford's priorities as well. The 1975 COPE report found consolation in the fact that if the labor movement had not worked so hard to build a liberal majority in the 1974 elections, "the President would have had a virtually free hand in imposing negative and regressive policies upon the nation."[11] Gearing up for the 1976 elections, the AFL-CIO stressed Ford's "abuse" of the veto power and his desire to "impose minority rule," calling for the election of Jimmy Carter and "a Congress to back him up."[12] Labor got the electoral victories, but the legislative victories once again proved elusive.

The Arrival of Carter

Jimmy Carter was the first presidential nominee to be selected almost entirely through the primary process. The AFL-CIO leadership opposed the Democratic Party's shift to primaries and remained neutral in the 1976 contest because of the lack of a consensus candidate in a crowded field.[13] But many of the affiliates got involved, and the UAW and AFSCME played an important role in building momentum behind Carter's nomination.[14] As a Georgia governor with no experience in national politics, Carter ran against Washington and had very few connections with the Democratic Party establishment. Although he was not their first choice, liberals, labor, and minorities joined in support of Carter's candidacy as it gained momentum, hoping he would appeal to the electorate as a fresh voice untainted by the corruption of Washington in the aftermath of Watergate. Carter tried to woo liberal and labor support by selecting Walter Mondale as his running mate. Several planks were also put into the Democratic platform to build labor's enthusiasm in the election, including support of national health insurance, indexing of the minimum wage to inflation, repeal of 14(b), and strengthening of the National Labor Relations Act. Hoping to capitalize on the liberal gains in Congress that had been checked by Ford's veto, the AFL-CIO threw its support behind Carter after the Democratic convention.

Numerous conflicts emerged between Carter and labor, but Congress imposed greater limits on labor's legislative objectives than the administration did. Labor leaders, particularly George Meany, were frustrated with missteps by the Carter administration and the lack of advance consultation before the release of major proposals. There were also tensions over wage and price controls, just as there had been with Truman and Johnson, and labor felt Carter worried too much about inflation in devising proposals on its legislative priorities. While these conflicts often led labor leaders to be publicly very critical of Carter's leadership, many of labor's problems in accomplishing its legislative goals were actually in Congress. The concessions necessary to get bills through the legislative process were greater than those demanded by the president. Labor would learn during the Carter years that even a reformed Congress would challenge its legislative priorities.

The Impact of Congressional Reform

The Shifting Institutional Base of Conservative Power

For labor, the biggest change in the 1970s was the shift from the House to the Senate as the main source of obstruction. The conservative coalition in the House was weakened by committee reforms and the increasing percentage of non-Southern Democrats in the Democratic Caucus, making it more likely that liberal policy proposals would make it to the House floor. The conservative coalition continued to appear regularly in floor votes, but the success rate declined from the highs of the 1940s and 1950s (table 2.1). No longer able to count on legislation being scaled back by the House, conservatives became more assertive in the Senate, increasingly resorting to the filibuster or filibuster threats to shape legislation. The filibuster's use had largely been limited to civil rights legislation in the postwar years, but the range of legislation subjected to filibusters expanded and the number of filibusters creeped up in the 1960s and grew faster in the 1970s.[15] The number of cloture votes, which were typically unsuccessful, grew correspondingly (see figure 6.7). Whereas the House had often pulled legislation to the right in conference committees during the heyday of the conservative coalition, now the Senate was becoming the conservative force in negotiations.

A Power Vacuum

Another prominent change in the legislative process in the 1970s was growing decentralization.[16] The proliferation of subcommittee chairs and staff and the heightened role for the caucus reduced the power of committee chairs as brokers in the legislative process. A power vacuum emerged because party leaders did not fully assume the role once played by committee chairs in directing legislation.[17] Because of continuing division within the Democratic Caucus, largely along regional lines, there was not enough party unity for liberals to take full advantage of the reforms passed earlier in the decade that held the potential to strengthen the caucus and the leadership.[18] As Bruce Oppenheimer notes, a "new obstructionism" developed in Congress in which many members, rather than a few powerful committee chairs, now had the power to "delay or defeat" legislation unless their own particular demands were met.[19] The reforms also confused committee jurisdictions, creating an ambiguity that fed institutional rather than ideological power struggles between committees and committee chairs. The various sunshine reforms that opened up the workings of the committees and the caucus to public scrutiny, in combination with external political changes in the media and elections, also precipitated changes in the way Congress operated. Insider bargaining and the brokering of compromise legislation became more difficult under the scrutiny of interest groups, the media, and the public.[20] As a result of these changes, the House occasionally descended into a state bordering on chaos in the first years of the postreform Congress.

For organized labor, these changes made lobbying more complicated and legislative outcomes more unpredictable. Although in many instances the institutions of the prereform Congress served to limit labor's political influence, labor lobbyists learned to function in the old system. Labor's experience in the mid- to late seventies demonstrated that an "insider" lobbying strategy of consulting with committee chairs, a few key committee members, and the party leadership was not as effective. Andrew Biemiller, the AFL-CIO legislative director, noted upon retirement in 1979 that "more than ever before, you have to see practically every member of Congress if you are to have any hope of success."[21] In this more open system, party leaders continued to have difficulty delivering votes. Meany complained, "Quite a few new House members are not paying attention to their own leaders. . . . We just keep plugging away at what we think is good legislation, and we do have the cooperation of the leadership. But that doesn't mean that the leadership can automatically turn over to us the membership of either the House or the Senate."[22] One lobbyist within the AFL-CIO Department of Legislation during this period observed that after the "upheaval of the congressional seniority system where a lobbyist could deal with the chairman of a committee and cut a deal and votes would be delivered . . . you had to do more lobbying of the rank-and-file members. We found, after some hard lessons, that we could not rely on lobbying by a chief officer, we had to go deeper into the movement to broaden the pressure base of the organization."[23]

Meany mourned the decline of party discipline, but of course organized labor had always faced the recalcitrance of conservative Southerners within the Democratic Party. Yet since the 1940s labor had been able to count on most Democrats from industrial states as fairly reliable friends. But party unity among House Democrats declined slightly in the 1970s, and non-Southern Democrats on average were less likely to support liberal positions during the Carter years.[24] A number of scholars argue that Democrats were increasingly open to the pressure of a range of groups as labor's dominant position in the party was challenged by the "new politics" groups on the left and business influence on the right.[25] However, the new Democratic representatives were not reflexively antilabor as the conservative Southern and rural Democrats had been. Their votes were in play. These Democrats could not be counted on in the way many of the occupants of Northeastern and industrial Midwestern and Western seats had been counted on before. But as the discussion of labor law reform below illustrates, labor lobbyists could often win their votes if they fought for them.

The congressional reforms occurred under Republican presidents, and labor lobbyists hoped a Democratic president would fill the leadership vacuum in Congress. But Meany complained about Carter's ability to deal on the Hill after a series of legislative losses: "I don't think he has been able to deal with Congress the way you would normally expect the President to deal with the Congress in control of his own party. So, while I certainly don't blame President Carter for the setbacks, I think that if he were a stronger President, stronger in relation with Congress, I think he might have been helpful to us."[26] A stronger president might have been more helpful, but in many ways Carter's weakness was institutionally embedded and exacerbated by external circumstances such as the oil shocks and the staggering economy. The factors that complicated labor's efforts to persuade Congress, such as the growing decentralization of power, also made it more difficult for the president to lead.[27] Moreover, if Meany had reflected on labor's experience during the Truman administration, he would have realized Truman was not very "helpful" either, even with a Congress controlled by the Democratic Party. Even the legendary Johnson's success rate in Congress fell from its peak in 1965 to a figure on par with Carter's for the rest of his presidency.[28] Labor was very disappointed in the Carter presidency, but as the next sections illustrate, the record of legislative accomplishments on labor's issues was quite consistent with the postwar pattern.

Continued Incrementalism on the Minimum Wage

Incrementalism and the need to make repeated legislative attempts in order to improve the minimum wage continued into the 1970s. Since most jobs were now covered by the FLSA, the fight was over whether certain workers should have a subminimum wage. In 1972, the House passed a minimum wage increase that included a subminimum wage for teenagers, a provision strongly opposed by organized labor. When the Senate passed a much more liberal bill without the youth subminimum, the House twice voted against sending the measure to conference with the Senate. The members of the conservative coalition united on these votes because they were convinced that House conferees, who would be drawn from the increasingly pro-labor House Education and Labor Committee, would approve the Senate version. In the first session of the next Congress, a bill favored by labor passed both the House and the Senate. But Nixon vetoed it because the bill did not include a youth subminimum, and he viewed the size of the wage increase as inflationary. Although the House failed to override the veto, both the House and Senate passed a similar bill in the next congressional session by such substantial margins that Nixon signed it, convinced his veto would be successfully overridden.[29]

After years of skirmishes like these on the minimum wage, labor hoped to realize a longtime goal in the Carter administration of raising the minimum wage and permanently indexing it to inflation to allow automatic increases without new legislation. Labor supported a House bill increasing the minimum wage from $2.30 an hour to $2.85 and indexing it to 60% of the average manufacturing wage.[30] Two months into his administration, Carter called for a minimum wage increase to only $2.50 an hour and indexing to only 50% of the manufacturing wage. The administration failed to consult with labor leaders before the announcement, which was routine for Democratic presidents on long-standing issues of interest to the labor movement. This failure ensured that the relationship with labor would get off to a rocky start. A shocked George Meany termed the proposal "shameful."[31] By summer the disagreement was smoothed over, and the administration and labor reached a compromise. However, labor was unable to prevail in Congress on the indexing provision. The final version phased in a more generous increase to $3.35 an hour by 1981, but its value was eroded by high inflation. The minimum wage's value fell even further as conservatives gained power in Washington over the next decade, which contributed to rising income inequality.[32] In contrast to the incrementalism on the minimum wage, stalemate continued on labor law reform.

The Return of Labor Law Reform

Compared with earlier efforts, the committees that handled labor law reform in the 1970s were very responsive to labor, and the House Rules Committee no longer posed an obstacle. Instead the struggle over labor law reform emerged as an elaborate game of legislative "whack-a-mole" as labor lobbyists struggled to get victories in the House, Senate, and executive branch in one legislative session. A bill to deal with the common situs picketing issue in the construction industry fell victim to a presidential veto in one Congress and to a House floor defeat in another. A comprehensive package to reform the NLRA, pursued during the first years of the Carter administration, received the highest level of support in both the House and Senate that any pro-labor reform had received in the postwar period, but it was still defeated by a filibuster. The path of these legislative proposals indicated the new opportunities—and complications—for labor in building support in the reformed political system, as well as the impact of the enduring protections for the minority that allowed the conservative coalition to continue to exert veto power on legislation of interest to organized labor.

Common Situs

In 1975, labor decided to take advantage of recently implemented congressional reforms, large Democratic majorities in Congress, and a promise from

President Ford to sign a common situs bill if it contained certain other provisions dealing with collective bargaining. Common situs legislation provoked intense opposition from business interests, which correctly feared that its passage would spur labor's effort to pursue more comprehensive labor law reform including another effort at repeal of 14(b). Despite this opposition and the appearance of the conservative coalition on the vote, the House easily passed a bill that contained the provisions desired by Ford 230–178.[33] In the familiar pattern, 95% of non-Southern Democrats voted for the bill, compared with only 31% of Southern Democrats and 20% of Republicans. In the Senate, a filibuster on the motion to proceed to consideration of the common situs bill was broken by a 66–30 cloture vote. Opponents then launched a filibuster of the bill itself. The first cloture vote failed 58–31, but after an intensive labor lobbying effort focused on members of both parties, the second cloture vote succeeded 62–37. These victories would not have been possible without the recent cloture reform lowering the threshold from 67 to 60 votes. As in the House votes, the conservative coalition also appeared in the votes on cloture, weakening amendments, and final passage, but it only succeeded in thwarting the majority on the first cloture vote on the bill. The bill finally passed 52–45. Desperate to break organized labor's momentum, business groups launched a major lobbying effort that convinced Ford to reverse his position and veto the bill early in 1976.[34] Ford changed his position in part because he feared giving an issue to Ronald Reagan in the primary.

After the election of Carter, labor leaders decided to pursue the common situs issue again. The AFL-CIO saw the 1977 legislative session as an opportunity for significant gains on issues that had been held up by the committee system in the prereform Congress or vetoed by the Republican presidents of the previous eight years. However, when a common situs bill came up early in the 95th Congress, it was met with a surprising defeat in the House, where it had passed handily fifteen months before. The National Action Committee on Secondary Boycotts, an umbrella organization of business groups, initiated a massive campaign against the bill to generate grassroots contacts with Congress from constituents, primarily owners and employees of small businesses and nonunionized construction firms. As the date for floor consideration approached, the campaign chipped away at labor's support. Although the Education and Labor Committee had easily passed a bill on a party-line vote, Democrats on the committee worked with moderate Republicans to produce a new compromise acceptable to labor that might draw more support by exempting significant sectors of the construction industry from the law. However, even a weakened bill failed to pass (205–217), with 88% of non-Southern Democrats, 24% of Southern Democrats, and only 10% of Republicans voting for the bill.[35] If the same percentage of non-Southern Democrats had voted for the bill that voted for it in the Ford administration, it would have passed.

Fearing the loss, the Democratic congressional leadership had suggested pulling the bill off the floor schedule, but labor lobbyists felt confident that they had the votes.[36] However, rank-and-file Democrats, particularly electorally vulnerable freshmen, were open to the appeals of a resurgent business community, and labor was caught off guard by the need to fight for its agenda within the mainstream of the Democratic Party. While labor focused its lobbying on an expected Senate filibuster, the business community focused on the House. The National Association of Manufacturers targeted ninety-one congressional districts, sixty-eight of which were represented by freshmen.[37] Thirty-seven of these sixty-eight freshmen voted against the bill, including seven Northern Democrats and thirteen freshmen supported by COPE in the 1976 elections. Suggesting the success of the business lobbying effort, new members noted that the overwhelming balance of constituent mail opposed the bill and played a role in their final decisions.[38]

The defeat of common situs legislation convinced many within the AFL-CIO that support on a controversial measure even among "liberal Democrats" could no longer be taken for granted at any stage in the legislative process. The labor movement was outmaneuvered by the business community, and many members of Congress questioned whether union lobbyists' had the support of the rank and file.[39] Over the course of the late seventies, and particularly during the eighties, the AFL-CIO and many of the affiliated unions focused on improving their grassroots lobbying capacity. This effort began in earnest with the push for comprehensive labor law reform. After the common situs defeat, the AFL-CIO and its affiliates geared up for what was expected to be a tremendous battle with the business community and conservative organizations over reform of the NLRA later in the year and made a more concerted effort to mobilize union members. However, as occurred with repeal of 14(b), labor again ran into the obstacle of the filibuster.

Action on the Labor Law Reform Package

By the late seventies, the NLRA was no longer providing adequate protection for workers trying to organize. It became the standard practice for companies to hire "labor-busting" consultants to exploit weaknesses in the law.[40] The often lengthy period of time between employees' petition for a certification election and the actual election allowed employers to chip away at employee support for unionization. Employers had an advantage because they could hold employees as a "captive audience," using work hours to address employees and convince them to vote against union representation. In contrast, union organizers had to contact workers outside work hours and generally off the employer's property, making it virtually impossible to reach all employees at once, if at all. Moreover, employers were tempted to break labor laws, including harassing or firing union supporters, because the penalties were so minor. Even if a union was certified, it often struggled for months and sometimes years to get employers to bargain a first contract. Thus labor's goals went beyond repeal of 14(b) to a range of reforms to address these problems.

In the first months of the Carter administration, labor leaders and lobbyists, congressional allies, the Labor Department, and White House staffers engaged in extensive negotiations to develop a comprehensive labor law reform package that all could endorse. Although the Carter administration is often believed to have given only lackluster support to labor's policy goals, the administration made labor law reform a top legislative priority.[41] The administration worked hard to pass the bill and never backed away from its commitment because the administration saw labor law reform as key to building a good working relationship with labor. As Carter's chief domestic policy adviser, Stu Eizenstat, noted to the president, "It is difficult to overestimate the importance of this matter in terms of our future relationship with organized labor. Because of budget constraints and fiscal considerations, we will be unable to satisfy their desires in many areas requiring expenditure of government funds. This is an issue without adverse budget considerations, which the unions very much want. I think it can help cement our relations for a good while."[42]

The administration and labor finally agreed on a package of reforms in the summer of 1977. Over the course of the negotiations, labor dropped three of its most controversial goals—repeal of 14(b), a provision to allow certification of a union as a collective bargaining agent without a NLRB election based on signatures of support from employees (now known as "card-check" recognition), and a provision requiring the new owners taking over a company to honor existing union contracts.[43] These provisions were not supported by the administration, and they were certain to meet stiff resistance in Congress. The final package included several provisions to make it easier for unions to organize, including accelerated certification elections, a larger NLRB capable of process-ing cases more quickly, and union access to employees during work hours on company property. It also stiffened penalties for employers who violated labor laws by prohibiting them from receiving government contracts and requiring them to pay double back pay (rather than the existing provision of back pay) to employees illegally fired for organizing activity. The package also addressed the difficulty newly unionized employees had in getting recalcitrant employers to bargain by empowering the NLRB to award workers the wages the board esti-mated they would have earned under an average collective bargaining agree-ment if employers were found to have illegally refused to negotiate.

The administration-backed proposal sailed through the House. The House Education and Labor Committee quickly reported a clean bill with Republican amendments defeated on party-line votes. Shortly afterward the bill passed 257–163 on the House floor in a striking reversal of fortune compared with the defeat on common situs. Ninety-seven percent of non-Southern Democrats supported the measure, as did a sizeable minority of 41% of Southern Demo-crats along with 26% of Republicans. This time organized labor did not take support in the House for granted and launched a massive lobbying effort,[44] gaining support from many representatives who voted against common situs. In contrast with labor's previous experience with bills like Landrum-Griffin, floor consideration was structured to favor labor, largely because of the support of the congressional leadership and its ability to control the Rules Committee. The House adopted a rule that restricted amendments from congressional op-ponents. Those amendments that opponents did manage to offer that had a strong chance of passing were countered by more benign proposals from labor's supporters. These amendments gave House members cover and diverted sup-port from the more antilabor provisions. Votes on amendments that would have weakened various provisions of the bill were defeated handily, although close margins were expected. One labor strategist noted, "We never lost control of the bill."[45] After a year of many defeats and disappointments that led pundits to declare the demise of organized labor's political influence, the victory on labor law reform demonstrated that organized labor could still win in Wash-ington. But the real challenge would come in the Senate.

At the beginning of the 1978 session, the Senate Human Resources Com-mittee easily approved the administration's labor law reform package spon-sored by Senator Harrison Williams Jr. (D-NJ) and liberal Republican senator Jacob Javits (NY), in a bipartisan vote of 13–2. But Senate majority leader Robert

Byrd (D-WV) was reportedly reluctant to schedule the bill for fear the votes were not there to invoke cloture on an inevitable filibuster. Byrd wanted the administration's commitment that it would actively lobby the bill. White House staffers urged the president, "We believe the Administration should remain committed to go all out on this bill."[46] Byrd scheduled the bill for debate in mid-May, and the White House scheduled a number of public events to build momentum.[47]

Although Carter was often accused of abandoning labor, the administration saw it the other way around. In a meeting with George Meany, the president pledged to do everything he could to pass labor law reform but was urged by staffers to demand something in return. They felt the administration should be given more credit for its support of labor's legislative agenda in Meany's public statements and that the administration should get more cooperation from labor. As presidential adviser Landon Butler emphasized to Carter, "The relationship between the AFL-CIO and the Administration cannot continue to be a one-way street."[48]

Throughout the struggle, the administration and labor felt confident cloture could be invoked. The administration counted 53 "firm" votes, with another 6 who indicated they would "eventually" vote for cloture,[49] making it necessary to find only one more senator. They worried more about a likely "post-cloture filibuster" waged through endless amendments as labor's opponents, led by Senator Orrin Hatch (R-UR), had prepared roughly a thousand amendments to prolong consideration of the bill.[50]

But getting the 60 vote supermajority to invoke cloture proved to be harder than expected.[51] Although labor leaders had already made a number of concessions in negotiations with the administration, they agreed to more at various points in the Senate battle in the hope of picking up votes. In order to blunt the effects of a lobbying offensive by small business, Senator Byrd, with labor's concurrence, arranged for the introduction of an amendment that would exempt most small businesses from the law's protections.[52] Unlike Majority Leader Mansfield in 1965, Byrd was working hard to get the bill through.[53] But after three weeks of debate that shut down consideration of all other legislation, the first two cloture votes failed 42–47 and 49–41. These votes underestimated labor's support because five cloture supporters were absent and others had indicated they would support cloture on subsequent votes.

After negotiations with the administration and labor, the majority leader and Senators Williams and Javits announced a compromise proposal somewhat weakening the provisions to accelerate elections and to punish employers who violated labor laws in the hope of breaking the filibuster. However, the next cloture vote still failed 54–43. After picking up three Republicans targeted by labor and one absentee Republican supporter, the pro-cloture vote jumped to its highwater mark of 58 in the next two votes.[54] Ninety-five percent of non-Southern Democrats and a surprising 37% of Republicans supported cloture. But Southern Democratic support was disappointing at only 17%.

The efforts of the administration, congressional leaders, and labor focused on four Southern Democrats (Senator Dale Bumpers [AR], Senator Lawton Chiles [FL], Senator Russell Long [LA], and Senator John Sparkman [AL]), as well as two small state senators who had historically voted against cloture motions, regardless of the substance of the legislation, as a matter of principle (Senator Howard Cannon [NV] and Senator Edward Zorinsky [NE]). President Carter personally pressured a number of these senators to vote for cloture, plus he contacted Senator Ernest Hollings (D-SC), who was stirring opposition by the vehemence of his public criticism of the bill.[55] All parties made a feverish effort to pick up the remaining two votes. Senator Sparkman, a onetime labor supporter who had served in the Senate since 1946 and had been Adlai Stevenson's running mate in 1952, indicated he would support cloture on the sixth and final vote.[56] Everyone looked to Senators Chiles, Long, and Bumpers for the last necessary vote on the bill, with labor agreeing to drop the controversial provision granting unions' equal access to employees and promising to accept the Senate version over the more favorable House bill in conference in order to get one more vote.[57] It appeared that the filibuster might finally be broken with the support of Senator Long, but then Senator Ted Stevens (R-AL) started to waver.[58] It became clear that cloture could not be invoked.

The Senate voted to recommit the bill to the Human Resources Committee, where supporters attempted to reach a new compromise. Over the course of the negotiations, labor leaders realized that the compromises necessary to get the bill passed would make it virtually meaningless. Moreover, the end of the congressional session was approaching, making scheduling even a "bare bones" proposal difficult.[59] Labor and the administration finally abandoned the effort.

Just as political commentators had viewed passage of labor law reform in the House as a sign of labor's strength, failure in the Senate was viewed as a sign of labor's weakness. But the two peak cloture votes reflected roughly the same level of support in the Senate as the overwhelming victory in the House. Fifty-eight percent of senators voted for cloture, while 59% of House members voted for the labor law bill.[60] The bill's failure was also blamed on the stridency of the opposition of the business community and Carter's failure to make a successful public appeal.[61] But the bill's failure centered on a small handful of senators from conservative states with low unionization rates who were already predisposed to oppose the bill. Public appeals were unlikely to change these senators' position. Little had changed since the 1965 defeat on 14(b) repeal, except that labor had more support. The conservative coalition's ability to block legislation supported by a majority in the House had been all but eliminated by congressional reform. But an alliance of Republicans and Southern Democrats could still control the outcome on the labor law bill through the Senate filibuster—a tool they would increasingly turn to. As UAW president Douglas Fraser observed to President Carter, the defeat of labor law reform was "proof that because of the revival of the filibuster, no controversial legislation may be passed by a majority of the Congress. Apparently, now there must be 60 votes to pass such legislation."[62]

Journalists and pundits depicted the loss as an indication of labor's declining political power in the seventies. In a press conference following the final failed cloture vote, a reporter asked Meany to comment on the state of labor given that labor leaders had been "hit over the head on legislation." Meany responded: "I would put the labor movement just where it has been in the forefront fighting for liberal and social causes. As far as legislative situations are concerned, if you look up the legislative record, we have had setbacks in legislation for many, many years, but we keep right on and, when you look back over the years, the progress has always been in our direction in the long run. Now, when you say we have had a setback I suppose you are talking about Labor Law Reform. Actually the labor law is today what it was yesterday, what it was last month, what it was last year. There is no change in it."[63] Meany's response highlights the legislative experience of organized labor in the postwar period, slow and incremental progress in some legislative areas and stalemate in others. The 1977–78 legislative path of labor law reform had been somewhat different from previous labor efforts on 14(b) and common situs. Demonstrating the impact of congressional reform, the committee system no longer served as an impediment, and the party leadership utilized some of its tools to strengthen labor's position. The bill made it fairly easily through the legislative system until it met the filibuster. As in 1965, labor was able to build majority support for labor law reform but not the supermajority needed for cloture. Despite improvements in the legislative process, the outcome was the same—failure to alter the status quo. Conservative obstructionism in the Senate also played a major role on another labor priority, full-employment legislation.

The Return of the Full-Employment Issue

Unemployment reached the highest levels since the Great Depression during the mid-1970s. Throughout the decade, the AFL-CIO and many affiliates pushed for public works and other government spending programs to stimulate employment. The combination of high unemployment and high inflation known as "stagflation" flummoxed policy makers because treating one problem risked exacerbating the other and traditional policy tools did not seem to bring much improvement. The long postwar economic boom had dampened interest in economic planning. But the new economic situation led a few economists outside the mainstream of the discipline, some businesspeople, and organized labor to pursue a less interventionist version of the type of economic planning that had been considered and rejected in the United States in the postwar reconversion period. Several supporters of centralized economic planning joined in early 1975 to form the Initiative Committee for National Economic Planning headed by Nobel prize–winning economist Wassily Leontief and United Auto Workers president Leonard Woodcock.[64] Later in the year, Hubert Humphrey, the former vice president and then senator from Minnesota, joined Senator Javits (also the Republican cosponsor of the administration's labor law reform package) to sponsor legislation based on the recommendations of the committee to create new planning capacity in both the White House and Congress and new institutions focused on a longer-range outlook than those created in the Full Employment Act of 1946.

Humphrey soon joined forces with Representative Augustus Hawkins (D-CA), a leading member of the Congressional Black Caucus who had sponsored a full-employment bill guaranteeing a job to all who wanted to work. Civil rights leaders had long argued that civil rights legislation meant little without a comprehensive effort to end the economic isolation of blacks. Black unemployment was often double the rate of white and became a double-digit problem in many inner cities, particularly among young people. Several Great Society employment and training programs targeted black unemployment, but underfunded and perhaps poorly conceived, they failed to solve the problem. As the ratio of black to white unemployment edged higher in the 1970s, there was growing demand for government action by civil rights leaders and black politicians.

Congressional Democrats hoped to make full employment a major campaign issue in 1976. As the chair of the Joint Economic Committee of Congress, which was created by the Employment Act of 1946, Humphrey held a series of regional hearings throughout the country in the winter of 1975 on unemployment and the need to amend the 1946 legislation. In the spring of 1976, Humphrey and Hawkins cosponsored the Full Employment and Balanced Growth Act, which joined the planning approach of the earlier Humphrey measure with the commitment to full employment of the Hawkins proposal. The Humphrey-Hawkins bill set a goal of 3% adult unemployment to be reached within four years. The president, Congress, and the Federal Reserve were to cooperate with state and local governments to stimulate private-sector job creation. The government would serve as the employer of "last resort," creating public-sector jobs when necessary to achieve full employment. The AFL-CIO, affiliated unions, the UAW, and civil rights groups formed the core support for the bill. Demonstrating the cooperation of old liberals and new, the coalition picked up support from women's organizations, churches, and even an organization of environmental groups under the umbrella of Environmentalists for Full Employment, uniting the major organizational supporters of the Democratic Party.[65] But between the introduction of the Humphrey-Hawkins proposal in March 1976 and its final passage in October 1978, the full-employment bill would gradually be winnowed down to a largely symbolic commitment to reducing unemployment.

Critics of the Humphrey-Hawkins bill argued it would send inflation soaring even higher. At the insistence of organized labor, the first Humphrey-Hawkins proposal excluded wage-price controls and guidelines and included a provision requiring the public-sector jobs created as a result of the legislation to pay "prevailing wages." Prevailing wages in government contract work were often determined through collective bargaining and were generally considerably higher than minimum wage. Opponents charged that these public-sector jobs would lure workers away from lower-paying private-sector jobs and feed wage inflation. These concerns stalled the bill in Congress and shaped negotiations over full-employment language in the Democratic platform committee. The AFL-CIO indicated a new willingness to go along with some form of wage-price stabilization and to drop the "prevailing wages" provision in exchange for Carter's support of full-employment legislation and other labor priorities. Before the election, the House Education and Labor Committee reported a substitute proposal reflecting these changes, along with stronger measures to deal with inflation and the stipulation that the "last resort" public-sector jobs would primarily be low skilled and low paying.

Following his election, Carter felt obligated to support the bill, but the administration had numerous concerns, including the potential inflationary impact, possible redundancy with existing programs, and the effectiveness of the various proposals in addressing unemployment in a changing labor market. There was also an overarching fear the bill would "raise false expectations about the ability of the Government to remove the impediments to full employment quickly."[66] Given the fragmentation in economic policy-making authority recognized in the bill between the Federal Reserve, Congress, the executive branch, and the states, the president would not be given the institutional tools needed to plan *and* implement a full-employment policy effectively, but he would likely be blamed politically for not fulfilling the goals of the act.[67] Although Representative Hawkins was initially resistant to significant changes in the bill,[68] supporters both in and outside Congress, including representatives of the AFL-CIO and the UAW, spent months negotiating a compromise that Carter could endorse.

The Humphrey-Hawkins proposal was revised to give the president more room to maneuver. It set a target unemployment rate of 4% overall and 3% for workers aged twenty and over to be reached in five years rather than four. The measure still embodied the principle that every person willing to work was entitled to a job and that public-sector jobs should be created to reduce unemployment when necessary. However, the president insisted on the authority to revise the goals and timetables at a later date. He also demanded flexibility in how to go about expanding the number of jobs. In a gesture to labor, there was no specific provision for wage-price guidelines, and the bill merely stated that price stability should be sought as soon as possible. The independent and politically insulated Federal Reserve Board, which had been subject to intense criticism by organized labor as committed to restraining inflation regardless of the costs in increased unemployment, was also required to explain how its monetary policies would address unemployment targets. Many proponents of full-employment legislation felt the proposal had been rendered all but worthless, whereas opponents continued to argue it could be devastating to the economy.[69]

The House finally moved toward a vote in 1978. Following partisan wrangling within the House Education and Labor Committee, a modified bill reflecting a number of concessions to critics of the legislation was reported in February. On the House floor in March the bill was besieged with amendments.[70] After four days of tumultuous floor action, Humphrey-Hawkins finally passed 257–152, with more than 95% of non-Southern Democrats supporting the bill. More Southern Democrats supported Humphrey-Hawkins than the labor law reform bill in the House at 62%, while fewer Republicans voted for it at 18%.

As with labor law reform, Humphrey-Hawkins faced more trouble in the Senate. It was referred to two committees, which delayed final action. Although the more liberal Human Resources Committee reported a bill in May without major amendments, Humphrey-Hawkins faced more opposition in the Banking Committee. The committee finally reported a bill in late June with a number of amendments added by fiscal conservatives to establish a goal to eliminate inflation by 1983, to balance the budget, and to reduce the federal budget to 20% of gross national product. Meeting these goals would likely make it impossible to reach the unemployment targets. The committees failed to reach a compromise after two months of contentious negotiations, and instead of melding the two bills, each reported its version as a substitute for the original bill. With roughly a month left in the congressional session and a crowded Senate calendar, Majority Leader Byrd was reluctant to bring up the bill for fear of bogging down the Senate. Republicans were threatening to launch three possible filibusters—one on the motion to consider the bill, another on the bill itself, and a postcloture filibuster through endless amendments (a tactic also threatened on labor law reform). To forestall these possibilities, Byrd repeatedly tried to negotiate a time agreement for consideration of the bill with Republican leaders to limit debate, but conservatives dug in their heels.[71]

Carter, fearing further deterioration of his relations with core groups in the Democratic Party, initiated a last-ditch effort to broker a compromise. He brought leading Republican opponents to the White House to "attempt to secure their agreement to allow the bill to be considered in an orderly manner" and called media attention to Republican obstructionism.[72] The White House launched a major lobbying effort to get the votes for cloture and fight off unfavorable amendments. White House staff also coordinated the efforts of interest group supporters to maximize pressure on targeted senators.[73]

The bill came to be derisively referred to as the Humphrey-Hawkins-Hatch Act because of the concessions supporters granted the leading Republican opponent, Orrin Hatch, to avert a filibuster. The labor–civil rights coalition struggled to maintain the integrity of the bill and threatened to pull its support if the Banking Committee's provisions on inflation and federal spending were in-

cluded. The coalition opposed making so many concessions to prevent a filibuster and preferred to take up the fight in floor votes. It finally got its wish. The
vote on the inflation measure came in an episode of legislative brinkmanship in
which the labor–civil rights coalition lobbyists again differed over strategy with
many of their congressional allies. Senate liberals feared that if they did not vote
for Hatch's inflation amendment, he would kill the bill through endless amendments. AFL-CIO lobbyists were convinced Republicans would not allow Hatch
to do this, but they failed to persuade enough senators to call Hatch's bluff.[74] A
vote on a weak inflation amendment backed by labor and sponsored by Humphrey's widow produced a tie. It was broken by several senators changing their
votes to no, and the Hatch amendment was adopted with the votes of several
liberals who favored the weaker approach. However, the coalition prevailed on
the federal spending issue when the stringent goals of fiscal conservatives were
rejected in favor of a vague commitment to reducing the federal share of the
economy.[75] The amended Humphrey-Hawkins bill passed 70–19 with Hatch
voting against it despite his role in shaping the final product. On the last day of
the congressional session the House accepted the Senate amendments on a
voice vote.

Just as organized labor had been disappointed with the final version of the
Employment Act of 1946, the AFL-CIO and its allies were disappointed with the
final version of the Humphrey-Hawkins Act. Ken Young, an AFL-CIO lobbyist,
tried to muster some enthusiasm after passage: "It does represent a small symbolic step forward but the Senate weakened it severely."[76] Like the Employment
Act of 1946, Humphrey-Hawkins committed the government to full employment in principle but provided no real way to achieve it. However, the barriers
to passage of a strong bill were quite different. Unlike Truman, Carter had
insisted on weakening changes in the bill to protect his own institutional and
political position. But in both cases, Congress insisted on a weaker bill than
the administration. However, in what was becoming the typical pattern of
obstruction, the Senate rather than the House emerged as the major obstacle to
Humphrey-Hawkins. Congressional reform and the changing composition of
the Democratic Party meant that conservative committee chairs no longer dictated the outcome in the House. The Senate's fiscal conservatives played a role
in weakening the bill in the Banking Committee, but the real challenge was the
threatened filibuster. Conservative opponents were never forced to prove they
had the 41 votes to maintain a filibuster. The labor–civil rights coalition begged
for the opportunity to call what they felt was a bluff by Republicans led by

Hatch. Instead, some of the coalition's allies in the Senate blinked first and caved to Hatch's demands. Liberals bore the burden of compromise because they wanted a bill and Hatch did not. The threat of a filibuster thus had a substantial impact on the bill, even though a filibuster was never actually launched. This calculus became a major feature of legislating with the rise of the filibuster in the postreform period in Congress.

The Renewed Push for National Health Insurance

After the passage of Medicare, labor resumed the pursuit of universal health care. But the situation that confronted advocates of national health insurance in the 1970s had become even more complicated than in the 1940s. By the 1970s, a set of problems that continue to plague the American health care system—and efforts to reform it—became apparent. Health care costs were increasing at rates far in excess of general inflation. American health care had tilted in favor of overutilization of expensive, high-technology care over prevention, and methods of reimbursement encouraged spiraling costs. Health care had also become a major sector in the economy with a diverse range of interested parties eager to protect their stake in the system. Most working-age Americans were covered by private insurance provided by their employers, but a substantial percentage, particularly among the unemployed, part-time workers, low-wage workers, and those working for small businesses, were uninsured. Many who had insurance were underinsured for sizable health costs and could still face bankruptcy from excessive medical bills.

Although almost everyone agreed that health care reform was needed, there was no consensus on the best way to address these problems. While some advocates of reform favored universal coverage that would guarantee that no one went without care, others favored a targeted approach focused on vulnerable populations such as mothers and children or low-income workers. Similarly, some advocates of reform felt that everyone should have coverage for a comprehensive set of benefits, whereas others felt the government should act only to protect people from catastrophic medical costs. As in the development of the Medicare proposal, those on the left advocated a national health insurance approach, in which the government would pay directly for medical care; conservatives and some moderates favored the expansion of private insurance coverage. There was also broad disagreement on how to control and distribute spiraling costs between the government, employers, and the individual. There was no consensus on what combination of reforms would preserve the best features of American health care while eliminating the worst. Organized labor stood on one end of the continuum in advocating a universal, comprehensive, government-funded health care system with no cost sharing for the individual (outside of the tax system) and cost controls imposed by health budgeting by the federal government.

Labor leaders understood that compromise on national health care would be inevitable given the realities of the American political system. However, labor struggled in the 1970s to find the right balance between how much needed to be sacrificed to reach a politically viable compromise and how much was too much to sacrifice in the interests of a legislative victory. Momentum behind health care reform grew and subsided in fits and starts during the 1970s, and at several points sweeping health care reform appeared all but inevitable. However, labor rejected what might have been a viable compromise in the Nixon years, and health care reform ultimately fell victim to sparring among reform advocates, jurisdictional struggles in the reformed congressional committee system, and growing budget woes during the Carter administration.

Efforts at Reform in the Nixon-Ford Years

Numerous proposals for health care reform circulated as the issue gained momentum in the 1970s. At the beginning of the decade, organized labor commenced a long-term partnership with Senator Edward Kennedy (D-MA) to push health care reform. The AFL-CIO, UAW, and the Committee for National Health Insurance (CNHI), an organization formed by labor to build support outside the labor movement, worked with Kennedy to prepare a bill for comprehensive national health insurance funded through payroll taxes and general revenues that was first introduced in early 1971. Labor and the CNHI worked on building a broader coalition in support of this approach with minority groups, religious groups, and state and local political leaders.[77] As part of a budding rivalry with Kennedy as the 1972 elections approached, President Nixon countered Kennedy's proposal with a plan based on a mandate on employers to cover 75% of the cost of government-approved health insurance plans for their employees. A new federal program would cover low-income families without access to employer plans. Other major bills introduced that year included a plan endorsed by the AMA to provide tax credits for the purchase of private health insurance with the size of the credit scaled to income. Hearings were held in a number of congressional committees on the various plans. The Health Subcommittee of the Democratic Policy Council, a division of the Democratic National Committee headed by UAW president Woodcock, held field hearings in numerous cities on national health insurance to build momentum for labor's position heading into the 1972 Democratic Convention. However, there was no movement in Congress before or after the election.

The prospects for passage of significant health reform improved considerably over the course of the 1974 congressional session.[78] As had initially happened with Medicare, the Ways and Means Committee was deadlocked with members split in support of different proposals. In a major breakthrough, it appeared that the stalemate might finally be broken when Ways and Means chair Mills, under threat that his committee's jurisdiction over health care might be taken away by a rebellious caucus, joined Senator Kennedy to develop a compromise measure announced in early April.[79] The Kennedy-Mills compromise required all employers and employees to participate in a new national program with a standard menu of benefits that would also be extended to Medicare and Medicaid beneficiaries. The program would be funded by payroll taxes and run by an independent Social Security Administration with a role for private insurers as financial intermediaries. Unlike in the original Kennedy-labor proposal, individuals would be responsible for deductibles and copayments. Shortly after the proposal was introduced, Ways and Means opened long-awaited hearings on national health care. At the same time, another proposal by Senators Russell Long (D-LA) and Abraham Ribicoff (D-CT) to cover catastrophic medical expenses funded by a small payroll tax appeared to have majority support in the Senate Finance Committee.[80] But the Nixon administration voiced opposition to the catastrophic approach, with Health, Education, and Welfare (HEW) secretary Caspar Weinberger arguing that "partial action" was as undesirable as "no action."[81] Mills later indicated similar feelings. Momentum was building behind a comprehensive approach.

As compromise between the administration and leading figures in the House and Senate seemed more likely, organized labor began to drag its feet. The CNHI refused to endorse Kennedy-Mills and criticized its approach as inadequate as compared with the more comprehensive national health insurance bill. Internal AFL-CIO documents suggest that by early April figures within the AFL-CIO and the CNHI were beginning to consider less comprehensive proposals including proposals with some of the compromise features of Kennedy-Mills and modified versions of the administration plan.[82] But publicly the position of the AFL-CIO and other labor supporters of national health insurance hardened in opposition to the Kennedy-Mills compromise. Two factors played into this strategy. Labor was willing to settle for Kennedy-Mills, but labor leaders and lobbyists feared that if they softened their position this early in the legislative process, an even more watered-down proposal would be likely to emerge in the final legislative product.[83] Clearly this had happened to labor numerous times before, and past experiences encouraged labor leaders and lobbyists to dig in to preserve organized labor's goals of universal and comprehensive coverage in the face of proposals like the Long-Ribicoff catastrophic bill. There was also the fear on the part of labor leaders like Woodcock that it would be hard to shift their stance after spending years selling their memberships on a comprehensive, government-funded approach. The other major factor was the growing likelihood of liberal gains in the 1974 congressional elections as the Watergate scandal heated up, which labor leaders assumed would improve the prospects for a bill more to their liking.[84] This created a great deal of strategic uncertainty.

When Ford assumed office, he urged quick action on health care, but the Ways and Means Committee remained divided on whether health insurance should be compulsory and how it should be financed. A vote on the AMA's limited proposal for tax credits for health insurance premiums tied 12–12 with five Southern Democrats joining all but three Republicans in support.[85] The conservative coalition's hold on important committees had been loosened but clearly not eliminated. Subsequently, the committee tentatively adopted 12–11 a staff-engineered compromise with many of the features of the Nixon proposal, but Mills refused to report the bill, believing the narrow committee margin implied trouble on the floor.[86] Supporters of a broader bill including organized labor fended off further action in a lame-duck legislative session called after the November elections, safe in the knowledge that a whole new class of liberals would arrive in the 94th Congress. Labor did not realize that the window for national health insurance was closing rather than opening wider.

Political analysts felt action in the next Congress was inevitable, but a growing federal budget deficit complicated the picture. Critics of national health insurance have always tarred it with the label of "socialized medicine," but moderates and even some liberals were far more open to the criticism that national health insurance would create a vast new entitlement program that was financially unsustainable.[87] In the two months between the election and the opening of the 94th Congress, the growing tensions over the cost of national health insurance spilled into negotiations between labor lobbyists, representatives of the CNHI, Senator Kennedy, and Representative James Corman

(D-CA), who had become the chief sponsor of the labor-endorsed proposal in the House. In one meeting, Kennedy, acting in what was described as "almost a belligerent manner," stated that he resented charges made against him that he was "selling out on the health issue" but insisted he did not want to reintroduce the national health insurance bill in its present form because it would be "saddled" with its "$90 billion cost."[88] Representative Corman and the AFL-CIO's Andrew Biemiller disagreed with Kennedy and argued that a national health insurance bill should again be introduced even though compromises would eventually be necessary. Corman and Biemiller won out, but the CNHI continued to develop and evaluate alternative proposals to utilize in future negotiations, including the possibility of phasing in national health insurance coverage by demographic categories such as children and mothers.[89]

As the economy sagged and spending on entitlements grew precipitously, the federal budget deficit (though nothing compared with what it would become in the eighties) became a greater problem, giving opponents of national health insurance ammunition. The Ford administration announced a moratorium on new federal spending at the beginning of the 94th Congress, while congressional proposals became entangled in jurisdictional conflicts in the House, precipitated by the decentralization of power in the reformed Congress. The health subcommittees of the Ways and Means and Commerce committees both claimed jurisdiction, and both held hearings. Efforts to build consensus between the two committees, including negotiations led by a DSG task force, proved futile in 1975 and 1976. The divisions between the committees were so deep that a consensus could not be reached on a stopgap measure to provide health insurance for the rising number of unemployed, which was viewed as a legislative dress rehearsal for broader health care reform.[90] There was no further action on benefits for the unemployed or national health insurance in 1975 or 1976 as presidential election year politics again entered the picture.

Health Care Reform in the Carter Administration

As a candidate, Carter pledged his support of national health insurance, but in recognition of budget constraints, the 1976 Democratic platform called for phasing in reform. In office, the administration first focused on a hospital cost containment bill, arguing that holding down health care inflation was a necessary precursor to national health insurance. Labor and Senator Kennedy made every effort to push the administration to develop an acceptable health reform approach while they prepared a new, somewhat compromised version of their own proposal released in spring of 1978.[91] But disagreement between the administration and Senator Kennedy and organized labor persisted over cost sharing, cost containment, and the role for private insurers.[92] There were signs of trouble by Carter's second year in office. As Eizenstat noted in a memo to President Carter to prepare him for yet another meeting with Senator Kennedy and labor representatives:

> In our discussions with labor, we assume that their support is probably indispensible to passage of NHI legislation, since most other interest groups are satisfied by the status quo. On the other hand, the type of bill that labor is supporting cannot possibly be enacted and may well be ill-advised substantively. The goal therefore must be to persuade labor to accept a viable bill.
>
> We may be able to reach an acceptable compromise with labor. However, we are by no means certain of this. NHI is not a "bread and butter" issue for labor. Most unions have good health insurance; many (including the UAW) have excellent coverage. Thus, labor can afford to be ideologically pure on NHI. At the same time they have invested years in educating their workers on the desirability of the Kennedy/Corman Bill. Labor may not be as willing to compromise on this issue as it has been on such "bread and butter" issues as labor law reform.[93]

While Kennedy and labor pressed the administration to introduce a proposal in time for hearings to be held prior to the 1978 elections, other key members of Congress urged the administration to hold off. Al Ullman (D-OR), the new chairman of the House Ways and Means Committee, believed that submitting a national health insurance bill would "destroy" Carter's presidency because it ran "so counter to the fight on inflation."[94] The president's advisers argued, "Although the UAW may believe otherwise, the climate is not right to make national health insurance a major campaign issue. More time is also required to educate the public that the national health plan is needed to bring health expenditures under control and is not simply another expensive benefit program."[95] The administration decided to release a set of principles for health reform in July, with the understanding that legislation would be introduced in the 1979 congressional session. Labor and Kennedy were losing faith that the administration would act.[96]

Internally the administration continued to struggle with how comprehensive its proposal should be. Labor leaders were opposed to a phased-in approach because they feared it would alleviate the pressure on Congress to take further action, whereas the Carter administration was convinced that an incremental proposal was the only approach that had a chance of passing Congress.[97] The administration also debated the merits of a "targeted" approach of adding limited coverage for certain vulnerable populations versus a "broad" approach of universal, comprehensive health care for all. While recognizing the importance of fulfilling the administration's campaign pledge on national health insurance and its commitment to labor and Senator Kennedy, Secretary of Health, Education, and Welfare Joe Califano struggled with finding the most effective strategy in Congress:

> Passage of a National Health program that follows the broad approach will not be easy in either this or the next session of Congress. Indeed, given the strong congressional sentiment against a broad approach, there is the very real danger that the Administration will be criticized for, once again, proposing broad, comprehensive legislation that has little chance of passage when it could have submitted a more modest bill (following the targeted approach) that does have reasonable chances of Congressional success and will effect important reforms.
>
> But it is highly unlikely that a targeted approach *that included the types of cost containment and system reforms that the Administration is likely to propose* would have an easier passage through Congress than a broad approach. Moreover, adoption of the broad approach allows you to educate the American people more fully on the health system as a whole and puts you in a position to compromise if Congress decides to accept only the initial phases of a broad bill (phases that might be similar to a targeted approach).[98]

The administration was struggling to pass its hospital cost containment bill—which was ultimately gutted in the House and dropped in the Senate because of a filibuster threat—and it recognized the difficulty of getting any meaningful legislation through Congress.[99]

By the fall, organized labor and Kennedy finally broke with the administration and again pushed their own proposal. The Kennedy-labor proposal, however, had come a long way. The proposal was no longer based on a system of federally funded national health insurance but was instead a mixed system based on an employer mandate to provide highly regulated private insurance to employees and their dependents. Unlike in previous versions of the bill, employees could be asked to share the costs of premiums, but there would still be no deductibles or copayments. A government-funded program would cover the unemployed, the poor, the disabled, and the elderly. There were a lot of similarities to the Nixon plan that labor had rejected four years earlier as inadequate.

The Carter administration reached out beyond Kennedy and labor to consult with other health care leaders on the Hill. In summer of 1979, Carter finally announced a detailed proposal that was essentially a catastrophic health plan that offered limited coverage to everyone. Employers would be mandated to pay 75% of the premiums for a high-deductible policy. The elderly, disabled, and poor would be joined in a new, comprehensive fully federal program. The proposal was considerably smaller than what Carter had campaigned on, but the administration was trying "to occupy the middle ground in a polarized situation" and to thread the needle in Congress.[100] It hoped to win over Senator Long, chair of the Senate Finance Committee, whom they saw as key to passage of any bill, and other moderates. The administration presumed liberals would eventually find it hard to vote against a measure that significantly expanded health coverage. Anticipating labor's criticism, Carter's press secretary advised the president to emphasize in his public discussions of the proposal that "we believe that the time has come to concentrate on actually getting something done to help Americans and that this is more important than adhering to some semi-sacred ideological principle."[101]

The longtime supporters of national health insurance led by organized labor and Kennedy, who was widely expected to challenge Carter for the Democratic presidential nomination, were highly critical of Carter's plan as unfair to low- and middle-income families. Labor leaders refused to give any public indication of a willingness to accept a catastrophic health bill. While the AMA and insurers expressed qualified support for Carter's plan, businesses attacked it as imposing new costs on employers who did not already provide insurance, thus encouraging inflation and further burdening business in a time of high unemployment and economic stagnation.[102] Even this pared-down proposal was considered by many in Congress to be too expensive. The Senate Finance Committee worked on a catastrophic bill, and there was considerable interest in a catastrophic proposal in Congress. However, providing too little to attract liberal supporters and costing too much to attract conservatives, catastrophic health care reform languished on Capitol Hill.

Another episode in the efforts of organized labor to obtain universal, comprehensive health care came to a close. The election of Ronald Reagan as president pushed the issue off the agenda for more than a decade. Many observers and scholars believe the United States came closer to comprehensive health care reform in 1974 than it ever had before.[103] Policy makers, including organized labor, may have pulled back from negotiating a compromise at a critical moment. Because of events beyond their control, supporters of universal health care lost momentum after the 1974 elections when they expected to gain it. The American labor movement is often criticized for being too willing to compromise on legislation, but in this instance they were not. Had organized labor been willing to accept the Kennedy-Mills compromise and more willing to make concessions, perhaps a program of universal health care would have passed in lieu of labor's preferred program of federal national health insurance. But supporters of national health insurance knew substantial concessions would likely be made to get even the Kennedy-Mills compromise through the legislative gauntlet. From this perspective it was not unreasonable to wait for the 1974 congressional elections to fortify liberal ranks, which might have given labor more leverage in the negotiations, if other problems like the deteriorating economy had not intervened.

There were many factors that contributed to failure of national health insurance in the 1970s, and, as in the 1940s, legislative institutions did not prevent a committed majority from acting. But they did complicate reformers' strategic calculus and create an inhospitable environment for reform. House committee obstruction was replaced with obstruction by the filibuster in the Senate, while the conservative coalition remained a force in both chambers. The greater fragmentation in the legislative process in the early postreform period in the absence of strong leaders and a unified caucus also made it more difficult to build legislative majorities. Having seen moderate proposals like labor law reform, Humphrey-Hawkins, and numerous other initiatives, including hospital cost containment, stalled or gutted in Congress, the Carter administration struggled to find a health reform proposal that might be politically viable, but in the process he lost labor's support.

Conclusion

The enfranchisement of African Americans and congressional reform did not produce the legislative outcomes labor had hoped for in the mid- to late seventies. The position of labor and liberals in Congress was improved in many respects, particularly in the declining power of the conservative coalition in the committee system. But the immediate decentralizing effects of congressional reform and confusion of committee jurisdictions further complicated efforts to build viable legislative coalitions and made the chamber more unpredictable. Furthermore, the parties did not instantly realign in the wake of civil rights, and the conservative coalition, though weakening, still cropped up on labor-backed legislation. Most important, while obstruction in the House declined, obstruction in the Senate became more prominent, as conservatives increasingly turned to the filibuster. Even though the filibuster had been reformed to lower the cloture threshold in the mid-seventies, overcoming it still required an often elusive supermajority. Although viewed as a sign of labor's declining political influence in the 1970s, labor's legislative failures were shaped by this larger institutional context.

Government's failure to address pressing public policy problems in the 1970s, like the lack of access to health care and high levels of unemployment, further threatened labor's policy agenda as the public increasingly came to question the ability of government to deliver on its promises. Legislation like Humphrey-Hawkins was touted as a solution for unemployment, but it was so watered down that it had little effect. Carter and congressional liberals ran on pledges of universal health care that they never delivered on. Income inequality increased as the minimum wage failed to keep pace with inflation. Government's inability to act coherently in the face of widespread problems undermined public trust and made many in the public quite receptive to the criticisms of government made by Ronald Reagan and a subsequent generation of conservatives.[104]

6

The More Things Change, the More They Remain the Same

With the exception of a brief period during the first two years of Democratic president Bill Clinton's administration, the labor movement would find itself on the defensive from the election of Ronald Reagan in 1980 through President George W. Bush's last year in office in 2008. At many points during this almost thirty-year period, it looked as if the foundations of the limited welfare state that labor had fought so hard to establish would be washed away by a conservative, antigovernment tide. Reagan railed against "big government," and even Clinton asserted four years into his presidency that "the era of big government is over."[1] George W. Bush pledged to create an "ownership society" by privatizing government programs. Unified Republican control of the government during most of his two terms in office posed the greatest threat to labor's policy accomplishments in the postwar period. But by the time Bush left office, many of labor's most cherished programs were barely changed. Social Security, the third rail of politics, escaped with minimal modifications.[2] A Medicare prescription drug benefit provided through private insurers had been created, and some Medicare recipients were now covered by government-paid private health insurance policies, but most of the elderly remained in the targeted national health insurance program. The collective bargaining rights of a number of government workers were imperiled after their jobs were subsumed into the new Homeland Security Department, but for the most part labor laws remained unchanged.[3] Meanwhile, even some incremental policy gains advocated by organized labor were realized.

The limited American welfare state remained largely intact because it is just as difficult to get rid of a program as it is to put one in place, as long as there are influential advocates to protect it.[4] Labor was able to defend these programs during a period of conservative ascendancy for many of the same reasons it had difficulty realizing its most ambitious policy goals during periods of liberal strength. Labor benefited from the separation of powers and the enduring protections for political minorities in the legislative process. It also took advantage of its own improved position within the congressional Democratic Party as a result of the long-term impact of the reforms that labor pushed in the 1960s and 1970s. Underlying the limited changes in public policy were significant changes in the party system and the operation of Congress. These changes produced two countervailing trends for labor—the Democratic Party became more ideologically cohesive and more uniformly receptive to labor's policy agenda, despite declining union density, while the Democrats became less dominant in elections, throwing the presidency, for most of this period, and eventually the Congress into Republican hands.

This chapter looks at the fallout of the institutional and electoral reforms of the 1960s and 1970s and their effects on the public policies organized labor advocated from 1980 to 2008. The first part of the chapter outlines the realignment of the Democratic Party and the impact of these changes on the way Congress operates and the support of congressional Democrats for organized labor. The second part looks at public policy battles over these three decades, again focusing on the areas of labor law reform, universal health care, and workers' income security programs. In most of these policy struggles, labor was able to defend against conservative attacks on the welfare state and to make a few incremental gains. But even during the brief period when Democrats controlled both the White House and Congress (1993–94), labor continued to come up short in its efforts to pass pro-labor policies and significant expansions of the welfare state. During this period, the more things changed, the more they remained the same.

The Fallout of the Reforms of the 1960s and 1970s

The Realignment of the South

When Lyndon Johnson signed the Civil Rights Act of 1964, he predicted that the Democrats "have lost the South for a generation." Instead, it took roughly a generation for the Democratic Party to lose its hold on the South—and likewise for the South to lose its grip on the Democratic Party. Over the course of the late sixties and seventies, the South became a two-party region. Although the Democrats lost the Deep South at the presidential level in the Democratic landslide of 1964, Southern states largely followed national patterns, and a few Southern states remained competitive for the Democrats through the Clinton years. But in the 2000 and 2004 presidential elections, the solid South became solidly Republican. The South also gradually shifted to the Republicans in congressional elections. The percentage of Southern seats held by Democrats fell off considerably in the 1970s and 1980s but dropped below a majority in the House and Senate only after the 1994 midterm elections gave Republicans control of Congress (table 6.1). The Southern contingent in the House Democratic Caucus gradually declined to a low point of 23.2% in the 2006 election, which returned control of Congress to the Democrats.

Over time, the Democratic contingent of the old antilabor conservative coalition became Republican. While more and more conservatives entering politics decided to run for office as Republicans, a number of prominent conservatives who had spent their careers as Democrats switched parties, such as Strom Thurmond of South Carolina in the 1960s, Newt Gingrich of Georgia in the 1970s, and Phil Gramm of Texas in the 1980s. Over the years Gramm repeatedly said in speeches to his conservative, once Democratic constituents, "I had to choose between [Speaker] Tip O'Neill and y'all and I decided to stand with y'all."[5] Continuing this trend, Alabama senator Richard Shelby announced he would switch party allegiance to the Republicans the morning after the 1994 elections. Five House members followed his example.[6]

The Demise of the Conservative Coalition

As Southern conservatives moved into the Republican Party, the remaining Southern Democrats gradually became much more like their non-Southern peers in their voting patterns. As Polsby notes, the percentage of "Dixiecrats," or conservative Southern Democrats, in the House Democratic Caucus declined

Table 6.1.   Decline of the South in the Democratic Caucus

	House		Senate	
Year	Percentage of Southern Seats Held by Democrats	Percentage of Democratic Caucus from the South (Size of Caucus)	Percentage of Southern Seats Held by Democrats	Percentage of Democratic Caucus from the South (Size of Caucus)
1937–38	98	29.8 (334)	100	28.9 (76)
1949–50	98.1	39.2 (263)	100	40.7 (54)
1961–62	93.4	37.8 (263)	100	33.8 (65)
1973–74	68.2	30.4 (242)	63.6	25.0 (56)
1981–82	63.9	28.4 (242)	*54.4*	*23.9 (46)*
1989–90	67	29.3 (260)	68.2	27.3 (55)
1991–92	66.4	28.8 (267)	68.2	26.8 (56)
1993–94	61.6	29.8 (258)	59.1	22.8 (57)
1995–96	*48.8*	*29.9 (204)*	*36.4*	*19.1 (47)*
1997–98	*43.2*	*26.1 (206)*	*31.8*	*15.6 (45)*
1999–2000	*43.5*	*25.6 (211)*	*36.4*	*17.8 (45)*
2001–2	*42.4*	*25.1 (212)*	36.4	*16.0 (50)*[a]
2003–4	*41.9*	*26.8 (204)*	40.9	*18.8 (48)*
2005–6	*37.4*	*24.4 (202)*	18.2	*9.1 (44)*
2007–8	41.2	23.2 (233)	22.7	10.2 (49)

Source: Based on figures from *Vital Statistics on Congress.* Size of House Democratic Caucus found at www.clerk.house.gov. Numbers in italics indicate Democrats are not in control of the legislative body.
   [a]The Senate was 50/50 and controlled by the Republicans until Republican senator James Jeffords of Vermont switched to caucus with the Democrats in the summer of 2001.

precipitously from 27% in 1970 to 5% in 1990, while "mainstream Democrats" came to dominate the Southern contingent of the Democratic Caucus.[7] Several factors contributed to the changing ideological orientation of Southern Democrats. The enfranchisement of African Americans, redistricting to group minority voters together in congressional districts, and growing urbanization increased the number of liberal-leaning House districts in the South. Two-party competition also encouraged a class cleavage in voting among Southern whites, and vote choice increasingly corresponded with positions on social welfare issues, which aligned the South with national patterns.[8] This trend made it possible for Southern Democrats to move to the left, just as labor strategists had expected. As figures 6.1 and 6.2 indicate, the support of Southern Democrats in both the House and Senate for the Democratic Party position in votes that divided the parties increased considerably, and the gap between Southern and non-Southern Democrats narrowed. As a result, by the 1980s, the conservative coalition of Southern Democrats and Republicans that had controlled out-

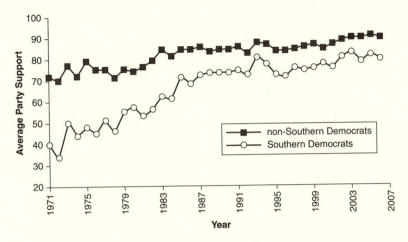

Figure 6.1. House Sectional Party Unity in Democratic Caucus. Average party support on party unity votes in which a majority of one party aligns against a majority of the other party. *Source:* Party unity support scores from *Congressional Quarterly.*

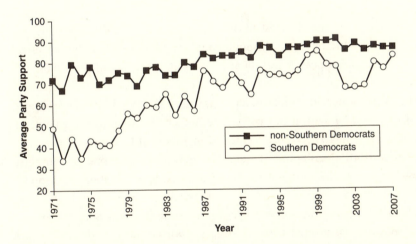

Figure 6.2. Senate Sectional Party Unity in Democratic Caucus. Average party support on party unity votes in which a majority of one party aligns against a majority of the other party. *Source:* Party unity support scores from *Congressional Quarterly.*

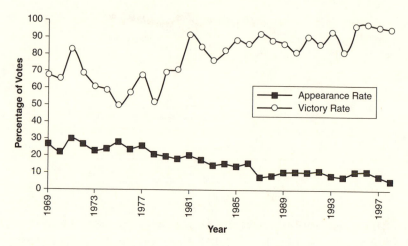

Figure 6.3. Decline of Conservative Coalition in Congress. Votes in the House and Senate are combined here. *Source:* Statistics from *Congressional Quarterly.*

comes on legislation of interest to organized labor for decades gradually declined as a force in Congress,[9] although on those occasions when the conservative coalition did appear, it was on average more successful in the 1980s and 1990s (fig. 6.3).

The shift among Southern Democrats was also reflected in increased support for labor's position in roll call votes. The AFL-CIO's Committee on Political Education compiles the voting records of members of Congress on the AFL-CIO's top-priority legislation. The average lifetime COPE scores of Southern House Democrats almost doubled from 45.5% in support of labor's position in 1970 to 88.2% in 2007.[10] Some of the most liberal members in the House, with lifetime COPE ratings in excess of 95%, now come from the South. Many of these Southern Democrats with strong pro-labor voting records are African Americans elected from districts with substantial minority populations.[11] Although, on average, Southern Democrats in the Senate remain less supportive of labor than those in the House, the gap has closed in recent years. In 2000, the eight Southern Democratic senators had an average lifetime COPE score of 70.8%, compared with the Southern average of 80.7% in the House. In 2007, the five Southern Democratic senators had an average lifetime COPE score of 85.6%, compared with a regional average of 88.2% in the House. Whereas only one Southern senator, aspiring presidential candidate John Edwards of North

Carolina, had a lifetime average over 75% in support of the AFL-CIO's position in 2000, all five Southern Democratic senators did in 2007.

Party Competition and Party Polarization

The price that Democrats and organized labor paid for greater party cohesion was less success in the electoral arena. As Larry Bartels observes, the net decline in support for Democratic presidential candidates associated with the demise of the New Deal coalition "is *entirely* attributable to partisan change in the South."[12] The growing competitiveness of the Republicans in the South corresponded with the growing dominance of the Republican Party at the presidential level with the election of Presidents Nixon, Reagan, George H. W. Bush, and George W. Bush. Carter and Clinton, both Southerners, were temporary diversions from this trend. While many Southern states and congressional districts became Republican strongholds in the 1990s, a number of Northeastern and Midwestern states and districts remained competitive, making it more difficult for the Democrats to win both the presidency and control of Congress. This trend certainly hurt labor's overall political position, but in many ways it improved organized labor's position in the Democratic Party.

Given the narrow partisan balance from the mid-1990s through the 2008 elections, organized labor remained a very valuable constituency in the Democratic Party. Despite declining union membership, labor was a pivotal player in industrial swing states like Michigan, Ohio, Pennsylvania, and Wisconsin and an important force even in swing states like Florida.[13] As Peter Francia documents, labor successfully ramped up its electoral mobilization beginning in 1996.[14] In the 1996, 2000, and 2004 presidential elections, voters from union households represented about a quarter of the electorate, and significant majorities voted for the Democratic candidates in both the presidential and congressional races.[15] Even though union membership continued to decline, labor's efforts to mobilize union members and allied constituencies improved.

In recent election cycles the most highly unionized states have been more likely to go Democratic, and the least unionized states have been more likely to go Republican.[16] Of the twenty-seven states with union density over 10% of the workforce, twenty-four went for Democratic nominee Barack Obama in the 2008 election. Of the twenty-three states with union density under 10%, only five went for the Democrat. There is a fairly strong correlation of the percentage of the workforce unionized in a state with the percentage of the vote that went for the Democratic presidential candidate in 2008 (r = .61). In the wake of the 2008 elections, only one of the twenty-seven states with union density over 10% was represented by two Republicans in the Senate, compared with thirteen of the twenty-three states with union density under 10%.[17] As a result, unions now find more support in the congressional Democratic caucuses, which are more heavily weighted with members from comparatively high union density areas in the Northeast, industrial Midwest, and Pacific Coast region. Labor's electoral mobilization has no doubt contributed to this regional realignment of party strength, but so has the shifting regional appeal of the parties based on ethnicity, religion, cultural issues, and policy positions.[18] The rising dominance of Southern conservatives in the Republican Party has further alienated moderate voters outside the South in recent election cycles.[19] The impact can be seen in the near extinction of Northeastern Republicans in Congress. Historical regional attachments to the Democratic and Republican parties dating from the Civil War have been replaced by party preferences that are more closely linked to policy preferences.[20]

Another consequence of these changes is that both parties have become more ideologically cohesive and polarized from each other. From a low point in the late 1960s and early 1970s, party unity in both parties in both the House and Senate has gradually risen to postwar highs in recent years (figs. 6.4 and 6.5). The ideological distance between the two parties has also grown, with measures of party polarization reaching postwar highs as well. The parties have developed more distinct policy agendas, which are more likely to be supported by a larger percentage of each party's caucus in Congress than in the period from the 1940s to the 1970s.

Although labor issues have always been quite partisan, they have become even more so. Through the 1970s, it was common to have a number of pro-labor Republicans from high union density areas, such as Senator Jacob Javits of New York, who cosponsored and fought for the labor law reform bill during the Carter administration. These Republicans have all but disappeared. By 2008, there were only a handful of Republicans from more heavily unionized areas who tended to vote with labor in the House. The lone labor-friendly Republican remaining in the Senate, Pennsylvania's Arlen Specter, became a Democrat in 2009. Because of the importance of labor to the national Democratic Party, there are strong party pressures on all Democrats to support labor on its legislative priorities. Members from areas with low union density are still more likely to resist this pressure, but as the discussion of congressional support for labor

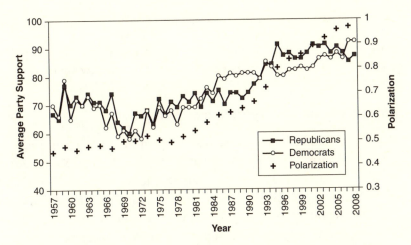

Figure 6.4. House Polarization and Party Unity. *Sources:* Party unity scores from *Congressional Quarterly.* Polarization is the difference between the Democrats' and Republicans' means on Poole and Rosenthal's nominate scores on the liberal-conservative dimension; Poole and Rosenthal's scores obtained from www.polarizedamerica.com.

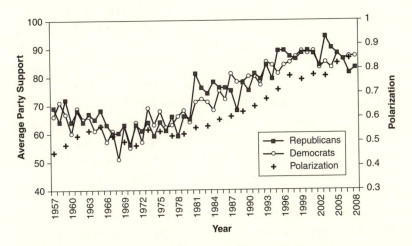

Figure 6.5. Senate Polarization and Party Unity. *Sources:* Party unity scores from *Congressional Quarterly.* Polarization is the difference between the Democrats' and Republicans' means on Poole and Rosenthal's nominate scores on the liberal-conservative dimension; Poole and Rosenthal's scores obtained from www.polarizedamerica.com.

law reform below illustrates, support for labor among all Democrats increased considerably from the eighties through the first decade of the new millennium.

Repercussions for the Operation of Congress

These changes in conjunction with the reforms from the 1970s opened new opportunities for organized labor, the liberal majority within the Democratic Party, and the congressional Democratic leadership to exert influence in congressional politics, particularly in the House. David Rohde argues that the growing homogeneity within the Democratic Party in the eighties made possible the emergence of "conditional party government" in the House whereby majority party leaders are able to use the powers granted them by the congressional reforms of the seventies to pursue a partisan legislative agenda.[21] The leadership tries to establish party priorities and to build a national record for the parties' candidates to run on.[22]

Interest group pressures emerged as an important informal resource for party leaders. As Democratic leaders became more activist, the relationship between congressional party leaders and labor grew closer. As Taylor Dark points out, these changes helped organized labor pursue its agenda in Congress.[23] Jim Wright (D-TX), who assumed the speakership in 1987, set a new standard as an activist Speaker in the postwar period. Wright was eager not only to seize the initiative on issues on which there was already a consensus but also to try to generate consensus on more contentious issues by coordinating grassroots pressure with interest groups such as labor to bring wavering Democrats, and even some Republicans, into line. In return for labor's cooperation on the Democratic leadership's priorities, Wright and Majority Leader Tom Foley (D-WA) put some of labor's priorities on the House's agenda, despite the opposition of rank-and-file members from competitive districts.[24] The relationship between House Democratic Party leaders and the AFL-CIO was so strong that by 1987 the AFL-CIO Department of Legislation was hosting teleconference planning sessions with its field staff, state federation officers in target states, and congressional leaders to develop strategies for pressuring representatives to vote for shared legislative priorities.[25]

The reforms of the seventies in the Senate were much more limited, and, unlike in the House, the leadership was given few new tools to encourage party discipline. The leadership played an important informal role in trying to build party consensus, but the minority has considerable power in the Senate because

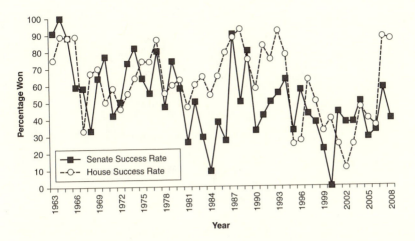

Figure 6.6. Success Rate on COPE Votes.

of the filibuster threat. Despite the commitment of the Democratic leadership in the Senate to many of labor's legislative priorities, it had a much harder time delivering on them. Labor has typically prevailed on a smaller percentage of COPE votes in the Senate than in the House when both were under Democratic control (fig. 6.6). But while filibusters made it hard for labor to pursue its agenda when the Democrats were in power, they also made it hard for labor's opponents to pursue theirs when the Republicans controlled the Senate for much of the period from 1980 to 2006, as elaborated later in this chapter.

Growing partisanship, along with reforms that allowed the Senate to take up other business while filibusters were being conducted, encouraged both individual senators and the minority party to resort to the filibuster more frequently.[26] As figure 6.7 indicates, efforts to invoke cloture picked up in the seventies, spiked in the late eighties when the Democrats took back control of the Senate, and remained at a high level throughout the contentious nineties and into the new century.[27] By 2008, almost 2 out of every 5 votes required a 60 vote supermajority.[28] Cloture fights on issues on labor's legislative agenda have become routine. For example, of the 5 COPE votes that labor won in 2006 in the Republican-controlled Senate, 3 were failed cloture votes that prevented legislation labor opposed from coming to a vote. In 2007 and 2008, when the Democrats controlled the Senate, the circumstances were reversed. Of the 8 COPE votes that labor lost in 2007, 6 were failed cloture votes that prevented legislation labor supported from coming to a vote. All the 6 COPE votes that labor lost

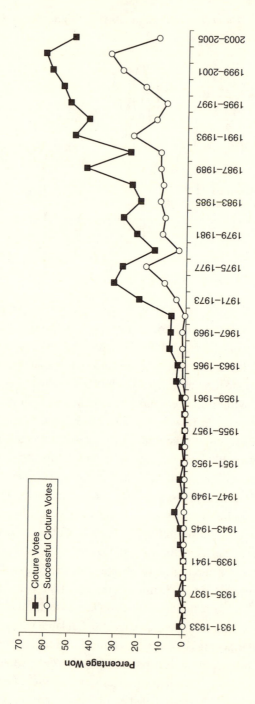

Figure 6.7. Number of Cloture Votes. *Source: Vital Statistics on Congress.*

in 2008 were failed cloture votes (the only 2 losses in the House were failed veto overrides that required a two-thirds supermajority).

All these changes had an impact on the legislative process and the way public policy decisions were made. Ironically, the growing liberalism of the Democratic Caucus came just as the public policy discussion moved to the right in the 1980s. By the 1990s, the Democrats and Republicans held more distinct approaches to the role of government, and both sides often fought to a stalemate on many of the issues on labor's legislative agenda.[29]

Incrementalism and Stalemate in Public Policy

Divided government, in which one party controlled the White House and another controlled one or both houses of Congress, prevailed for twenty-one and half years out of the twenty-eight years from 1980 to 2008. Democrats controlled both branches for two years during the Clinton administration, but while they held fairly substantial majorities in Congress, they did not have enough seats in the Senate to invoke cloture against filibusters. Thus the Republican minority had an effective veto in the legislative process. The Republicans controlled both branches for four and a half years during the George W. Bush administration, but they also did not have filibuster-proof margins in the Senate. Particularly from the early nineties forward, the close partisan balance fed even greater partisanship in Congress as each party jockeyed for advantage in the upcoming election (see figs. 6.4 and 6.5). In this context, labor saw incremental adjustments on the minimum wage and emergency extensions of unemployment insurance but continued stalemate on labor law reform and universal health care, while full-employment planning moved off the agenda.

The Turn against Government

After the expansion of the welfare state from the 1930s through the early 1970s, there was a marked shift against government. Vietnam, Watergate, the intractable economic crisis of the 1970s, declining U.S. competitiveness in the global economy, and the Iranian hostage crisis all fed a crisis of confidence in the government. Ronald Reagan's message in the 1980 presidential campaign that government was the cause of rather than the solution to the nation's problems resonated with many voters. Reagan pledged to shrink or eliminate many of the programs that organized labor had spent the past fifty years building up.

The conventional wisdom holds that Reagan's presidency was the last gasp for organized labor. Membership slid, and unions were forced to make contract concessions to hold on to members' jobs. Reagan's decision to fire striking air traffic controllers in 1981 and issue an executive order preventing them from ever being hired by the federal government again exemplified his administration's assault on labor. Congressional Democrats, sensing a conservative, antigovernment turn in public opinion and the emergence of a new electoral force in the "Reagan Democrats," are believed to have rolled over. But, as Dark argues, the conventional wisdom of labor's political demise in the eighties generalizes the experience of the first half of the decade to the entire decade. Dark finds "a surprising resiliency in labor's relationship with congressional Democrats," noting that "in some respects, labor's position in the party actually improved over the course of the decade."[30] As the number of conservative Democrats declined, liberals used their power within the House and Senate Democratic caucuses to challenge the Reagan and Bush administrations in the latter half of the decade.

Reagan and his business and conservative supporters hoped to scale back the welfare state and regulations that protected workers and unions. Presidential appointment of pro-business conservatives to executive departments and agencies, shifting budget priorities, a rising deficit, and the continuation of a trend toward deregulation begun in the Carter years made some headway toward these goals. But in terms of antilabor legislation, the Reagan years left a small legacy. The biggest accomplishment was a major regressive and pro-corporate tax cut the first year of Reagan's presidency. Labor had only a marginal impact on Reagan's tax package and the administration's 1981 and 1982 budget proposals, which cut social spending and increased defense spending. But after the Democrats picked up twenty-six House seats in the 1982 elections, the situation for organized labor improved.

Labor's opponents, while benefiting from the ideological shift of the eighties, were no more successful in reaching their most ambitious legislative goals than labor had been when liberalism was ascendant. Although labor's legislative priorities stalled, it defended past accomplishments. Labor's experience for most of the Reagan presidency was summed up in COPE's 1986 Report on Congress: "For workers, progress on key bills was stymied in the right-wing controlled Senate where a long list of key bills has been buried. Meanwhile, the House continued to prevent Senate-inspired, anti-labor initiatives from seeing the light of day."[31]

Labor Law

Reagan's appointments to the NLRB, his firing of the Professional Air Traffic Controllers Organization (PATCO) strikers, and weak enforcement of existing labor laws had a chilling effect on organizing and collective bargaining, but Congress never passed major labor law changes.[32] Plans to restrict the protections of the NLRA went nowhere. Conservatives found it difficult to make even less controversial changes—labor defeated nine efforts between 1981 and 1992 to restrict Davis-Bacon protections that guarantee prevailing wage rates on federal construction contracts. On another front, organized labor defeated repeated attempts in 1982, 1984, and 1985 to prohibit unions' use of funds for political activities including voter registration, get-out-the-vote drives, and voter education. Labor's friends in the Senate also led a successful filibuster against an attempt to amend the Hobbes Act in 1986 to apply stiff fines and prison sentences to strikers involved in picket line violence. Legislation requiring employers to offer employees sixty days' notification in advance of a plant closing was initially vetoed by Reagan but subsequently passed by veto-proof margins at the end of 1987 and became law without Reagan's signature. Thus, not only were conservatives unsuccessful at rolling back the legal protections for labor through legislation, but by the conclusion of Reagan's term they had suffered a mild defeat in the passage of a law pushed by organized labor.

Unemployment, Health Care, and the Minimum Wage

The major problem for advocates of an activist government in the Reagan years is that pressing social and economic problems went unaddressed. Unemployment surged as the Federal Reserve focused on reducing inflation and the economy slipped into a recession.[33] The number of medically uninsured continued to creep up. The trade imbalance spiraled out of control as whole manufacturing industries disappeared from the United States, with some companies going out of business and others moving manufacturing to low-wage countries. Facing stiff international competition, core industries such as steel struggled to survive and went through a wrenching transformation that hurt thousands of workers and their communities.[34] As a consequence, manufacturing employment fell steeply, and millions of comparatively high-wage jobs that served as the steppingstone for workers and their families to the middle class were eliminated. Many of these lost jobs were unionized, accelerating the long-term decline in the unionized percentage of the workforce. Real wages for most Americans fell, the value of the minimum wage plummeted, and income inequality grew during the eighties.[35]

In response to these conditions, labor's political allies in the House passed extensions and expansions of unemployment compensation, increases in the minimum wage, protectionist trade measures, and tax reforms to reverse the benefits extended to high-income groups in 1981. But many of these labor-backed House bills were either not taken up, filibustered, or voted down in the Senate, or were vetoed by Reagan. The status quo again worked against the political position of organized labor.

The George H. W. Bush Years: Obstruction and Incrementalism

During Bush's entire term, the Democrats controlled both houses of Congress, and partisanship was very high. Bush vetoed a wide range of labor-backed legislation over the four years from protectionist trade measures to legislation dealing with a labor dispute at Eastern Airlines. On several bills a veto override failed in the Senate by only 1 or 2 votes, demonstrating the support for labor-backed legislation in Congress but not the supermajority support needed to counter a hostile president. However, legislative compromises were reached on several bills that Bush signed after vetoing earlier versions, such as a minimum wage increase, an emergency extension of unemployment benefits, and civil rights legislation endorsed by the AFL-CIO designed to reverse several Supreme Court decisions that shifted the burden of proving discrimination by employers to the employees. In one of the few areas of agreement with the Bush administration, labor backed the first significant expansion of federal government regulation since OSHA in the Americans with Disabilities Act.

Policy Stalemate in the Clinton Administration

Frustrated with the obstruction and incrementalism of the Bush years and eager to depose the Republicans from the White House and break the legislative stalemate, labor worked diligently for the election of Democrat Bill Clinton in 1992. As in 1976, the Democratic nominee was not the first choice of much of the labor movement but instead a centrist, relatively unknown Southern governor who appeared to be the Democrats' best shot at recapturing the presidency.

Like Carter, Clinton made overtures to organized labor as a key Democratic constituency and pledged to back labor's legislative priorities including universal health care, labor law reform, and economic stimulus.[36]

For the first two years of Clinton's administration, Democrats again tried to expand the welfare state and pass legislation favorable to labor. When Clinton came to power in 1993, a small wave of legislation that had been vetoed by Bush was quickly passed and signed into law, including the Family and Medical Leave Act, enabling employees to take unpaid leave to care for a new child or ill family member; the Motor Voter bill, allowing people to register to vote when they applied for drivers' licenses or government benefits; and Hatch Act reform, allowing federal and postal workers to participate in partisan politics. In the typical postwar pattern, Clinton also signed two bills extending emergency unemployment benefits, instead of fundamentally reforming the system.

But major legislative proposals encountered difficulty on the Hill. With partisanship reaching postwar highs, Republicans were increasingly unwilling to compromise and eager to challenge many of the president's initiatives. While Clinton still had to fight for his most contentious proposals in the House, the Senate was the major obstacle. Without the party margins to invoke cloture, Clinton had to gain the support of a few Republicans in the Senate and hold every Democrat. The likelihood of obstruction in the Senate also made it difficult to force Democrats to take tough votes in the House on legislation they feared would never make it into law. Thus, even with unified Democratic control of the government, rising Democratic Party unity, and greater support for liberal initiatives among Democrats in Congress, the most ambitious goals on labor's agenda like labor law reform and universal health care again failed to make it into law. Despite significant political change, the pattern of postwar policy making changed very little. After a series of legislative failures in Clinton's first two years of office, the antigovernment tide returned to Washington when the Republican revolution was launched in the 1994 congressional elections.

An Inauspicious Beginning

Clinton encountered major problems when he tried to legislate his economic plan. The first casualty was an economic stimulus package strongly supported by labor. Even though a scaled-back version easily passed the House, Clinton was forced to make more concessions to fend off a filibuster by two fiscally conservative Southern Democrats in the Senate. With only fifty-seven Democrats in the Senate (one of whom would soon become a Republican), he needed the support of a handful of Republicans to get around the filibuster. Despite heavy labor lobbying of Northeastern Republicans such as Al D'Amato of New York and Arlen Specter of Pennsylvania, the Administration failed to get their votes. Clinton was forced to concede defeat, arguing in frustration that "democracy and majority rule [was] being undermined" by the Senate filibuster.[37] This fight set the tone for the beginning of his administration.

Clinton barely succeeded in getting his first budget through Congress, a massive deficit reduction package that included tax increases, budget cuts, and spending increases for Clinton's priority programs. Tax increases prevented him from attracting any Republican support and jeopardized support from conservative members of his own party. But because the budget resolution and reconciliation bills were not subject to filibuster, he did manage to get a bill after making major concessions. The budget included some consolation prizes for liberals, including tax increases on the wealthy and the expansion of the Earned Income Tax Credit targeted at the working poor. Vice President Al Gore was needed to cast a tie-breaking vote in the Senate.

The one major area in which organized labor and the Clinton administration differed was the North American Free Trade Agreement (NAFTA), which lowered trade barriers between the United States, Canada, and, most controversially, Mexico. The grassroots lobbying operation that the AFL-CIO and many of the affiliates had developed during the Reagan and Bush years was utilized and expanded to fight NAFTA. One Clinton administration staffer noted of the union effort, "They almost took it across the goal line. We [on the pro-NAFTA side] had all the editorial pages controlled, the economists, the think tanks, the intelligentsia all over this town was on the pro side, and they almost won."[38] But in the days leading up to the vote in Congress, the business community and the Clinton administration launched a major effort to ensure passage.[39] The NAFTA fight strained the relationship between labor and the administration and many congressional Democrats. Labor leaders blamed their defeat on Clinton's promises of pork barrel projects and other goodies to wavering legislators. In retribution, labor pledged to fight pro-NAFTA Democrats in the upcoming primaries, and it cut off funding for the Democratic National Committee (DNC) for six months. Although NAFTA caused a lot of bitterness, if labor wanted to achieve any legislative goals, it had to put the trade bill behind and move on to areas of agreement with the administration, such as labor law and health care.

Labor Law Reform

In the area of labor law, Clinton did what he could as chief executive by making labor-friendly appointments to the NLRB, reversing Reagan's executive order prohibiting the rehiring of former striking PATCO members, and appointing a commission led by former secretary of labor John Dunlop to study labor policy and make recommendations for changes. Labor hoped to build momentum for broader labor law reform by first passing a bill to prohibit the permanent replacement of striking workers. The problem stemmed from a 1938 Supreme Court decision that interpreted the NLRA to permit the permanent hiring of replacements for strikers. During the recession of the early nineties, many locals were broken by employers who replaced their striking workforce. Some companies intentionally and illegally used this tactic to get rid of a union in their workplaces by essentially refusing to bargain in good faith, provoking a strike, and then replacing all the workers. Union leaders argued that the tactic undermined the economic power of the strike and scared many workers into accepting unfair contracts. A striker replacement bill passed the House in 1991 but stalled in the Senate as labor came 3 votes short of invoking cloture against a filibuster in 1992.

Clinton pledged to work for and sign the bill, and organized labor immediately set out to pass it at the beginning of Clinton's term. Even though a group of conservative Democrats petitioned the leadership not to take up the controversial legislation so soon after the difficult vote on Clinton's budget,[40] the Democratic leadership was eager to get Democrats on record in support of one of labor's top priorities. The striker replacement bill passed the House 239–190 in the summer of 1993 with all but one non-Southern Democrat voting for the bill, compared with 62% of Southern Democrats and 10% of Republicans. The Senate finally took up the legislation a year later, but as in 1992, Republicans launched a filibuster. This time organized labor could muster only 53 votes for cloture. The vestiges of the conservative coalition and the enduring regional deviations from party positions were apparent on the cloture vote. Every non-Southern Democrat voted for cloture; all but three Republicans (D'Amato, Specter, and Mark O. Hatfield of Oregon) and six of fourteen Southern Democrats voted against it. Although the vote could have been expected, it was salt in labor's wounds. Union leaders argued that if Clinton had worked as hard for the striker replacement bill as he did for NAFTA, it would have passed. But it is virtually impossible to envision how Clinton or organized labor could have gotten 60 votes. Neither had much leverage with Republicans, other than the three who voted for cloture, but the support of one more Republican and all of the Southern Democrats would have been necessary to cut off debate.[41] No compromise, short of entirely gutting the bill, could garner this level of support. The defeat on striker replacement dashed labor's hopes of broader labor law reform. As during the Johnson and Carter years, labor simply could not muster the supermajority support necessary to get favorable labor law reform passed. This also proved true on health care reform.

The Return of Universal Health Care Reform

Labor activists believed another window of opportunity had opened for health care reform in 1993. Employer-based health coverage was declining, health care costs were spiraling out of control, and businesses argued that these costs put them at a competitive disadvantage with companies in other countries. Unions were concerned about both the international competitive disadvantage and the prevalence of nonunionized firms that did not provide health insurance. All these problems led to consistently high levels of support in polls for health care reform.[42] Indicating the popular appeal of the issue, Harris Wofford, a dark horse Democratic candidate in a special election to fill an open Senate seat in Pennsylvania in 1991, was largely credited with winning because of an ad he ran that argued if an accused criminal had the right to a lawyer, every American citizen should have the right to see a doctor.[43] Clinton's victory, greater party unity among Democrats, the decline of the conservative coalition, and stronger congressional party leadership strengthened prospects for reform on Capitol Hill. However, as the battle unfolded, Democrats struggled to find a compromise that could hold the support of Democrats and attract a few Republicans, giving the minority party the ability to obstruct legislation in the Senate.

Shortly after taking office, Clinton charged his wife, Hillary, with developing a detailed plan for universal health coverage.[44] Hillary Clinton and her task force advisers held extensive sessions with experts and stakeholders including organized labor. After months of work, the president unveiled his plan and promised to veto any bill that did not contain universal coverage in a dramatic nationally televised speech before a joint session of Congress in September 1993. Clinton's plan was based on a novel, hybrid concept of "managed competition" in which heavily regulated private insurers would compete for customers in government-run regional health care alliances that would offer individuals a choice from a range of plans.[45] Employers would be required to cover 80% of the cost of their employees' premiums, and the government would subsidize the premiums of the poor, the unemployed, and others traditionally without access to group insurance plans.

Although organized labor was initially divided over what type of proposal to endorse, most of the labor movement coalesced behind Clinton's approach, convinced that more far-reaching reforms like single-payer, national health insurance had no shot of making it through Congress.[46] Fearing that intransigence might result in a replay of the failures of the 1970s, the AFL-CIO and most of the affiliates were willing to drop the idea of a government-run system and were open to compromise as long as universal coverage was the goal and the comprehensiveness of existing health coverage for most union members with employer-sponsored insurance was not scaled back. Labor hoped a moderate proposal based on the existing system would draw a wider range of support, including business groups, that might be capable of breaking the decades-long impasse on health care reform. The Clinton plan also included several specific proposals to keep labor on board. During the task force stage, labor lobbyists succeeded in killing a proposal to tax employer-provided health benefits beyond the basic plan established by government regulators.[47] In response to a request by unions and automakers, the plan included a provision for government subsidization of 80% of the cost of early retirees' health premiums. Postal workers, unlike other federal employees, were also exempted from the regional health alliances and allowed to keep their union-run plans. The AFL-CIO Executive Council officially endorsed the Clinton plan the day before Clinton's televised speech.

Labor ultimately played a major role in pushing for Clinton's health care plan in Congress, even though tension over the NAFTA fight lingered and some labor leaders questioned the administration's commitment.[48] Some leaders feared labor had caved too soon in supporting Clinton's plan and lost valuable negotiating room. After watching Clinton compromise away his agenda in Congress, they feared that he might drop some of the core provisions of his plan, which already involved substantial compromises. As Congress and the administration entered into negotiations over the health proposal late in 1993, union leaders made it clear that they would not be willing to compromise over the employer mandate and warned the administration against making concessions early in the debate. The Clinton administration pledged to maintain the mandate. To keep labor on board and to try to smooth over the split produced by the NAFTA fight, Vice President Al Gore and an unprecedented number of administration officials were dispatched to the AFL-CIO's February Executive Council meeting in Florida to confer with labor leaders on health care legislation.[49] The AFL-CIO pledged to spend $10 million on the health care battle, including $3 million on media.[50] However, this spending was eventually dwarfed by opponents of the Clinton plan, which included small businesses and small and medium-size insurers that stood to lose their customers. The labor effort began with a campaign of political education of union members and grassroots lobbying in the districts of twenty-four swing members on the three key House committees that would initiate action on the bill.[51] The AFL-CIO also joined and funded several coalitions pushing for health care reform such as the Health Care Reform Project, which included the AARP, several provider organizations, and prominent large companies such as Ford.

Yet there was substantial opposition among conservatives in Congress, and several influential interest groups were determined to kill the Clinton plan, in particular the National Federation of Independent Business (NFIB) and the Health Insurance Association of America (HIAA). Notably absent from the early opponents of the Clinton plan was the American Medical Association, which was at least rhetorically committed to reaching universal coverage. But as Steinmo and Watts point out, over time the opposition to Clinton's plan grew: "Opponents of reform, we should remember, have always been careful not to argue against any kind of health care reform. Instead, opponents of Clinton's plan did exactly what opponents of the Truman, Nixon, Ford and Carter health plans did: They said, 'Oh yes, we *do* need reform. But there are particular things about *this* reform plan that we don't like.' Then they slowed the reform inside the congressional labyrinth. This left time for the media and the industry's public (dis)information campaigns to frighten voters and members of Congress about the details of the administration plan."[52] Public support began to slide under the advertising onslaught launched by interest groups and conservatives. A March 1994 poll found that 45% of respondents opposed the "Clinton plan" and only 37% supported it. The same poll asked if respondents favored a plan with a list of characteristics that described the Clinton plan, but did not label the plan as Clinton's, and 76% of respondents expressed support.[53]

Congress and Clinton's Plan

Scholars and pundits have suggested a number of reasons for the health care plan's failure, including a lack of adequate leadership from Clinton, the unpopularity of Hillary Clinton, neglect of Congress, lack of outreach to Republicans, the strength of the organized opposition, the poor quality of the pro-reform public relations effort, and the weakness of organized groups that supported reform including labor.[54] But the filibuster threat and the need for supermajority consensus in a partisan environment on such a complex issue exaggerated the effects of these factors and were just as critical to the outcome.

A summary of legislative action on the bill in *Congressional Quarterly* noted, "At every point in the congressional process, health care proved too difficult for the institution to digest."[55] To begin with, Speaker Foley chose to put off the jurisdictional fight by referring the bill to multiple committees. The bill was taken up by three major committees in the House (Ways and Means, Education and Labor, and Energy and Commerce), two major committees in the Senate (Finance and Labor and Human Resources), and a host of secondary committees in both houses. On each of the committees the familiar splits arose between liberals who supported a single-payer national health insurance proposal, others who supported the administration's plan, still others who favored a more incremental approach, and conservatives who preferred nothing. Multiple referrals made it more likely that a diversity of approaches would be reported and that a single powerful committee like Ways and Means or Finance would not control the outcome. But it also meant that the committee process did little to generate a viable floor bill.

The House committees produced a range of bills. The Education and Labor Committee endorsed an expanded version of Clinton's plan, but in order to get the votes of the more liberal members to report the modified Clinton bill, the committee chair agreed to reporting a single-payer, traditional national health insurance bill as well. The House Ways and Means Committee reported a patchwork bill full of provisions and concessions necessary to build a narrow committee majority. The bill abandoned the regional alliances in the Clinton bill and relied on an employer mandate and an expansion of Medicare to reach universal coverage. Only the House Energy and Commerce Committee, chaired by John Dingell, the son of the legendary champion of national health insurance and cosponsor of the multiple Wagner-Murray-Dingell bills back in the forties, could not produce a bill. Viewed as a bellwether of congressional opinion because of its ideological and regional mix of members, the committee could not reach a consensus that would hold together liberals and the large number of Democratic moderates on the panel.[56]

On the Senate side, the two bills reported by the main committees were quite different. The Senate Labor and Human Resources Committee, chaired by Senator Kennedy—who, like most labor leaders, was a convert to the Clinton plan—reported a modified version of Clinton's proposal. In contrast, the Senate Finance Committee was the only committee to produce a bill that could reasonably be called bipartisan.[57] To reach this consensus, the goal of universal coverage and the employer mandate had to be dropped in favor of a goal of health coverage for 95% of the population by 2002, to be reached through insurance regulations and government subsidies for the purchase of health insurance.

The proliferation of proposals during committee consideration fragmented the legislative process with individual members and interest groups developing allegiances to their favorite among the competing bills. As Representative David Skaggs (D-CO) noted, "Typically, the committee process clears out the underbrush on legislation. That didn't happen on health care."[58] Because none of the committee bills was considered viable for floor consideration in either the House or the Senate, the leadership in both houses asserted its growing role in the legislative process by trying to craft a compromise.

By this point most Republicans were convinced of the political wisdom of letting health care die and were not willing to come to the table. Conservative strategists, most notably Bill Kristol, argued for months that passage of universal health care could present serious problems for the Republican Party by strengthening the attachment of the middle class to government programs and their Democratic defenders.[59] Kristol argued that if the Republicans refused to cooperate there would be no way for the Democrats to get a bill passed but the Democrats, in control of both the White House and Congress, would likely be held responsible for inaction in the 1994 elections. Newt Gingrich, who had been laying the groundwork for a Republican takeover of the House for more than a decade, saw the health care issue as the perfect way to portray the Democrats as ineffectual, out of touch, and wedded to inefficient, big government programs.

This highly partisan atmosphere complicated the congressional leadership's task. House majority leader Dick Gephardt (MO) cobbled together a plan, but House Democrats did not want to take the difficult vote until the Senate deadlock was broken. As the Senate took up debate in August, Majority Leader George Mitchell (ME) struggled to devise a compromise that could attract Republican and Democratic moderates without losing the liberals. A few Republican moderates still seemed willing to work on legislation in the Senate (Lincoln Chafee of Rhode Island, David Durenberger of Minnesota, John Danforth of

Missouri, William Roth of Delaware, and James Jeffords of Vermont). Because of Republicans' filibuster threat, the leadership would have to hold all the Democrats, including several (mostly Southern) moderates who did not see much political payoff in the health care issue, and pick up four of the five Republicans to invoke cloture. It became clear that a filibuster-proof majority could not be built around a bill that maintained quick implementation of the employer mandate and universal coverage. Clinton began to lay the groundwork for conceding on these points by talking about "functional" universal coverage. However, in dropping these commitments, the leadership risked losing the support of liberal members of Congress and organized labor. After a bitter, partisan fight on Clinton's crime bill that suggested the political environment was not ripe for compromise, Congress went away for its August recess without either house voting on a health care bill. Mitchell continued to negotiate into September but could never count 60 votes for any given compromise. He officially announced the demise of health care reform on September 26, noting, "Even though Republicans are a minority in Congress, in the Senate they're a minority with a veto. They have the ability to block legislation and they have chosen to do so."[60] Once again the window of opportunity for significant health care reform closed.

The 1994 Elections

The first two years of the Clinton administration proved to be a short detour in the march of American politics to the right. The 1994 elections brought Republican control in the House for the first time in forty years and Republican control in the Senate for the first time in eight years. Scholars such as Theda Skocpol have argued that the Republican surge that dashed so many of labor's legislative expectations for the Clinton administration was in large part a result of the spectacular failure of Clinton's proposal to ensure universal health care.[61] In a vision shared by many labor leaders, Clinton hoped that his health care program would create an enduring boost for the Democratic Party, much as Social Security had decades earlier. It had the opposite effect, giving Republicans a campaign issue on which to attack the ineffectiveness of the Democrats, even though the Republicans had played a major role in defeating the plan. It is hard to determine how much of an effect health care had on the 1994 elections, but the outcome certainly had a profound impact on future policy debates and the labor movement.

The overwhelming majority of Republicans running for House seats, both incumbents and challengers, ran on the Contract with America, a ten-point platform developed by Gingrich, Republican Conference chairman Dick Armey (D-TX), and other conservatives. Echoing the conservative themes of Reagan, the contract pledged to restrict the role and spending of government (except on defense), shift federal responsibilities to the states, unfetter the private sector through deregulation and tax cuts, and emphasize personal responsibility. But as journalists George Hager and Eric Pianin suggest, Gingrich was Reagan at "warp-speed."[62] Reagan was opposed to many of the programs of the Great Society, but he was not very interested in taking on safety net programs for the middle class like Social Security and Medicare. Gingrich and his followers wanted not only to roll back the Great Society but also to push back the New Deal.[63] Almost every piece of legislation organized labor had pushed in the past seven decades was a target. Many of the insurgents wanted to drop the progressive income tax, privatize Social Security, convert Medicare to subsidized private insurance, eliminate federal departments such as Education and Energy, and replace regulatory regimes such as OSHA with voluntary programs. Many of the old-line Republicans in the Senate did not share the commitments of the Gingrich revolutionaries in the House, but even the Senate experienced an influx of conservative freshmen.

Far more ominous than the election of Ronald Reagan in 1980, the 1994 elections were an earthquake for liberals that shook the entire labor movement. The loss of the House to the Republicans was particularly disheartening. Through the dark years of the Reagan and Bush administrations, the labor movement had always found protective allies in the House. Given Clinton's low public approval ratings in the immediate aftermath of the 1994 election, labor leaders feared the 1996 election might bring unified Republican control of all three branches of the government and labor would have nowhere to turn. Many of the leaders of the affiliates began to question openly the competence and commitment of the leadership of the AFL-CIO that was primarily responsible for directing organized labor's political activity. The result was the first contested election for the AFL-CIO's presidency in the federation's history, in which the existing leadership was ousted and John J. Sweeney, the president of the growing and occasionally militant Service Employees International Union (SEIU), was elected. Sweeney pledged to reinvigorate the labor movement through a greater federation role in organizing and more effective political mobilization.

The first priority for the AFL-CIO under the new leadership was to stop the conservatives in Congress and push the political agenda back toward issues of economic fairness and a strong government safety net. Owing to the lobbying efforts of organized labor, in combination with the protections of the minority and the bias toward the status quo in the legislative process, labor was able to play a fairly effective role in defending the core of the welfare state against conservative attacks during the Clinton administration. Much like the Reagan revolution, the Gingrich revolution fizzled out as the conservative agenda worked its way through the legislative process.

The Republican Revolution and the Attack on the Welfare State

The 1994 election furthered the process of partisan realignment and polarization that had been accelerating since the 1980s. On average, the Democratic incumbents who won were more liberal than the Democratic incumbents who lost.[64] All Republican incumbents won in 1994, and the victorious Republican freshmen who joined them were on average quite conservative. The pool of moderates shrank considerably. As noted above, there was a marked shift in Southern seats in both the House and the Senate, with Republicans finally winning a majority of seats from the South in both bodies. The 1994 elections also brought Southerners back to dominance of the leadership ranks with Trent Lott of Mississippi becoming the majority whip in the Senate and Gingrich of Georgia and Texans Dick Armey and Tom Delay taking the top leadership slots in the House. The South rose again and pushed the Republican Party further to the right.

With the exception of term limits, the provisions of the Contract with America sailed through the House over the opposition of a unified Democratic Party. The Senate was a different story. Many of the contract proposals died in the Senate or were significantly compromised. The presidential veto and the filibuster became effective weapons as liberal groups such as labor turned to President Clinton and the Senate to protect past legislative gains. In 1995, Republicans set up a showdown with President Clinton by passing a filibuster-proof budget reconciliation bill that included extensive changes and cuts in Medicare, Medicaid, welfare, farm policy, and a host of other public policy areas, including areas that directly affected labor such as job training and OSHA funding. In dramatic fashion, Clinton vetoed the bill with the same pen Lyndon

Johnson had used to sign Medicare into law.[65] Vetoes and veto threats prevented much labor-opposed legislation from becoming law. Given the strong party unity among Democrats, it was almost impossible for the Republicans to override Clinton's vetoes. Only two were overridden in Clinton's two terms in office. Labor was now in the position its political opponents had occupied for years under Republican presidents and Democratic Congresses. The ability of organized labor to stop antilabor legislation was particularly apparent in the contentious area of labor law and worker protections.

Conservatives Take Up Labor Law Reform

Conservative Republicans developed an agenda of labor law reforms designed to offer businesses greater flexibility and scale back protections for workers and unions. Most of these proposals either died in the Senate or were vetoed. After the failure of the striker replacement bill, Clinton issued an executive order in March 1995 to bar federal contractors from permanently replacing strikers. Democrats successfully filibustered Republicans' efforts to deny funding for enforcement of the executive order.[66] An effort to pass a national right-to-work bill in the Senate that would have made union dues voluntary was also successfully filibustered. In the perennial effort to repeal Davis-Bacon, the Republicans passed an amendment to the budget reconciliation bill to end the provision, but it died when Clinton vetoed the underlying bill. Repeated efforts in the 104th (1995–96) and 105th (1997–98) Congresses to scale back OHSA either died in committee or were successfully filibustered. A top priority for the Republican leadership was a bill to allow employers to offer employees "comp time," time off for overtime hours worked, rather than the time-and-a-half pay mandated in the Fair Labor Standards Act. While advocates argued that the bill would give employees greater flexibility, unions argued that employers would coerce employees into taking the comp time and the income of many hourly-wage workers would fall considerably. The bill passed in the House in both 1996 and 1997. Clinton threatened to veto the bills, but Democratic filibusters kept them from reaching his desk.[67]

Clinton vetoed another Republican leadership priority, the TEAM Act, allowing companies to set up worker-management groups to address workplace issues by repealing a provision in the NLRA that bars "company unions." Republicans argued that the bill would allow companies to address workers' concerns and become more competitive. Unions argued that the act would allow companies to set up company-controlled unions and discourage workers from joining independent unions. Frustrated with their inability to get legislation enacted and angered by labor's efforts to target Republicans in the 1996 elections, House Republicans launched a $1.4 million study of labor law and workplace regulations and an investigation into union political activity, but very little came of it. Republicans were again defeated by a filibuster in one final effort to pass a bill in the 105th Congress (1997–98) to fight off what companies feared might be a new wave of union organizing under Sweeney's leadership of the AFL-CIO. The bill banned the practice of "salting," whereby union organizers or supporters gain employment in a nonunionized company with the intention of building support for unionization. As a consequence of the filibuster, the veto, and the narrow Republican majority, six years of Republican control of Congress brought no appreciable labor law changes.

Incremental Gains: The Minimum Wage and Targeted Health Care Reform

Although labor was primarily on the defensive for the remainder of the Clinton years, there were some incremental gains. Under Sweeney's leadership the labor movement geared up for an unprecedented mobilization in the 1996 elections, with a special effort to target vulnerable Republican freshmen and call attention to public policy issues like the minimum wage and patients' rights in HMOs. The value of the minimum wage when adjusted for inflation was approaching a forty-year low. After consulting with the AFL-CIO on a proposed increase, Senator Kennedy led Democrats in the Senate in creating procedural havoc by trying to attach a minimum wage increase to almost every bill that came up on the Senate floor.[68] The Republican leadership in both the House and the Senate tried two strategies: avoiding taking up the minimum wage on the floor and trying to bundle it with other policy proposals the Democrats and organized labor would not support. But moderate Republicans got nervous they were going to pay a price in the elections, and the leadership ultimately conceded to a vote. Labor ran ads in thirty Republican congressional districts to build support for the bill, and fifteen of these House members ultimately changed their position to vote for the increase.[69] To save face the Republicans packaged the wage increase with business tax cuts and a short-term youth subminimum training wage. Despite these concessions, organized labor considered the bill the biggest accomplishment of the 104th Congress. A perennially popular issue, the minimum wage came up again in 1998, 1999, and 2000 but fell victim to strategic brinkmanship between Democratic and Republican party leaders.

Faced with swallowing substantial tax and spending cuts as the price for getting a minimum wage increase, organized labor and Democratic leaders favored saving the issue for the 2000 election.

In health care, labor turned to a few popular, targeted measures. Labor supported legislation passed in 1996 to prevent insurers from denying coverage for preexisting medical conditions if a new applicant had recently been covered by a group policy. As with the minimum wage, labor also tried to shape the debate around Medicare by running a massive ad campaign in the 1996 elections accusing Republicans of trying to kill the popular program. The public reaction muted Republicans' interest in transforming the program, although congressional leaders did get the Clinton administration to agree to some cuts in Medicare and Medicaid in the 1997 budget agreement. Clinton accepted these cuts in exchange for a new federal-state program at the top of the AFL-CIO's legislative agenda to expand health coverage for the children of the working poor, known as the State Children's Health Insurance Program (SCHIP).[70] These policies fell far short of labor's goals, but they added to the patchwork of protections in the American welfare state.

The George W. Bush Administration: Labor's Last Stand?

Perhaps no other political event in the post–World War II period more vividly illustrates the challenges to labor's influence posed by American political institutions than the outcome of the 2000 presidential election. Organized labor launched a record drive to elect the Democratic candidate Al Gore and helped produce a Gore victory in a series of swing states as well as the popular vote.[71] However, Bush, one of the most antilabor presidents in recent history, won the electoral college vote. Given the disproportionate weight of small states in the electoral college and the winner-take-all allocation of electoral college votes in most states, labor's impact on the outcome was reduced because union members are concentrated in high-population, and in many cases high-voter-turnout, states. Labor had long advocated the elimination of the electoral college and direct election of the president, but the senators from small states had blocked these changes.[72] The AFL-CIO and civil rights groups organized public demonstrations to protest electoral irregularities in Florida amid the recount in that highly contested state, but once the U.S. Supreme Court spoke in a controversial 5–4 decision ending the Florida recount, there was little labor could do. George W. Bush assumed the presidency. In the wake of the election, the AFL-CIO set up a voter protection program across the country to avoid some of the problems at the polls in 2000.

The first defeat for organized labor came quickly in the elimination of sweeping new ergonomics regulations dealing with repetitive stress injuries issued in the final days of the Clinton administration. The ergonomics rules had already been the subject of skirmishes during the Clinton years as Congress repeatedly and unsuccessfully tried to deny funding to OSHA to issue the rules.[73] In a surprise move at the beginning of the 107th Congress (2001–2), Republicans invoked an obscure law known as the Congressional Review Act. The act allowed Congress to invalidate major rules by a simple majority vote within sixty days after the rules were formally reported to Congress. The resolution invalidating the rules passed narrowly in early March. If it had been procedurally permissible to filibuster the bill, it would have been very difficult for the Republican leadership to have found the 60 votes for cloture. However, because the resolution required only a simple majority vote, labor was unable to exercise its defensive role, and the ergonomics rules, more than ten years in the making, were repealed before they went into effect.

The next major defeat for labor and liberals was passage of Bush's centerpiece tax legislation in May, which, as part of budget reconciliation, was also not subject to filibuster. The bill included significant tax cuts for the wealthy that labor feared would create revenue shortfalls that might be used to justify cuts in social spending. The administration also pushed ahead with other priorities like a Medicare prescription drug bill, patients' rights legislation, and education reform, all in forms opposed by labor. But progress was slowed as the president encountered more resistance on the Hill. It appeared that labor's defensive role would be strengthened when Democrats gained control of the Senate because Republican senator James Jeffords of Vermont, frustrated with the strong-arm tactics and conservative orientation of the administration, decided to become an independent and caucus with the Democrats. The trajectory of the Bush administration might have been very similar to that of the Reagan administration —the accomplishment of a major tax cut in the first year followed by more incremental changes and stalemate. By summer of 2001, gridlock appeared to be returning to the Capitol. Then September 11 changed the political environment. Although there was a brief period of unity and peace on the Hill, bitter partisanship returned as Congress approached the 2002 elections. The position of President Bush was transformed from the loser of the popular vote to the national leader in a time of war. Emboldened, the administration became even less interested in compromise with its opponents than it had been before.

Legislation to create a Department of Homeland Security produced the greatest clash of the Bush administration with organized labor and its Democratic allies. The Bush administration initially opposed a proposal by Democratic senator Joe Lieberman to create a cabinet-level homeland security department but later switched course and adopted the idea as its own in the summer of 2002.[74] The administration bill consolidated all or part of twenty-two federal agencies responsible for counterterrorism activities and sought maximum flexibility in managing the more than one hundred thousand federal government workers expected to become a part of the department. When debate on a version of the administration's proposal commenced in the House in July, a bitter fight erupted when Democrats and moderate Republicans from labor-oriented districts tried to insert protections for existing union representation and collective bargaining rights of federal government employees. This effort was defeated, and the final version of the House bill did not include the protections.

The Democrat-controlled Senate, however, took up debate in September on Lieberman's version of the bill that included these protections. But Senate Republicans wanted a vote on a Republican bill without the union protections. Neither side in the 51–49 Senate had the votes to avert a filibuster. An effort to invoke cloture on the Lieberman bill produced an almost purely party-line vote of 50–49. The only Democrat to vote with the Republicans was Zell Miller, the soon to be infamous Democratic senator from Georgia who would rail against the Democrats' position on national security in primetime at the 2004 Republican National Convention. The only Republican to vote for cloture was moderate senator Lincoln Chafee of Rhode Island. Unfruitful bipartisan negotiations among moderates continued until Majority Leader Tom Daschle pulled the bill from the floor as the regular session came to a close before the 2002 congressional elections. Senate Democrats all but unanimously defended organized labor's position until the end—a factor repeatedly pointed to by Republicans in the campaign. Democrats like Vietnam veteran Senator Max Cleland of Georgia were savaged as undermining national security, largely because of their votes on cloture. Losing Cleland's seat and one other, the Democrats lost control of the Senate. Defeated, the Democrats gave up the fight in a lame duck session after the election and passed the bill in the form favored by the administration.

Labor's ability to work with its congressional allies to play a defensive role in the legislative process declined in the next Congress. The conservatism of the House in alliance with the conservatism of the administration became the dominant legislative force. Whereas conference committees had previously been an arena in which the final version of legislation was most often pulled in the more moderate Senate direction, the more conservative positions of the House and administration frequently prevailed in conference over the objections of moderate Republicans, who were increasingly unlikely to challenge the administration's position. The Democrats, who had been attacked in the elections as obstructionists, also appeared chastened. In the 108th Congress (2003–4), with Republican strength bolstered by the midterm elections, Republican leaders and the administration managed narrowly to push through priorities that had stalled in the previous Congress, including additional tax cuts and a version of the Medicare prescription drug benefit opposed by organized labor that benefited private insurers. By threatening vetoes, the administration prevailed in conference negotiations, winning its version of policies strongly fought by organized labor on outsourcing federal jobs, restricting worker eligibility for overtime pay, and allowing workers to be offered comp time by their employers instead of overtime. These were the very types of policies that labor was able to fend off in earlier administrations.

Because of its experience under the Bush administration, organized labor worked diligently to elect John Kerry in 2004, viewing it as a matter of political life and death. Despite labor's successes in getting its voters to the polls, once again the labor effort was not enough. Six months before he would pull his union out of the AFL-CIO to form a rival federation, SEIU president Andrew Stern argued in a postelection meeting of the AFL-CIO Executive Council that organized labor was too geographically concentrated and its membership had fallen too much to allow it to shift the political balance of power.[75]

But Bush's second term was not as productive as the first. Following the 2004 election, the president asserted that he had earned political capital and he was going to spend it. Emboldened, conservative Republicans in the Senate even proposed a major institutional change to prohibit filibusters of judicial nominees to allow President Bush to shape the federal judiciary unimpeded by Democrats' obstruction.[76] But the president's declining popularity as a result of the Iraq War and the administration's poor handling of Hurricane Katrina, as well as the disaffection of many congressional conservatives who were increasingly critical of a growing government and deficit spending, ate away at Bush's effectiveness on the Hill. Gridlock returned as Bush administration proposals such as making his massive tax cuts permanent and overhauling immigration policy bogged down. Bush was also forced to drop serious talk of reforming Social Security. Labor activists considered this defeat to be at least partially a result of their efforts to fight the privatization proposals.[77] The changing political tide was reflected in the 2006 elections when the Democrats won back control of both the House and the Senate and ended twelve years of Republican rule.

Old Patterns and New: The 110th Congress

Organized labor's efforts played an important role in many of the Democratic victories in the 2006 elections, and the new Congress was much more supportive of labor's agenda. The elections reflected a continuation of the trends discussed in the first section of this chapter. While the Democrats picked up one Southern seat in the Senate (Jim Webb in Virginia), the remainder of the pickups came from more heavily unionized areas. Many of the gains in the House were also from more heavily unionized regions. Even many of the moderates among the Democratic freshmen ran as economic populists, and they were supportive of most of labor's policy positions. The actions of the 110th Congress also reflected the trends discussed earlier in this chapter. Partisanship remained high. The Democratic congressional leadership also worked hard to deliver for organized labor. The success rate on COPE votes surged to 88% in the House in 2007 and 87% in 2008 (see fig. 6.6). Four of the five defeats in the two-year period were failed veto overrides requiring a two-thirds supermajority. The success rate also increased in the Senate and would have been comparable to the House rate except for the large number of defeats on cloture votes against Republican-led filibusters, in which labor had majority, but not supermajority, support.

As expected, legislative accomplishments on labor's priorities were limited by filibusters and President Bush's vetoes. After exercising only one veto in his first six years in office, Bush issued eleven vetoes in the 110th Congress. In the typical postwar pattern, successes were largely incremental. For example, after almost a decade of deadlock on the minimum wage, the Democrats managed to attach an increase to an emergency war spending bill that the president was unlikely to veto. Demonstrating the continued impact of the minority Republicans in the Senate, this compromise proposal had to include five billion dollars in business tax breaks in order to attract enough Republican votes to avert a filibuster.

Table 6.2.   Party Support on Labor Law Votes in the House

Legislation	Date of Vote	Percentage of Democrats Voting For (Vote)	Percentage of Republicans Voting Against (Vote)
14(b) repeal	July 28, 1965	70 (200–86)	85 (21–117)
Labor law reform package	October 6, 1977	79 (221–59)	74 (36–104)
Striker replacement	July 17, 1991	88 (230–33)	90 (16–149)
	June 15, 1993	87 (221–33)	90 (17–157)
Employee Free Choice Act	March 1, 2007	99 (228–2)	93 (13–183)

Source: Congressional Quarterly.

Although the bill did not become law, the growing support for organized labor in the Democratic caucus was best illustrated in a vote on labor law reform in the 110th Congress. The top legislative priority for organized labor, the Employee Free Choice Act (EFCA), would allow unions to circumvent the cumbersome NLRB union certification election process in favor of a procedure known as "card check." Under card check, a union can be certified as the collective bargaining agent once it obtains signatures of support from more than 50% of employees. Labor agreed to drop this controversial provision from the package of labor law reforms pursued during the Carter administration, but like the 1970s proposal, EFCA would also impose stiffer penalties on employers who violate labor laws and make it easier for unions to force employers to negotiate first contracts. Employers have become increasingly sophisticated in fighting organizing drives during the drawn-out election process, and many willfully violate the labor law because the penalties are so negligible.[78] Organized labor viewed the EFCA as the key to more successful organizing and to reversing the steep slide in unionization rates. Most employer associations, including the National Association of Manufacturers and the Chamber of Commerce, were adamantly opposed to the bill. Even though Bush pledged to veto the bill, the Democratic leadership wanted to assure labor of its support and get members on record by bringing the bill to a vote in both the House and the Senate. Once again, the legislative path followed the typical pattern for labor law reform since the 1960s. The bill passed comfortably in the House but was successfully filibustered in the Senate.

The EFCA fight demonstrated an unprecedented level of Democratic support, as well as how partisan labor law reform had become. As indicated in tables 6.2 and 6.3, there was nearly unanimous support among Democrats in

Table 6.3.   Party Support on Labor Law Votes in the Senate

Legislation	Date of Vote[a]	Percentage of Democrats Voting for Cloture (Vote)	Percentage of Republicans Voting against Cloture (Vote)
14(b) repeal	February 8, 1966	67 (45–22)	81 (6–26)
Labor law reform package	June 14, 1978	72 (44–17)	63 (14–24)
Striker replacement	June 16, 1991	91 (52–5)	88 (5–37)
	July 13, 1994	89 (50–6)	93 (3–41)
Employee Free Choice Act	June 26, 2007	100 (50[b]–0)	98 (1–48)

Source: Congressional Quarterly.

[a]When multiple cloture votes were taken, the vote reflecting the highest level of support for cloture is included here.

[b]The ill Tim Johnson (D-SD) was incapable of actively serving in the Senate at this time and did not vote, but he was a cosponsor of the legislation and would have almost certainly voted for it. Table includes the votes of independents Bernard Sanders (VT) and Joe Lieberman (CT), who caucus with the Democrats.

the House and unanimous support among Democrats in the Senate, compared with historically high levels of opposition among Republicans. In contrast with earlier efforts at labor law reform, the conservative coalition had finally disappeared, and Democrats from all regions and ideological persuasions went on record in support of a strong, pro-labor bill. All but eight Democratic House members were cosponsors of the legislation,[79] and forty-seven of forty-nine Democratic senators, plus two independents that caucused with the Democrats, were cosponsors. The partisan nature of the vote marked considerable change from the 1970s, which was actually the highpoint of congressional support for labor law reform because of much greater support among Republicans. The changing pattern of roll call votes on labor law reform clearly demonstrates the patterns discussed in the first section of this chapter—growing party unity, growing party polarization, and growing Democratic support for organized labor. Despite all these changes, the 2007 filibuster of the EFCA and the threatened presidential veto also demonstrated the continuing obstacles for labor in the legislative process.

At the end of the session Republicans also used a filibuster to kill an effort to extend government loans to GM and Chrysler to keep the companies out of bankruptcy. Reflecting the continued antagonism between Southern conservatives and organized labor, a number of Southern Republican senators led a direct attack on the UAW in the final days of the Bush administration. Writing in the mid-eighties, political scientist Richard Bensel observed that "the now-dominant labor wing of the Democratic party has rediscovered what many New Deal congressmen recognized fifty years ago, that class conflict was as much an intersectional phenomenon as a characteristic of northern, urban center politics. A United Auto Worker in Detroit takes home an annual salary greater than all but a small percentage of the population in Mississippi."[80] This intersectional class conflict has only been intensified by the location of nonunion, foreign-owned auto plants throughout the South since Bensel wrote. As the price for dropping their filibuster of the auto loans, a handful of Southern senators demanded that the UAW agree to cuts in pay and benefits to bring GM and Chrysler in line with the compensation offered by foreign-owned plants. The UAW refused the offer. UAW president Ron Gettelfinger noted of the Southern senators, "They thought perhaps they could have a twofer here maybe: Pierce the heart of organized labor while representing the foreign brands."[81] Ultimately the Bush administration extended emergency funds to the auto companies from a fund created to stabilize the banking industry, thus buying time to allow the incoming Obama administration to make its own decision about how to handle the failing automakers.

Conclusion

The reforms that labor sought from the 1940s through the 1970s had a profound impact on the evolution of the political system from the 1980s through the first decade of the new millennium. Implementation of civil rights legislation, congressional reforms, and the decline of historical regional attachments to the political parties resulted in the gradual disappearance of labor's old archenemy, the conservative coalition. Labor had hoped this outcome would open up the political system to pro-labor policies and welfare state initiatives. Instead of producing a more powerful liberal coalition, the changes labor fought for contributed to Republican dominance of the political system for several decades. Throughout this period, organized labor was able to use the institutional protections for the minority in the legislative process to protect many of its past policy gains. But in standing still, workers were also losing ground.[82] As Hacker has suggested, new public policies were not adopted to address changing "social risks," so most workers became more insecure.[83]

The political system has been in a long period of what Brady and Volden term "revolving gridlock," in which, regardless of the partisan control of the elected branches, there is little significant policy change.[84] Increased party polarization in conjunction with institutional veto points for the minority has contributed to greater inertia in the policy-making process.[85] As McCarty, Poole, and Rosenthal observe, "increased policy differences exacerbate the incentives to engage in brinksmanship so that even feasible policy compromises might not be reached."[86] Narrow partisan majorities, like those of the past decade, make this situation worse.

But over this period of time, the Democratic Party also rebuilt some of its strength, forming a new electoral coalition that is strongest in areas with comparatively high rates of unionization. As a result, labor's influence in the Democratic Party is no longer contested as it was in the early postwar period. Just as it seemed that organized labor's influence over public policy might fall to near insignificance at the beginning of Bush's second term, the Republicans' fortunes declined and the Democrats' fortunes surged.

Conclusion

Organized labor entered the postwar period with an ambitious policy agenda to ensure workers' security. However, labor leaders encountered numerous obstacles in the legislative process that forced them to scale back their demands and settle for incremental policy advances. While organized labor has not been able to mold this patchwork of policies into a comprehensive welfare state, labor, as part of a larger labor-liberal coalition, has contributed to a gradual transformation of the political system in pursuit of its agenda. Although labor's political influence is widely believed to have declined steadily from a highpoint either in the 1940s or the 1960s through the present, organized labor was not as politically powerful in the past, or as weak today, as is widely assumed because labor's political influence has always been shaped by the larger political and institutional context. As a result, organized labor has been able to sustain political influence, even as its power in the economy and society ebbed. In fact, with the election of Obama and sizable Democratic majorities in the House and Senate in 2008, labor was arguably in the strongest political position it had been in since the Great Society years. This chapter briefly looks at the limits on labor's political influence in the past, its accomplishments in the first years of the Obama administration, and its prospects for the future.

The Missing Opportunity

Many labor activists and scholars see the potential for labor to have built a more social democratic politics in the early postwar period, but this period was not a *missed* opportunity as much as a *missing* opportunity.[1] At the peak of its power in the workforce in the 1940s and 1950s, it was hard for the labor movement to translate its strength in numbers into commensurate power in the political system. The structure of the legislative process, the disenfranchisement of African Americans, malapportioned congressional districts, regional alignments in the party system, and the failure of labor organizing in the South all interacted to restrict labor's political influence at a critical juncture in the development of both the labor movement and the welfare state coming out of the New Deal. Labor has been criticized for clamping down on worker militancy, for failing to take on segregation, and for abandoning the idea of a third party in the 1940s— all of which might have transformed American politics.[2] But worker militancy produced a powerful conservative backlash in the public and Congress, labor faced a great deal of racism not only in society but within its own ranks, and, given the limited strength of liberal Democrats in the early postwar period, there is little reason to believe a third party could have effectively controlled the government. Instead, the labor-liberal coalition committed to realigning the political system by pushing for civil rights, working through the Democratic Party, and reforming the legislative process to make it more hospitable to liberal policies.

As this process proceeded unevenly, labor faced a changing constellation of institutional constraints on its policy agenda in Congress. One-party rule in the South, seniority, and the House Committee system, including the powerful Rules Committee, empowered the conservative coalition of Southern Democrats and Republicans to stop or weaken policies advocated by labor from the late 1930s through the 1960s. Although in decline, the conservative coalition remained a force on the House floor in the 1970s and, to a lesser degree, into the 1990s on some issues. Only sizable liberal congressional majorities, such as those produced by the 1964 election, could overwhelm conservative obstruction. But even in the Great Society years there were limits on what could be achieved. The period from the 1930s through the 1960s, viewed by most scholars to be the heyday of liberalism, corresponded with the period of the greatest strength of the conservative coalition in Congress, which limited liberals' policy accomplishments. After the passage of civil rights legislation, the reapportionment of congressional districts, and congressional reform, the Senate emerged as the major obstacle to labor's agenda. The filibuster and equal state representation made liberal supermajorities necessary for labor's most ambitious policy goals, but these were difficult to build given the uneven regional distribution of labor's strength. However, labor's influence has not been limited to policy advocacy, as it has also played a role in shaping contemporary politics.

By the late New Deal period, it was clear that old institutions could not accommodate new social forces, which resulted in a series of evolving conflicts that influenced political development over the next seventy years. Legislative institutions, the party system, and the organized constituencies supporting it including labor collided in what Orren and Skowronek term "multiple-orders-in-action" or "intercurrence," which ultimately produced a reordering of the party system and the legislative process.[3] During the 1930s and 1940s, organized labor became more fully mobilized in the political system, largely through the Democratic Party. This resulted in conflict within the party between agrarian, conservative Southern and urban, liberal interests that spilled into conflicts over the institutions of the legislative process that privileged the former. These conflicts also encouraged conservative Democrats to ally with Republicans to pass public policies restricting labor that helped confine it geographically, placing boundaries on labor's ability to further transform the political system. Yet, as the labor-liberal wing of the party gained ground within these boundaries, it managed to reform a number of institutions in the legislative process, acting either alone or in coalition with other interests that desired change. The labor-liberal coalition continued to push the realignment of the Democratic Party, in part through the mobilization of new social forces such as African Americans in the South. As the parties became more cohesive and polarized, the reformed institutions of the legislative process were used in new ways. The majority party came to dominate the House, while the use of the reformed filibuster skyrocketed. These changes in the operation of the legislative process, in turn, fed greater partisanship and polarization.[4] The labor-liberal coalition's legislative agenda has faced continued inertia and incrementalism under this new political configuration, leading to more calls for reform.

Despite the many changes in the political system in the postwar period, the limits on welfare state development across the areas of labor law reform, full-employment planning, workers' income security, and national health care have endured. Labor law reform has repeatedly been defeated by Senate filibusters, even though labor had majority support in both the House and the Senate. In both the 1940s and the 1970s, Congress passed largely symbolic full-employment legislation that neither committed the government to full employment nor created the policy-making infrastructure necessary to achieve it. The Employment Act of 1946 was watered down in the House Committee system, and thirty years later the Humphrey-Hawkins Act was watered down to survive a filibuster threat. The minimum wage, which applied to only a fifth of the workforce when it was passed in 1937 in order to overcome the resistance of Southern conservatives, has gradually been expanded to cover almost all workers. Labor also overcame conservative resistance to increasing the minimum wage in repeated battles over the past seventy years—in House and conference committees and against veto and filibuster threats—but its value has often lagged considerably behind inflation. The unemployment compensation system is another area in which Congress has resorted to short-term, emergency fixes because of conservatives' commitment to preserving a role for the states. A consensus approach to national health care that could attract a viable legislative coalition eluded reformers from the 1940s through the 1970s, and by the 1990s the filibuster made that consensus even harder to reach. The nature of the legislative process demands compromise, and this has repeatedly forced labor to scale back its ambitions. Health care policy is a good illustration.

Organized labor has been committed to universal health coverage throughout the postwar period, but it has supported a range of proposals to reach this goal. When national health insurance failed in the 1940s, labor decided to pursue universal health care incrementally by targeting the elderly in the Medicare program, which finally passed in 1965. In contrast, when labor held out for its ideal position, it often got nothing, as it did in the 1970s when it continued to support a single-payer health care system when a compromise based on private insurance might have been more achievable. By the 1990s, most labor strategists came to realize that building the supermajority consensus necessary to accomplish such far-reaching reform as a single-payer health care system was politically unrealistic, and most segments of the labor movement agreed to support reforms building on the system of employer-sponsored health insurance. This strategy, of course, ultimately succeeded in the Obama administration.

Was labor fighting an uphill battle trying to pass policies like universal health care or full employment that the public—and even many union members—did not support with their votes? Congressional historian Julian Zelizer notes that labor and its liberal allies operated under the assumption that "unfair institutional protections" allowed a small contingency of conservatives to block progressive policies that most Americans supported. But he questions whether the public really was supportive of the liberals' agenda.[5] It is hard to prove either way. Americans elected conservative majorities to Congress during this period, but they also elected presidents who ran on liberal agendas, such as Truman, Kennedy, and Johnson. Different local and national party identities, the various ways the electorate is configured into different constituencies for the purposes of electing House members, senators, and the president, and the role of the individual candidates themselves all make it very difficult to read the policy mandate behind electoral returns.

As labor leaders repeatedly emphasized to party leaders, the lack of party responsibility also made it difficult to turn out union members in elections and to build a larger liberal coalition. It was hard for Democrats to cultivate a progressive image outside the South when racist, conservative Southern Democrats were so prominent and powerful in Congress. Moreover, both parties ran on policy agendas that they could rarely deliver once in office because of the power of legislative minorities to obstruct majority rule. As Alan Ware argues, one of the main ways a party generates a loyal electorate is by implementing public policies favored by a group of voters. Yet this requires the party to control the policy-making process, which is unusual in the United States because of the dispersion of power across political institutions.[6] The broken promises, watered-down programs, legislative gridlock, and congressional wrangling that have been the norm in the postwar period feed public cynicism toward the parties, politicians, and the government. Steinmo argues that the cynicism produced by a dysfunctional political system has contributed to Americans' skepticism toward government solutions to national problems.[7] It has also likely had an impact on election returns. Certainly many potential voters have not bothered to participate at all. But labor has never given up.

Progress on Labor's Agenda in the Obama Administration

The resilience of the labor-liberal coalition was evident in the election of Barack Obama and large Democratic majorities in Congress. Although various scholars have argued that the labor-liberal coalition either declined or dissolved in the late 1940s, the late 1960s, or the 1980s, its constituent elements—organized labor, minorities, and middle- and upper-class liberals—remain the base of the Democratic Party and helped return control of the House, the Senate, and the presidency to the Democrats for the first time in sixteen years.[8] The major splits in the coalition were gradually smoothed over as Vietnam receded and women and minorities gained ground among unionized workers. As noted in Chapter 4, labor and New Left groups, including environmentalists and consumer protection advocates, often worked together in the legislative arena, despite occasional differences. Today these groups cooperate very closely in electoral politics and increasingly share a similar agenda that revolves around the expansion of the role of government.[9]

The major change in the past few decades is that the labor-liberal coalition no longer contends with Southern conservatives for control of the Democratic Party. Obama managed to carry Florida, North Carolina, and Virginia, all states with substantial in-migration from other regions, but the Southern percentage of the Democratic congressional caucuses hovered around all-time lows, and most congressional gains came in the North and West.[10] In the non-Southern states, Obama had a 14% advantage over John McCain, the third-highest margin in history following the landslides for Johnson in 1964 and Roosevelt in 1936.[11] The Democrats picked up substantial majorities in the House and briefly held sixty seats in the Senate. It took roughly five decades, but labor's goal of reorienting the Democratic Party away from Southern conservatism to its more liberal, urban wing was largely achieved, and the realigned Party finally won control of the government. The question was whether this long-term political strategy would finally pay off.

As has been true under every Democratic president in the postwar period, the fragmented American political system and its protections for the minority posed formidable challenges to organized labor in reaching its policy goals during the Obama administration. The early years of the Great Society, the most productive legislative period since the New Deal, demonstrated what labor could and could not accomplish when the conservative coalition was destabilized but still influential. The first years of the Obama administration offer a similar test of the boundaries on labor's power in a political system that has changed considerably since the 1960s. Liberals may be more influential in the party, but the larger Democratic majorities were made possible only by the election of a number of Democrats from moderate districts and conservative states. These Democrats would be especially problematic in the Senate, where 60 votes has become the de facto requirement for controversial legislation. A

2009 AFL-CIO convention resolution on political action warned, "On issue after issue, whether it's the Employee Free Choice Act or health care reform, tough choices must often be made to build a winning coalition."[12] Labor would still have to make painful compromises.

The opening days of the Obama administration reflected consistencies with past patterns in the legislative areas this study has highlighted. The federal government became intricately involved in management of certain areas of the economy in its efforts to restore the soundness of the financial system and the American auto industry. However, the sort of full-employment economic planning considered, but not adopted, during the 1940s and 1970s was still largely off the table. Instead, like previous administrations, the Obama administration pushed targeted government spending and tax incentives in the stimulus package to temporarily protect and generate jobs.

The stimulus bill also followed past patterns in extending emergency unemployment benefits. Though it included temporary federal incentives to the states to expand unemployment insurance coverage for additional workers like part-time employees, the plan made no effort to nationalize a patchwork system that excludes many categories of workers and varies considerably in terms of benefits and eligibility from state to state. Once again, Southerners led the charge against efforts to expand the program.[13] Although many more heavily industrialized states already covered the new categories of workers addressed in the stimulus bill, most Southern states did not. Several Southern governors—from Alabama, Louisiana, Mississippi, South Carolina, and Texas—made national headlines in refusing stimulus money for expanding unemployment compensation, arguing it would lead to higher taxes on employers in the future. South Carolina's governor, Mark Sanford, went further by threatening to reject almost a third of the stimulus funds available to his state. Texas's governor, Rick Perry, even suggested Texans might become so fed up with the growing federal government that they would want the state to secede. Southern conservatives remained the most vocal critics of the labor-liberal agenda. After the passage of the stimulus bill, the focus shifted to health care reform, which consumed Washington for the next thirteen months.

The passage of the health care bill is perhaps the best illustration of the limits and possibilities for labor's achievements in the legislative process. As with full employment and unemployment insurance, the labor movement had considerably scaled back its proposals from the 1940s. Although the AFL-CIO continued to support the goal of a single-payer system, it committed to working for a comprehensive, universal plan based on existing, employer-provided, private insurance.[14] However, it did support the creation of a "public option" that would provide a government-run insurance program to compete with private insurers. The AFL-CIO, many of the affiliates, the SEIU, and Health Care for America Now, a coalition of labor and community groups, led the effort to mobilize support for reform, spending millions on advertising, organizing local events, coordinating letter-writing and call-in campaigns to Congress, and commissioning polls to convince wavering lawmakers that health care reform was popular.[15] When conservative activists overwhelmed the town hall meetings representatives held in their districts over the August 2009 recess, unions dispatched their members to show support for reform. The SEIU alone dedicated four hundred full-time staffers to health care mobilization, which they modeled on their efforts in presidential elections.[16]

In the final months of 2009, Congress took its first votes ever on a program significantly expanding health coverage to the working-age population. In November, the House narrowly passed (220–215) a bill strongly supported by most of the labor movement with only one Republican vote. It included a public option, tax subsidies for low- and middle-income families to buy coverage, and a tax on upper-income earners to raise necessary revenue. But despite intense labor and liberal pressure on the Senate leadership to produce a comparable bill, Majority Leader Harry Reid (NV) could not secure the 60 votes for a plan containing the public option. The bill the Senate passed in December also provided less generous tax subsidies for the purchase of insurance and included a tax on high-cost employer-provided "Cadillac plans" that was staunchly opposed by many unions. The bill passed on a purely party-line vote with the support of all sixty Democrats, including disappointed liberals who hoped the final bill would be pulled toward the House measure. Various measures were added to entice moderate Democrats, such as special Medicaid provisions for Nebraska and Louisiana that became known as the "Cornhusker kick-back" and the "Louisiana purchase." Uninterested in compromise and shut out of the negotiations by this point, Republican leaders were relentless in their criticism of both the bill and the process. The bickering, wheeling, and dealing corresponded with an erosion of support for the plan in public opinion polls and a steeper increase in opposition.[17]

With the outcome on health care reform still far from certain, labor set its sights on the House-Senate negotiations. Congressional leaders and the administration decided not to utilize a formal conference committee, which would have posed additional procedural hurdles, choosing instead to work behind closed doors to reconcile the significant differences between the House and Senate bills. Labor drew a line in the sand over the tax on high-cost plans, while abortion emerged as a major sticking point for socially conservative House Democrats. At this point, President Obama got personally involved and brought congressional and labor leaders to the White House in January to work out a compromise on the benefits tax that exempted plans negotiated through collective bargaining until 2018 and raised the cost threshold, reducing the number of plans subject to the tax. Republicans assailed the deal as another reward for special interests. Despite the tense environment, negotiations were moving forward to craft a bill that could hold a House majority and still sustain the support of all sixty Democrats in the Senate. Right at the brink of victory, the whole reform effort was suddenly thrown into jeopardy when Republican Scott Brown was elected to fill the recently deceased Ted Kennedy's seat in late January. The race was not on liberals' radar screen until the final days, and while labor made a last-minute effort to elect the Democratic candidate, it was too late.[18] The administration, congressional Democrats, and labor leaders were taken aback. The administration contemplated a scaled-back bill.[19]

In early February, the new AFL-CIO president, Richard Trumka, called on Democrats to use the special budget reconciliation procedure, which would preclude a filibuster, to get a final version of the bill passed.[20] As the dust settled on the new fifty-nine-seat majority in the Senate, the reconciliation route gained support. Negotiations finally produced a compromise between the House and Senate that phased in the benefits tax for everyone, not just union members, and eliminated many of the other special provisions that had been included to secure 60 votes, as well as the public option. It also moved in the direction of the House bill, providing more generous tax subsidies for the purchase of insurance and stiffer penalties on employers who did not offer insurance. But only certain measures could be handled through reconciliation, which presented a procedural challenge. In order to get a comprehensive bill, House Democrats first had to vote for the extremely unpopular Senate bill, sending it to Obama to sign into law, and take the leap of faith that the feckless Senate would pass a package of "fixes" through the reconciliation procedure that would amend the original Senate bill. Nervous House Democrats hesitated, and Speaker Nancy Pelosi (CA) was not sure she could deliver the votes.[21] This was the final stage in a sixty-year quest for universal health care, and despite misgivings, most of the labor movement came on board, urging Democrats to support the compromise and the strategy.[22] With labor leaders working for votes down to the last minute, the House passed the bill. Action moved back to the Senate, which needed to pass the compromise reconciliation package. Although Republicans tried to throw the effort off track with a series of amendments, the bill ultimately passed 56–43. Three Democrats, Senators Mark Pryor and Blanche Lincoln of Arkansas and Ben Nelson of Nebraska, voted against it. Without the reconciliation procedure that allowed the bill to pass with a simple majority, the biggest expansion of social policy since Medicare would not have been possible.

As with health care, it appeared that some version of labor law reform finally had a chance of passing before the Democrats lost their Senate supermajority. The Employee Free Choice Act, which passed the House but was filibustered in the 110th Congress (2006–7), still appeared to have substantial support in the House with 231 cosponsors. But support fell off in the Senate, dropping from forty-six cosponsors in 2007 to forty in 2009 when the legislation actually had a chance of being signed into law. Business groups ran ads targeted at vulnerable senators and House members, typically in areas with low levels of unionization, arguing that the bill would deny workers their rights to choose union representation in elections and undermine recovery from the recession. In contrast to 2007, Bill Nelson (D-FL) was the only senator from the South who signed on. The lone Republican supporter, Senator Specter, also backed away from his position under the threat of a conservative primary challenger, but after he became a Democrat, he became more eager to embrace labor. While several moderate Democrats went to great pains to avoid taking a public stand on the issue, Blanche Lincoln, up for a tough reelection fight in 2010, stated she could not support the bill in its current form. If a bill was going to pass, labor, as always, would have to make concessions.

Senator Tom Harkin (D-IA) took the lead in trying to negotiate a compromise with labor that might attract 60 votes. Harkin suggested he was close to an agreement in July, but Kennedy, the sponsor of the legislation, was too sick to travel to take the vote, so moderate senators were not brought into the negotiations.[23] Labor would likely have to give up the two most controversial provisions, the "card check" procedure and mandatory arbitration when employers and unions were unable to reach a first contract in a reasonable period of time.[24] A compromise was widely expected to focus on accelerated elections, so employers would have less of a chance to wear down employees' support for unionization, and stiffer penalties for labor law violators. No Republican ever indicated a willingness to support a compromise measure, so with the loss of

Kennedy's seat, the issue was put on hold. We will never know if the Senate could have reached a viable compromise if the Democrats had held on to their supermajority through the 2010 elections. The best approximation of labor's support in the 111th Senate on a pure labor issue was a cloture vote to end a filibuster against the nomination to the NLRB of Craig Becker, an attorney for the SEIU and the AFL-CIO, whom Republicans consider to be too close to labor. The vote of 52–33 was taken in February 2010 in the midst of a blizzard that virtually shut down Washington, with a handful of likely pro-labor votes absent because of the storm. Two of the Democrats who voted against the final health care bill, Lincoln and Nelson, also voted against cloture. But a handful of Democrats from states with low unionization rates cast a tough vote in support of labor. Once again, labor had majority but not supermajority support.

On issues like labor law reform, party discipline can only go so far in delivering the support of members of Congress from states with low rates of unionization. Frustrated unions tried to send a message to Senator Lincoln by encouraging a challenger, Bill Halter, to take her on in the 2010 Democratic primary and spending millions on his campaign. He narrowly lost, and while many observers viewed the loss as a major defeat for labor, it did serve notice that labor was willing to challenge Democrats who stray from their positions.[25] But the reason Lincoln voted against labor was because of her vulnerability in the general election in a conservative state. Union money cannot compensate for the weakness of the liberal coalition in a state like Arkansas, where only 4.2% of the workforce is unionized.[26] In challenging moderate Democrats in primaries in conservative states, unions risk the election of Republicans in the general election—a long-standing conundrum for labor.

Labor activist and writer Kim Moody cites "the gutting of the Employee Free Choice Act" and "the utter destruction of meaningful health care reform" as examples of labor's "waning power."[27] But both issues reflect the challenges labor has faced in the political system throughout the postwar period, particularly since the rise of the filibuster beginning in the 1960s. That labor had as much impact as it did on the bills is a testament to its enduring political influence. A number of Democrats from conservative states with small union memberships forced moderation of the health care bill and pulled their support for card check. Labor's regional concentration was a major factor, but the impact of labor's weakness in the South and agrarian Plains states is exaggerated by the filibuster and equal state representation in the Senate, which give these states disproportionate weight in the political system. The effect of these legislative institutions is most evident in the contrast of labor's experience in the Senate with its experience in the House. While there are also a number of moderate Democrats in the House who often vote against labor's position, because the body is governed by majority rule, Democratic majorities have often passed legislation favored by labor, especially after congressional reform and the rise of party unity in recent decades. Labor's power has hardly waned in the House, and compared with much of the postwar period, it has grown.

As has happened with every other Democratic president, liberals blamed Obama for failing to lead when their priorities inevitably met resistance in the legislative process. Obama faced criticism from liberals and some quarters of the labor movement for not standing firm. But others pointed to political reality. As the seasoned chief lobbyist of the AFL-CIO, Bill Samuel, argued, "it's total partisan warfare" and "if you don't have 60 senators who feel exactly as you do, it's pretty hard to insist on getting your way," so whether Obama "draws a line or not, he doesn't have the votes for the things that he might want that we agree with."[28] Given everything it took to get the health care bill passed, it is hard to imagine that Obama or labor could have gotten much more, and they could have gotten a lot less.

Unable to deliver on labor law reform in Congress, Obama took a number of executive actions. Upon taking office he issued several executive orders reversing Bush administration labor policies. Although liberals criticized Obama for some of his choices for his economic team, labor advocates were placed in important positions in the Labor Department and began to ramp up enforcement of health and safety laws and labor standards, which was backed up with larger budget requests and a commitment to using the procurement process to punish violators of labor and other federal laws.[29] In the most significant overture to labor, Obama made a recess appointment of Becker and another labor lawyer to the NLRB, which was crippled for more than two years with three of its five seats empty because of partisan stalemate in the Senate. This could have a substantial pro-labor impact on the enforcement of the NLRA in the absence of labor law reform.[30]

Prospects for the Future

This book has not given much attention to unions' electoral mobilization, in part because it has been covered thoroughly elsewhere, but it is an important source of support for the Democrats that ensures labor's influence within the party.[31] Labor provides votes, money, and ground troops.[32] But labor has never been able to dictate electoral outcomes, even at the peak of union membership. As Al Barkan, the director of the AFL-CIO's Committee on Political Education, noted in the mid-sixties, "We are always conscious of the fact that we are a minority, but we are a minority which can provide the winning margin when there is not a real tide in the other direction."[33] This has hardly changed.

National electoral outcomes determine labor's influence over public policy, but they are often dictated by the larger political environment including the state of the economy, international affairs, and the attractiveness of individual candidates. Thus labor helped maximize the vote for Lyndon Johnson and Democratic congressional candidates in 1964, but Kennedy's assassination, the strong economy, and the Republicans' nomination of conservative Barry Goldwater gave him the advantage. Four years later, Vietnam and social unrest created an inhospitable political environment for Democrats that could not be overcome by labor's efforts. In 2008, Obama and Democratic congressional candidates benefited from labor mobilization in swing states, but the state of the economy, growing opposition to the Iraq War, and the unpopularity of President Bush influenced the outcome in many races. Largely because of voters' continuing dissatisfaction with the economy, especially the high unemployment rate, and frustration with Washington, the 2010 elections returned control of the House to the Republicans as this book was completed. Despite considerable spending and mobilization on the part of unions, voters from union households declined from 22% to 17% of the electorate.[34] Although union activity likely helped preserve a number of Democratic Senate seats, unions simply could not counteract the disaffection among their members and other potential Democratic voters or match the intensity of conservatives in many races. This will make it that much harder for labor to get favorable public policies passed through Congress.

But over the longer term there are some promising trends that may benefit Democrats, and as long as labor sustains its influence in the national Democratic Party, anything that contributes to Democratic electoral victories will help organized labor. In the absence of organizing breakthroughs, labor's political future will be determined by the size and strength of the broader labor-liberal coalition. Just as African Americans were viewed by labor in the 1940s and 1950s as an electoral ally that could broaden the Democrats' base, Latinos are a growing segment of the electorate who are trending Democratic. The coalition of labor, African Americans, and Latinos that has helped make California a Democratic stronghold might one day be possible in Southwestern states like Nevada where growing service-sector unions and Latinos are an important part of the Democratic base.[35] As a 2009 AFL-CIO convention resolution laying out future political strategy noted, the labor movement has been "in the vanguard of constructing an electoral coalition of union members, African Americans and Hispanics" for the past fifty years, and demographic trends are "increasing the strength of this coalition."[36] As a result, a number of right-to-work states have moved into play, and the federation resolved that the labor movement should focus its organizing efforts and political mobilization on the states where this coalition was most likely to grow. In fact, making inroads into these areas is necessary to sustain the current power balance because union strongholds in the Northeast and industrial Midwest will lose representation after the 2010 census. Immigration reform giving citizenship status to at least some illegal immigrants currently in the country, which most of the labor movement now supports, would assist this effort, but prospects for such reform are dim in the Senate.

Labor may benefit from these trends, but the preceding chapters suggest the limits on what labor can realistically expect to accomplish through the policy process. Supermajorities are rare in American politics, and the major policy issues on labor's agenda require them. Liberals and labor leaders would like to reform the filibuster to allow for majority rule, which could have a substantial impact on the policy process. The majority's rising frustration with Senate obstruction and the inability to get virtually anything done in a highly partisan environment have led to new calls for reform in Congress.[37] These calls may grow louder as more and more groups see their policy priorities, from addressing climate change to immigration reform, stymied by the filibuster. Rising pressure may one day lead to reform. But procedural hurdles, the close partisan balance of recent decades, and senators' desire to maintain their own individual power complicate the prospects for changing the cloture threshold. However, the majority may increasingly resort to procedures like reconciliation to circumvent the 60 vote requirement when possible.

Given the difficulty of achieving labor's policy goals, reversing the decline in union membership is central to unions' ability to create a more equitable society. Collective bargaining remains an important tool for improving workers' standard of living. Because American workers' security is so dependent on employer-provided benefits, the decline of unions that has occurred across most advanced, industrialized countries has had greater consequences in the

United States.[38] The statistics on union growth are not encouraging. After years of consistent decline, union membership went up slightly in 2007 and 2008. But the recession reversed that trend, and union membership again fell to 12.3% of the workforce and just 7.2% in the private sector.[39] In 2009 the number of government employees outnumbered private-sector workers in unions for the first time.

There are formidable obstacles to unionization. Global and regional economic competition and the rise of large, multinational corporations have posed new challenges to labor unions. Employers wage sophisticated antiunion drives and often resort to illegal tactics, which is why the labor movement has placed so much emphasis on labor law reform. An estimated 25–30% of employers targeted by organizing drives have fired workers for prounion activity.[40] Yet given that EFCA is unlikely to pass in the foreseeable future, the fate of the labor movement depends on the ability and commitment of unions to work through —or around—NLRB procedures. There are successful models for organizing. The SEIU, one of the most aggressive organizers, has built its membership in a number of cities including Houston with its Justice for Janitors campaign, which has focused on building supportive local coalitions of religious, community, and political leaders.[41] Various unions have also waged elaborate "corporate campaigns" in which employers are often pressured by negative publicity, investigations, litigation, and corporate shareholder activism to remain neutral in organizing drives or to allow union recognition through card check. The most effective drives require substantial human and financial resources, and there is a shortage of expertise in the labor movement.[42] Yet Kate Bronfenbrenner and Robert Hickey argue there is significant room for improvement, even within the hostile economic and legal climate unions confront.[43]

Labor's future remains uncertain. Every national effort to invigorate union organizing, from the election of insurgent candidate John Sweeney to the presidency of the AFL-CIO in 1995 to the creation of the rival Change to Win Federation a decade later, has failed to produce sustained growth. If private-sector unionization rates continue to fall over the long term, organized labor may lose its leverage in a number of states where it is still quite influential today. If so, an important voice for American workers will be lost. But so far labor has managed to sustain influence in the Democratic Party and a broader labor-liberal coalition. For the foreseeable future, organized labor is likely to remain an important advocate for expanding the limited American welfare state, within the substantial constraints of the American legislative process.

NOTES

Abbreviations

CF	Confidential File
GMMA	George Meany Memorial Archives, Silver Spring, Maryland
HSTL	Harry S. Truman Library, Independence, Missouri
JCL	Jimmy Carter Library, Atlanta, Georgia
LA	Labor Subject Files
LBJL	Lyndon Baines Johnson Library, Austin, Texas
LE	Legislation Subject Files
OF	Official File
PHF	Presidential Handwriting Files
PSF	President's Secretary's Files
UAW	United Auto Workers
WHCF	White House Central Files
WSU	Archives of Labor and Urban Affairs, Wayne State University, Detroit, Michigan

Introduction

Epigraphs: Reuther quoted in June 28 UAW press release endorsing filibuster reform, UAW President's Office, Walter P. Reuther Collection, box 577, folder 9, WSU. "Labor Looks at Congress, 1963," Support Services Department, AFL-CIO Publications, Series 1, GMMA. Andrew Stern, interview by Jonathan Cohn, Dec. 18, 2009, *New Republic*, www .tnr.com/node/72017.

1. Although most of the literature refers to Southern and Northern Democrats, I use the term "non-Southern Democrats" to refer to Democrats from all other regions.

2. For range of American exceptionalist explanations, see Lipset and Marks, *It Didn't Happen Here.*

3. Hartz, *Liberal Tradition;* Lipset, *American Exceptionalism.*

4. Katznelson, *City Trenches.*

5. Brecher, *Strike!*

6. Steinmo, "Rethinking American Exceptionalism."

7. Lipset and Marks, *It Didn't Happen Here*, chap. 2.

8. Oestreicher, "Rules of the Game."

9. The Knights of Labor briefly posed a reformist challenge in the 1870s and early

1880s but never approached the size or reach of the AFL and CIO in the late 1930s and 1940s.

10. As Walter Reuther told a British journalist about labor's strategy in the New Deal and postwar periods, "We felt that instead of trying to create a third party—a labor party . . . that we ought to bring about a realignment and get the liberal forces in one party and the conservatives in another." Quoted in Brandon, "Conversation with Reuther."

11. Some scholars suggest that in some ways the United States was ahead of other "liberal" welfare states such as Great Britain and Canada going into World War II. Quadagno and Street, "Ideology and Public Policy," 62.

12. This criticism is shared by scholars associated with the New Left of the late sixties and seventies such as Ronald Radosh, Stanley Aronowitz, Christopher Tomlins, George Lipsitz, and Nelson Lichtenstein. In a new introduction to his book *Labor's War at Home*, rereleased in 2003, Lichtenstein has modified his position somewhat. Some social activists in and outside the labor movement also view labor's alliance with the Democrats as a strategic failure that has limited labor's political power throughout the postwar period; see, for example, Mike Davis, *Prisoners of the American Dream*, and Kim Moody, *An Injury to All*.

13. Davis, *Prisoners of the American Dream*.

14. Greenstone, *Labor in American Politics*, xiv.

15. Goldfield, *Decline of Organized Labor*, chap. 2.

16. Vogel, *Fluctuating Fortunes*.

17. Gottschalk, *Shadow Welfare State*.

18. Madison, Federalist 10.

19. As Madison noted of the national government in Federalist 10, "Extend the sphere and you take in a greater variety of parties and interests: you make it less probable that a majority of the whole will have a common motive to invade the rights of other citizens; or if such a common motive exists, it will be more difficult for all who feel it to discover their own strength and to act in unison with each other."

20. Lee and Oppenheimer are among the few scholars to investigate the impact of unequal representation in the Senate on policy outcomes. Lee and Oppenheimer, *Sizing up the Senate*.

21. Dahl, *How Democratic?* 49.

22. Weaver and Rockman, *Do Institutions Matter?*; Pierson, *New Politics;* Huber, Ragin, and Stephens, "Social Democracy."

23. In the measure of fragmentation used by Huber, Ragin, and Stephens in "Social Democracy," the United States ranks as the most decentralized.

24. Immergut, "Institutions, Veto Points, and Policy Results" and *Health Politics*.

25. Steinmo and Watts, "It's the Institutions, Stupid!"

26. Steinmo, "Rethinking American Exceptionalism."

27. Krehbiel, *Pivotal Politics;* Brady and Volden, *Revolving Gridlock*.

28. Brady and Volden, *Revolving Gridlock*, 35.

29. McCarty, Poole, and Rosenthal, *Polarized America*, chap. 6.

30. The issue of free trade, particularly in the 1990s, is an exception. While organized labor and most Democrats supported free trade as long as the United States was the dominant manufacturer in the world, labor's support started to slide in the 1970s. Although many congressional Democrats shared labor's growing opposition to free trade agreements, both Democratic and Republican presidents have strongly supported it.

31. Orren and Skowronek, *Search for American Political Development*, 78.

32. Forbath, *Law and the Shaping of the American Labor Movement;* Hattam, *Labor Visions.*

33. Lowi, "Why Is There No Socialism?"

34. See call for more attention to Congress in the field of APD in Katznelson and Lapinski, "Congress and American Political Development." Several scholars in the APD tradition have focused on Congress, including Richard Bensel, Eric Schickler, Gregory Wawro, and Julian Zelizer. Scholars like Jacob Hacker and Christopher Howard have also demonstrated how congressional institutions encourage the development of certain types of policies over others. A number of congressional scholars have also taken a historical approach, such as Sarah Binder, Joseph Cooper, Nelson Polsby, and Steven Smith, just to name a few.

35. Farhang and Katznelson, "Southern Imposition."

36. See, for example, McCarty, Poole, and Rosenthal, *Polarized America;* Poole and Rosenthal, *Ideology and Congress;* and Theriault, *Party Polarization in Congress.*

37. Pierson, "Increasing Returns."

38. See, for example, Pierson, *Politics in Time;* Steinmo, "What Is Historical Institutionalism"; and Thelen, *How Institutions Evolve.*

39. Steinmo, Thelen, and Longstreth, *Structuring Politics*, 15.

40. In the following chapters, there is also a fair amount of material from the United Auto Workers archives when Walter Reuther was the president of the CIO.

CHAPTER ONE: The Rise of Organized Labor and the Conservative Coalition

1. AFL leaders felt they were not adequately consulted and represented on New Deal boards. Louis Stark, "Grave Labor Issues Facing White House," *New York Times*, Mar. 3, 1935.

2. Plotke, *Building a Democratic Political Order*, 101–2.

3. "President Orders Speed on NRA and Wagner Bills," *New York Times*, May 25, 1935.

4. Skocpol, Finegold, and Goldfield, "Explaining New Deal Labor Policy," 1300–1301.

5. Louis Stark, "Union Labor Reforming Its Line of Battle," *New York Times*, June 2, 1935, and "Labor Demands New NRA, Scoring Any Surrender," *New York Times*, June 7, 1935.

6. Zieger, *American Workers*, 55.

7. Horowitz, *Political Ideologies*, 234–36.

8. Statistics from Bureau of Labor Statistics as reported in Goldfield, "Worker Insurgency," 1267.

9. Quoted in Lichtenstein, "From Corporatism to Collective Bargaining," 135.

10. Cohen, *Making a New Deal*, 333–49.

11. Brody, *Workers in Industrial America*, 217.

12. Brinkley, *End of Reform*, 219–24.

13. Ibid., 219.

14. Quoted in Josephson, *Sidney Hillman*, 395.

15. Brinkley, *End of Reform*, 223.

16. Horowitz, *Political Ideologies*, chap. 8.

17. Cohen, *Making a New Deal*, 359.

18. Zieger, *American Workers*, 68.

19. Ibid., 67.

20. On labor in the war, see Lichtenstein, *Labor's War at Home*.

21. Zieger, *American Workers*, 84.

22. Dubofsky, *State and Labor*, 192.

23. Mills, *New Men*.

24. Turner finds a Northern-Southern split among Democrats on labor issues going back to the 1920s. Turner, *Party and Constituency*, 176.

25. Although as Plotke notes, "This sweeping approval is misleading, as many who would have preferred a different bill or no bill at all did not oppose it when passage seemed certain." Plotke, *Building a Democratic Political Order*, 101.

26. Paired and announced votes for and against the legislation as well as those not voting are included in the totals used to calculate the percentages.

27. Farhang and Katznelson, "Southern Imposition," 9.

28. Katznelson, Geiger, and Kryder, "Limiting Liberalism," 297.

29. Plotke, *Building a Democratic Political Order*, 104–6.

30. For the role of worker insurgency in the passage of the NLRA, see Goldfield, "Worker Insurgency," 1257–82, and Skocpol, Finegold, and Goldfield, "Explaining New Deal Labor Policy." While not challenging the importance of worker unrest, David Plotke argues that the leading actor in passing the legislation was a coalescing "progressive liberal political leadership." Plotke, *Building a Democratic Political Order*, 101–17.

31. Goldfield, "Worker Insurgency," 1270–77.

32. Communists controlled unions with 20–25% of the membership of the CIO, and Communist or Communist sympathizers occupied numerous staff positions. Bell, "Problem of Ideological Rigidity," 106.

33. Eric Schickler's analysis of Gallup and Roper polling data from the 1930s and 1940s, which he and Adam Berinsky have cleaned up and weighted to compensate for skewed samples, suggests deteriorating public attitudes toward organized labor over the course of 1937. The public became particularly critical of the sit-down strike, with 64% of the weighted sample favoring the use of force against the strikers by December 1937. Schickler, "Public Opinion," 11–15.

34. An American Institute of Public Opinion poll reported in the *Washington Post* that 52% of those with an opinion favored revision of the NLRA while another 18% favored outright repeal. George Gallup, "Fight on Measure Due in Next Congress," *Washington Post*, Nov. 13, 1938.

35. Farhang and Katznelson note that the "CIO's punitive electoral efforts" were repeatedly brought up by Southerners in debate on the Case bill. Farhang and Katznelson, "Southern Imposition," 24. Also see Patterson, "Failure of Party Realignment," 603.

36. Patterson, *Congressional Conservatism*, 135.

37. Quoted in *Time*, Aug. 23, 1937, cited in Patterson, *Congressional Conservatism*, 182.

38. Farhang and Katznelson, "Southern Imposition," 40.

39. Poole and Rosenthal, *Ideology and Congress*, 138.

40. Zelizer, *On Capitol Hill*, 26.

41. Turner, *Party and Constituency*, 173.

42. Patterson, *Congressional Conservatism*, 88.

43. Turner, *Party and Constituency*, 186.

44. Schickler, *Disjointed Pluralism*, 163–68.

45. Ibid., 165. Schickler notes that based on Poole and Rosenthal's nominate scores,

Cox and Dies were to the left of the average Democrat when they were appointed while Smith was just "a bit" to the right.

46. Ibid.

47. Congressional scholars who favor a "party cartel" approach to congressional parties argue that the Rules Committee served the majority party's interest by controlling what went to the floor. The blocking of controversial bills like civil rights legislation was a way to minimize damaging intraparty splits. Cox and McCubbins, *Legislative Leviathan*.

48. The old Gompersian position of the AFL had been that a minimum wage would become a maximum wage and would effectively cap what unions could obtain in collective bargaining. Labor leaders had largely abandoned this position, but both leaders of the AFL and John Lewis were apprehensive about the power of a board that was to be set up to implement the FLSA. Having been burned by government boards before and fearful the board's rulings might end up in the courts on appeal, AFL president Green insisted on changes to the structure and role of the board. See Horowitz, *Political Ideologies*, chap. 7. Others speculate that the AFL was afraid the board would favor the CIO. Fraser, *Labor Will Rule*, 405.

49. Fraser, *Labor Will Rule*, chap. 14.

50. Douglas and Hackman, "Fair Labor Standards Act."

51. Ibid., 514.

52. Fraser, *Labor Will Rule*, 411.

53. Maury Maverick, "Maverick Urges South to Join in Social Progress," *Washington Post*, May 9, 1938.

54. Poole and Rosenthal, *Ideology and Congress*, 138.

55. Fleck, "Opposition to the Fair Labor Standards Act," 49.

56. Schickler and Pearson, "Agenda Control."

57. See table in ibid., 468.

58. Ibid., 483.

59. Patterson, *Congressional Conservatism*, 318.

60. Dubofsky, *State and Labor*, 161, 173.

61. Roll calls are taken from Voteview. Percentages include all votes and members who were paired, who announced for or against the legislation, and those not voting.

62. Lichtenstein, *Labor's War at Home*, 185.

63. Dubofsky, *State and Labor*, 193.

64. McClure, *Truman Administration*, 68–69.

65. A statement by the United Steelworkers' International Wage Policy Committee issued on Jan. 23, 1946—after the union had agreed to the terms recommended by the Truman administration but U.S. Steel had refused—declared, "American industry has therefore deliberately set out to destroy labor unions, to provoke strikes and economic chaos, and mulct the American people through uncontrolled profits and inflation." Found in PSF, box 118, "Strikes: Steel" folder, Truman Papers, HSTL.

66. Bernstein, "Truman Administration," 796.

67. CIO president Philip Murray, "Issues Facing the Special Session of Congress," speech delivered on American Broadcasting Company Network, July 29, 1948, in WHCF-OF, box 779, 170 (1947–53) folder, Truman Papers, HSTL.

68. Lee notes that, despite the efforts of Secretary of Labor Lewis Schwellenbach to make the public aware of enormous corporate profits, the press repeatedly cited labor

costs as the source of inflation, which encouraged public opinion to blame organized labor. Lee, *Truman and Taft-Hartley,* 17–18.

69. Gallup poll, Apr.–May 1944, reported in Schickler, "Public Opinion," table 3.

70. Schickler and Pearson, "Agenda Control," 476.

71. A June 11, 1946, summation of the public mail coming into the White House on the Case bill noted approximately 40,000 telegrams (so numerous that they had not been broken down into those advocating or opposing the bill), 19,910 postcards, and 13,000 letters. Of the 6,064 letters addressing the issue of a veto, a majority of 3,440 urged the president not to sign the bill. PSF, box 98, "Case bill" folder, Truman Papers, HSTL.

72. Noted in President Truman to Senator Ball, Jan. 8, 1947, PSF, box 98, "Ca-Cl" folder, Truman Papers, HSTL.

73. A June 10, 1946, letter to President Truman from Representative Andrew Biemiller urged the president to veto the law and included a petition signed by ninety-six members of the House as well as a list of another thirty-one members who were unwilling to sign the petition but were committed to voting to uphold a possible veto. PSF, box 98, "Case bill" folder, Truman Papers, HSTL.

74. McClure, *Truman Administration,* 133.

75. One poll found that 64% of respondents thought the labor laws should be changed; 21% thought the laws gave too much advantage to employers versus 42% to labor. But the same poll found 34% agreeing that Truman was right to disapprove the Case bill versus 23% who thought he should have approved it. Gallup Poll (AIPO), June 1946, retrieved June 6, 2010, from the iPOLL Databank, The Roper Center for Public Opinion Research, University of Connecticut. On the value of the relationship between labor and Democrats, see, for example, Piven and Cloward, *Poor People's Movements;* Lichtenstein, *Labor's War at Home;* and Davis, *Prisoners of the American Dream.*

76. Philip Murray to President Truman, undated report, WHCF-OF, box 1122, file #407b, Truman Papers, HSTL.

77. Summaries of editorial content throughout the period prepared by the Division of Press Intelligence in the Truman administration consistently showed strong support for revision of the NLRA and extensive criticism of the labor movement, particularly the actions of John L. Lewis. As one summary prepared by the Government Information Service noted: "Labor is attacked for killing the goose that has been laying golden eggs. Government is condemned for being over liberal in attitude toward labor. The courts in turn come in for their share of criticism for not being just and fair to the employer and the public. Business, as the employer, escapes with comparatively little complaint." Jan. 2, 1947, summary of editorial content on topic of labor legislation prepared by the Division of Press Intelligence, PSF, box 109, "Legislation: Cabinet" folder, Truman Papers, HSTL.

78. Richter, *Labor's Struggles,* 67; Lee, *Truman and Taft-Hartley,* 47.

79. Truman, *Memoirs,* 505.

80. Goldfield, "Worker Insurgency"; Piven and Cloward, *Poor People's Movements.*

81. Lichtenstein, *Labor's War at Home.*

82. Lee, *Truman and Taft-Hartley,* 47.

83. Fiorina, *Retrospective Voting.*

84. Lee, *Truman and Taft-Hartley,* 72.

85. Gross, *Reshaping of the National Labor Relations Board.*

86. Richter, *Labor's Struggles,* chap. 4.

87. Lee, *Truman and Taft-Hartley,* 81.

88. Ibid.

89. Ibid., 87.

90. Collection of memoranda from labor relations experts submitted to President Truman in the summer of 1947, WHCF-CF, box 33, "Taft-Hartley" folder, Truman Papers, HSTL.

91. Lee, *Truman and Taft-Hartley,* 95.

92. These and subsequent roll call votes from *Congressional Quarterly.*

93. Farhang and Katznelson, "Southern Imposition," 2.

94. Ibid., 3.

95. There is some debate about the impact of right-to-work laws. For example, Lumsden and Petersen find that the effect is mostly symbolic, with little substantive impact on unionization rates, while Ellwood and Fine find that membership is reduced, primarily because of decreased organizing activity following the passage of such laws. Lumsden and Petersen, "Effect of Right-to-Work Laws"; Ellwood and Fine, "Impact of Right-to-Work Laws."

96. Box 57, folder 2, UAW Washington Office, Legislative Department, Donald Montgomery Files, WSU.

97. Farhang and Katznelson and Troy point to the potential impact of Taft-Hartley, particularly of right-to-work laws, on Southern organizing. Farhang and Katznelson, "Southern Imposition"; Troy, "Growth of Union Membership."

98. Troy, "Growth of Union Membership," 410.

99. Griffith, *Crisis of American Labor,* 162.

100. Farhang and Katznelson, "Southern Imposition."

101. Troy, "Growth of Union Membership," 407, 413.

102. For discussion, see Griffith, *Crisis of American Labor;* Troy, "Growth of Union Membership"; De Vyver, "Present Status"; and Friedman, "Political Economy."

103. Troy notes that Southern workers showed less support for union representation in NLRB-supervised certification elections than workers in the rest of the country. Troy, "Growth of Union Membership," 419–20.

104. Clark Clifford to Harry S. Truman, memo, Nov. 19, 1947, Clifford Papers, available at www.trumanlibrary.org.

105. Ibid.

106. Ibid. Clifford noted, "President Truman and the Democratic Party cannot win without the *active* support of organized labor. It is dangerous to assume that labor now has nowhere else to go in 1948. *Labor can stay home*" (emphasis in the original). An undated draft of a UAW resolution opposing the nomination of Truman indicated that labor's enthusiasm was certainly at stake. Resolution found in box 430, folder 19, UAW President's Office, Walter P. Reuther Collection, WSU.

107. In 1945, a frustrated Walter Reuther had asserted, "The time is now ripe for labor to divorce itself from the two old parties and resolve to build the base for an independent, indigenous national party." Quoted in Brody, *Workers in Industrial America,* 222. In contrast, a resolution adopted by the UAW in March 1948 rejected Henry Wallace's third-party candidacy because it would undermine "the vital political task" of repealing "the vicious Taft-Hartley Act." Resolution found in box 2, folder 13, UAW Political Action Department, Roy Reuther Files, WSU.

108. In fact, labor's experience with the 80th Congress in general pushed labor closer to Truman. Following a meeting with James Carey, secretary-treasurer of the CIO, Clark Clifford noted in a memo to Truman, "The President's Speech at the Convention made a great impression on labor as did the decision to call a Special Session of the Congress. The failure of the Congress to enact any legislation remotely beneficial to labor has helped crystallize the support of labor for the President." Carey advised that Truman bring CIO president Murray in for a meeting and expected that a CIO endorsement would soon follow. PSF, box 100, "Clark Clifford" folder, Truman Papers, HSTL. On Taft-Hartley's impact on labor's views toward Truman, also see Brody, *Workers in Industrial America*, 226.

109. Taft, "Political Activity," 170–72.

110. Many labor leaders were also opposed to Wallace because of their growing commitment to a staunchly anti-Communist foreign policy.

111. Savage, *Truman and Democratic Party*, 138.

112. Chen, *Fifth Freedom*.

113. Savage, *Truman and Democratic Party*, 139.

114. Ibid., 138.

115. In fact, prior to the New Deal, the 1928 election signaled a growing tension in the Democratic Party between the Southern and urban, liberal wings when the Democrats nominated Al Smith, the Catholic governor of New York, who lost a number of Southern states.

116. Greenstone, *Labor in American Politics*.

117. Lee, *Truman and Taft-Hartley*.

118. Schickler, "Public Opinion," 3. Ware points to a number of factors that preserved the Republican Party's strength outside the South during this period, including the strength of long-standing Republican Party organizations, the competitiveness of a moderate strain of Republicanism in the North, and the strength of the Republican Party in rural and suburban areas. The Democrats' appeal was very urban. Ware, *Democratic Party Heads North*.

119. Ware, *Democratic Party Heads North*, 231.

120. Troy, "Growth of Union Membership," 409.

121. Ibid., 407.

122. Friedman, "Political Economy," 386.

123. Poole and Rosenthal, *Ideology and Congress*, 54.

124. Although as recent scholarship has demonstrated, by the 1940s Republican state parties and members of Congress from non-Southern states had begun to show less enthusiasm for civil rights than Democrats from the same states, suggesting a changing dynamic on civil rights. Chen, *Fifth Freedom*, and Feinstein and Schickler, "Platforms and Partners."

125. Davis, *Prisoners of the American Dream*.

126. The only way this dynamic could have been overcome is if a more unambiguously pro-labor party generated more enthusiasm among liberal voters and significantly higher turnout. This is certainly a possibility, but far from likely. A poll found only 10% of respondents interested in joining a party formed by labor. Gallup Poll (AIPO), June 1946, retrieved June 6, 2010, from the iPOLL Databank, The Roper Center for Public Opinion Research, University of Connecticut.

127. Quoted in C. P. Trussell, "Poll Tax Repealer Taken Up in Senate," *New York Times*, May 10, 1944.

CHAPTER TWO: Labor, the Conservative Coalition, and the Welfare State

1. Paul Sifton to Walter Reuther, memo, June 5, 1950, box 23, folder 3, UAW Political Action Department, Roy Reuther Files, WSU.

2. Hattam, *Labor Visions;* Forbath, *Law and the Shaping of the American Labor Movement.*

3. Greenstone, *Labor in American Politics,* 67–70; Horowitz, *Political Ideologies,* 230.

4. Franklin D. Roosevelt, State of the Union Address to Congress, Jan. 11, 1944.

5. "Political Aims of Organized Labor."

6. McClure, *Truman Administration,* 11–12.

7. Shelley, *Permanent Majority,* 33.

8. Turner, *Party and Constituency,* 171–72.

9. Ibid., 187–88.

10. Ibid., 181.

11. Ibid., 89.

12. Key, *Southern Politics.*

13. Turner, *Party and Constituency,* 185.

14. Shelley, *Permanent Majority,* chap. 3.

15. Katznelson, Geiger, and Kryder, "Limiting Liberalism," 286–90.

16. Abram and Cooper demonstrate that deference to seniority in the selection of committee chairs had become the norm by the 1920s. Abram and Cooper, "Rise of Seniority," 80–81.

17. Louis Hollander, city chairman of the New York AFL-CIO, quoted in Clayton Knowles, "State Labor Asks Congress Reform," *New York Times,* Jan. 22, 1964, 34, accessed in ProQuest Historical Newspapers.

18. Andrew J. Biemiller, oral history interview by James R. Fuchs, July 29, 1977, HSTL.

19. From the adoption of Rule 22 in 1917 through 1964, only civil rights bills and proposals to reduce the cloture threshold were successfully filibustered. See Binder and Smith, *Politics or Principle,* 135.

20. Brinkley, *End of Reform,* 103.

21. Roosevelt, State of the Union, Jan. 11, 1944 (emphasis added).

22. Bailey, *Congress Makes a Law,* 80.

23. Ibid., 82.

24. Ibid., 123.

25. Quoted from the *House Hearings on H.R. 2202,* 390–91, cited in ibid., 141.

26. Sifton to Reuther memo, June 5, 1950.

27. Bailey, *Congress Makes a Law,* 153.

28. Ibid., 162.

29. Ibid., 167.

30. "Federal Supplement to State Unemployment Compensation," CQ Press Electronic Library, CQ Almanac Online Edition, cqal45-1403129; originally published in *CQ Almanac 1945.*

31. Known as the Knowland amendment, it put in place several procedures to delay penalties on states found in noncompliance with the limited federal standards in the unemployment program. The states had to be given ninety days' notice of noncompliance, and the federal finding of noncompliance had to have received final state court review before funds could be withheld. "Social Security Act," CQ Press Electronic

Library, CQ Almanac Online Edition, cqal50-1377221; originally published in *CQ Almanac 1950.*

32. "Unemployment Aid Extension," CQ Press Electronic Library, CQ Almanac Online Edition, cqal54-1357998; originally published in *CQ Almanac 1954.*

33. "Unemployment Benefits," *CQ Almanac 1958.*

34. Ibid.

35. Background in "Minimum Wages," *CQ Almanac 1949,* and Louis Stark, "Congress Agreed on 75C Basic Pay; Congress Acts Soon," *New York Times,* Oct. 15, 1949.

36. Stark, "Congress Agreed."

37. "Minimum Wage Bill Dies in Conference," *CQ Almanac 1960.*

38. Ibid.

39. Tynes, *Turning Points.*

40. Ibid., 116.

41. Ibid., 118. Federal workers were the only major occupational group left outside the program.

42. Quadagno, "Physician Sovereignty," 818.

43. "Social Security Extension," CQ Press Electronic Library, CQ Almanac Online Edition, cqal49-1399806; originally published in *CQ Almanac 1949.*

44. "Social Security Act," CQ Press Electronic Library, CQ Almanac Online Edition, cqal50-1377221; originally published in *CQ Almanac 1950.*

45. Quadagno, "Physician Sovereignty," 819.

46. Berkowitz, *Disabled Policy,* 75.

47. Quadagno, "Physician Sovereignty," 818; Berkowitz and Wolff, "Disability Insurance," 76–77. The age limitation also minimized the opposition of the insurance industry.

48. Berkowitz, *Disabled Policy,* 75.

49. Ibid., 76.

50. "Social Security," CQ Press Electronic Library, CQ Almanac Online Edition, cqal56-1349073; originally published in *CQ Almanac 1956.*

51. Berkowitz, *Disabled Policy,* 79.

52. Poen, *Harry S. Truman,* 60–61.

53. Ibid., 64.

54. Ibid., 118.

55. One sample in a July 1945 Gallup poll found that 53% of respondents favored a government plan and 34% favored a private-sector plan. Another sample in the same poll found that 47% favored a government plan while 40% favored a private-sector plan. Public opinion remained fairly evenly divided throughout the debate. There was never an indication that the public was either strongly for or against any particular measure.

56. Quadagno, *One Nation Uninsured,* 44–46.

57. "Health Reinsurance," CQ Press Electronic Library, CQ Almanac Online Edition, cqal54-1357935; originally published in *CQ Almanac 1954.*

58. Hacker, *Divided Welfare State,* 239–41.

59. Hacker also argues that government funding of research and hospitals before a system of cost controls was put in place made future health reform efforts even more difficult because of the soaring cost of health care. Hacker, "Historical Logic."

60. For summarization of the multiple explanations for the failure of national health insurance in the United States, see, for example, the introduction in Quadagno, *One Nation Uninsured,* and Hacker, "Historical Logic," 60–76.

61. Quadagno, *One Nation Uninsured;* Hacker, "Historical Logic."

62. Quadagno, *One Nation Uninsured.*

63. Ibid., 30–31, 34.

64. Hacker, *Divided Welfare State.*

65. Organized labor targeted congressional supporters of the Taft-Hartley Act in the elections. While the labor effort was unable to defeat the much hated Senator Taft, it did help replace seventy-five Republicans with Democrats in the House and eight in the Senate. Lee, *Truman and Taft-Hartley.*

66. This discussion is drawn from ibid., chap. 7.

67. Truman's threats on patronage discussed in Savage, *Truman and the Democratic Party,* 149.

68. William Green, "American Labor Must Be Strong and Free," speech in San Diego, Calif., Sept. 5, 1949, in *Vital Speeches of the Day* 15 (Sept. 14, 1949): 715.

69. This discussion is drawn from Gall, *Politics of Right to Work,* chap. 3.

70. Labor also launched a full-scale lobbying campaign to ensure this bill was recommitted and worked closely with the Senate Democratic leadership. Walter Reuther to International Union Presidents, memo, Apr. 7, 1954, box 422, folder 1, UAW President's Office, Walter P. Reuther Collection, WSU.

71. Witwer, *Corruption and Reform,* chap. 9.

72. Ibid., 188–91.

73. ORC Public Opinion Index, Nov. 1958 and Jan. 1959, retrieved June 13, 2010, from the iPOLL Databank, The Roper Center for Public Opinion Research, University of Connecticut.

74. Witwer, *Corruption and Reform,* 206. Republicans put out a pamphlet in 1956 entitled "The Labor Bosses: America's Third Party" that made this case.

75. Representative Bolling noted that others faced pressure from business not to bring up the bill because it contained a provision for increased oversight of management. Bolling, *House out of Order,* 157. Representative Udall noted the efforts on the House Education and Labor Committee. Stewart L. Udall Oral History Interview—JFK #1, Jan. 12, 1970, John F. Kennedy Library collection.

76. Bolling, *House out of Order,* chap. 8.

77. Much of this discussion is drawn from Bolling, *House out of Order,* "Congress Passes Anti-Corruption Labor Bill," *CQ Almanac 1959,* and McAdams, *Power and Politics.*

78. "Congress Passes Anti-Corruption Labor Bill."

79. Robinson, *George Meany,* 212.

80. Report of James McDevitt, national director of COPE, to Administrative Committee of AFL-CIO COPE, Feb. 10, 1960, Office of the President, George Meany Files, box 98, folder 8, GMMA.

81. CIO press release, Nov. 17, 1952, in WHCF-OF, box 779, 170 (1947–53) folder, Truman Papers, HSTL.

82. Bensel, *Sectionalism,* 175.

83. Walter Reuther to William Boyle, undated, box 23, folder 3, UAW Political Action Department, Roy Reuther Files, WSU.

84. Ibid.

85. Donald E. Montgomery to Walter P. Reuther, memo, Sept. 4, 1953, box 431, folder 8, UAW President's Office, Walter P. Reuther Collection, WSU.

86. Frustration highlighted in unsigned, undated memo, "Relations with the Demo-

cratic Party," box 24, folder 23, UAW Political Action Department, Roy Reuther Files, WSU.

87. Discussion of rift in Roscoe Born, "Labor Sits It Out," *Wall Street Journal,* Jan. 18, 1961, article found in Office of the President, George Meany Files, box 98, folder 8, GMMA.

88. AFL-CIO pamphlet, 1961, reprinted from article in *American Federationist* (Jan. 5, 1961), Support Service Department, AFL-CIO Publications, Series 1, GMMA.

89. Kennedy had also tried to include the common situs picketing provision in the Landrum-Griffin bill, but he lost the battle in conference committee.

90. Statistic from the Bureau of Labor Statistics.

91. For example, Kevin Boyle discusses the UAW's embrace of the "new liberalism" of the Truman years over its social democratic agenda and the UAW's adaptation to the Democratic Party's "truncated agenda." Boyle, *UAW,* 60, 84. Similarly, Alan Brinkley sees the period as the "end of reform" as a commitment to consumer Keynesianism replaced the desire to fundamentally transform capitalism among elements in the New Deal and the CIO. Brinkley, *End of Reform.* Nelson Lichtenstein discusses the "eclipse of social democracy" and the "forced retreat [that] narrowed the political appeal of labor-liberalism and contributed both to the demobilization and division of those social forces which had long sustained it." Lichtenstein, "From Corporatism to Collective Bargaining," 123. Ira Katznelson notes that "by the end of the 1940s labor's vision and potential contracted." Katznelson, "Was the Great Society a Lost Opportunity," 191.

92. Boyle, *UAW,* chaps. 3 and 4; Lichtenstein, *Labor's War at Home,* 240.

93. Plotke, *Building a Democratic Political Order,* 336, 363.

CHAPTER THREE: Possibilities and Limits in the Great Society

1. A display of all the signing pens from this period still hangs in the AFL-CIO's legislative office.

2. Incremental expansions of the welfare state do not necessarily follow this pattern, as indicated in the previous chapter's discussion of expansion of the minimum wage. Moreover, as scholars such as Christopher Howard have pointed out, in contrast to major spending programs, policy innovations like tax expenditures, which are adjustments to tax policy to encourage private-sector behavior like the mortgage interest deduction, have been pursued by bipartisan coalitions over extended periods of time. Howard, *Hidden Side.*

3. Quotes from 1963 AFL-CIO Convention resolutions in Harrington, *Socialism,* 264.

4. Boyle, *UAW,* 187–88.

5. Orren has further argued that labor lobbied for diverse programs to expand demand and increase government spending from Medicare to agricultural subsidies that forced the Federal Reserve to pursue an expansionary monetary policy. This facilitated sizable wage gains in collective bargaining and put downward pressure on unemployment. Orren, "Union Politics."

6. Kennedy was able to reward labor in some ways through NLRB appointments, the responsiveness of the Labor Department, and an executive order permitting federal employees to engage in collective bargaining.

7. Excerpts from report by the Textile Workers Union prepared by John W. Edelman,

"What Will the 1962 Congressional Election Mean to Labor and Liberals?" box 434, folder 3, UAW President's Office, Walter P. Reuther Collection, WSU.

8. Henry Wilson to Lawrence O'Brien, memo, July 18, 1962, box 4, Larry O'Brien folder 1/3, Office Files of Henry Wilson, LBJL.

9. Polsby, *How Congress Evolves,* 40–50.

10. "Helping to Write Your Nation's Laws," AFL-CIO pamphlet, 1963, Support Services Department, AFL-CIO Publications, Series 1, GMMA.

11. "Labor Looks at Congress, 1963," Support Services Department, AFL-CIO Publications, Series 1, GMMA.

12. Quote in Robinson, *George Meany,* 240–41.

13. Cooper and Bombardier, "Presidential Leadership," 1017.

14. Greenstone, *Labor in American Politics,* 55.

15. Quoted in Draper, *Rope of Sand,* 38.

16. Zieger, *American Workers,* 162.

17. Ibid., 183.

18. Area Conference Summary, 1962, Office of the President, George Meany Files, box 98, folder 9, GMMA.

19. Ibid.

20. In 1963 the AFL-CIO Executive Council decided to levy on the affiliates an assessment of five cents per member for a special voter registration fund. There was a massive registration drive going into the 1964 elections of union members and, as discussed in Chapter 4, of other liberal constituencies such as African Americans. COPE report, Office of the President, George Meany Files, box 98, folder 11, GMMA. A record number of international unions participated in the AFL-CIO's electoral efforts, and the affiliates released numerous upper-level staffers to work on the campaign under AFL-CIO direction. COPE report, Feb. 1965, Office of the President, George Meany Files, box 98, folder 12, GMMA.

21. Harrington, *Socialism,* 266; Greenstone, *Labor in American Politics,* xiii.

22. Greenstone, *Labor in American Politics,* xiv.

23. Harrington, *Socialism,* 266, 269.

24. Quoted in Brown, "Bargaining for Social Rights," 653.

25. Stevens, "Blurring the Boundaries," 137.

26. Gottschalk, *Shadow Welfare State.* Also see Klein, *For All These Rights,* and Stevens, "Blurring the Boundaries."

27. Press release on Case bill veto, WHCF-OF, box 1122, "Case Bill" folder, Truman Papers, HSTL.

28. In a May 15, 1946, memo to the president, the administrator of the Federal Security Agency underlined this point and suggested that "if the demands of the miners for a special welfare fund are incorporated into their contract, other unions will be encouraged to press for similar benefits." WHCF-OF, box 1256, folder 419b, Truman Papers, HSTL.

29. Operators' Negotiating Committee for the National Bituminous Coal Wage Conference to President Truman, May 16, 1946, PSF, box 118, Strikes: coal folder, Truman Papers, HSTL.

30. Stevens, "Blurring the Boundaries," 140–41; Brown, "Bargaining for Social Rights," 669.

31. Stevens, "Blurring the Boundaries," 141.

32. Brown, "Bargaining for Social Rights," 653.

33. Stevens, "Blurring the Boundaries," 146.

34. Hacker, *Divided Welfare State*.

35. Ibid., 61.

36. Lichtenstein, "From Corporatism to Collective Bargaining," 143.

37. Brown, "Bargaining for Social Rights."

38. Marmor, *Politics of Medicare*, 23.

39. Ibid., 14.

40. At this same time COPE showed growing interest in mobilizing senior citizens to vote. COPE research files contain numerous breakdowns by congressional district of the percentage of the population registered to vote and the percentage of the senior population registered to vote and voting with an eye to targeting districts for registration and get-out-the-vote drives.

41. Zelizer, *Taxing America*, 213.

42. Marmor, *Politics of Medicare*, 43.

43. Marmor notes that in 1963 eighteen states had still not set up programs under Kerr-Mills and the provision of funds varied widely from state to state. Marmor, *Politics of Medicare*, 36–37.

44. Marmor notes that a June 1961 Gallup poll found that two out of three people interviewed were in favor of increasing the Social Security tax to pay for medical insurance for the elderly. Ibid., 41.

45. Nelson Cruikshank to George Meany, memo, June 9, 1961, Office of the President, George Meany Files, box 52, folder 23, GMMA.

46. Quoted in Zelizer, *Taxing America*, 135–36.

47. Polsby, *How Congress Evolves*, 50.

48. Excerpts from report by the Textile Workers Union prepared by John W. Edelman, "What Will the 1962 Congressional Election Mean to Labor and Liberals?" box 434, folder 3, UAW President's Office, Walter P. Reuther Collection, WSU.

49. Noted in "Labor Looks at the 88th Congress," Oct. 1964, Support Services Department, AFL-CIO Publications, Series 1, GMMA. Ross Bass (D-TN) and Pat Jennings (D-VA) were appointed.

50. *CQ Almanac 1965*, 244.

51. "Senate Kills Social Security Health Care Plan," CQ Press Electronic Library, CQ Almanac Online Edition, cqal62-1326016; originally published in *CQ Almanac 1962*.

52. Henry Wilson to Lawrence O'Brien, memo, Apr. 20, 1964, box 4, Larry O'Brien folder 1/3, Office Files of Henry Wilson, LBJL.

53. Zelizer, *Taxing America*, 227.

54. Memo, Sept. 4, 1964, box 3, Medicare folder, Office Files of Henry Wilson, LBJL.

55. Lawrence O'Brien to President Johnson, memo, Sept. 13, 1964, box 3, Medicare folder, Office Files of Henry Wilson, LBJL.

56. Quoted in Zelizer, *Taxing America*, 229.

57. In stressing the need for the administration to pressure the House congressional leadership to ensure committee assignments were conducive to the president's program, one of Johnson's legislative staffers, Henry Wilson, noted, "Rearrangement of ratios on House committees and subcommittees, the assignment of members so as best to effectuate Administration programs, and, in the few cases where possible, the reshuffling of

subcommittee chairmanships and areas of authority can be as impt. as the level of the Congressional majority itself." Henry Wilson to Larry O'Brien, memo, Dec. 7, 1964, box 4, Larry O'Brien folder 1/3, Office Files of Henry Wilson, LBJL.

58. Trying to kill the social insurance bill, the AMA publicly attacked the plan's limited coverage, which, according to Wilbur Mills, actually pushed the Ways and Means Committee to find a way to expand the social insurance proposal rather than to dump it in favor of the AMA's "eldercare" approach. Wilbur Cohen, assistant secretary of health, education, and welfare, to Johnson staffer Douglass Cater, memo, Mar. 10, 1965, WHCF-LE, box 75, 3/1/65–5/31/65, LBJL.

59. Senator Abraham Ribicoff to President Johnson, Mar. 3, 1965, WHCF-LE, box 75, LBJL.

60. Poen, *Harry S. Truman,* 220.

61. Signatures on discharge petitions were not made publicly available, but House leaders and committee chairs could view them, so there was a chance of retribution but little chance of reward.

62. "Labor Looks at Congress 1965," Nov. 1965, Support Services Department, AFL-CIO Publications, Series 1, GMMA.

63. See Gall, *Politics of Right to Work,* 77–85.

64. Much of this discussion is drawn from a chronology of the 1965–66 battle over repeal of 14(b) prepared by Andrew Biemiller, the AFL-CIO's chief lobbyist, for President Meany. "Chronology," Legislation Department, Legislative Reference Files, box 48, folder 18, GMMA.

65. The administration apparently considered trying to trade votes for 14(b) for votes on the administration's farm bill to try to maximize the coalition for both pieces of legislation, but it found that the only Southerners willing to vote for 14(b) came from urban areas and that Northern Democrats weren't willing to trade a vote on the farm bill. A July 20, 1965, memo from Henry Wilson to Larry O'Brien concluded, "The proposal gets us not one vote for Repeal of 14-B and . . . it will seriously jeopardize many votes on the Farm bill." Box 9, Larry O'Brien folder, Office Files of Henry Wilson, LBJL.

66. "Chronology."

67. The AFL-CIO Department of Education even offered locals a film entitled "The Beat Majority" to stress to union members the importance of the "one man, one vote" concept and the need for proportional reapportionment of state and federal legislative districts.

68. "Chronology."

69. This is noted in ibid. as well as an Aug. 2, 1965, memo from Lyndon Johnson's aide responsible for the Senate, Mike Manatos, to his chief legislative representative, Larry O'Brien, box 9, Poverty folder, Office Files of Mike Manatos, LBJL.

70. Mansfield's pessimism described in several memos such as a Sept. 2, 1965, memo from Mike Manatos to Larry O'Brien, box 12, Mike Mansfield folder, Office Files of Mike Manatos, LBJL, and another from Sept. 9, 1965, noting that Mansfield had told Biemiller "he was in trouble on 14(b) because the votes are not available to invoke cloture." Box 2, Legislative 1965, Jan.–Sept. folder, Office Files of Mike Manatos, LBJL.

71. Numbers reported in various newspapers and AFL-CIO Department of Legislation documents.

72. AFL-CIO Executive Council Minutes, Oct. 28, 1965, GMMA.

73. A Jan. 15, 1965, memo from Biemiller to Meany estimated 53 votes in the Senate in

support of cloture reform. Thus, a filibuster of cloture reform was likely to be successful. Legislation Department, Legislative Reference Files, box 19, folder 38, GMMA.

74. A Jan. 25, 1966, memo to Marie Fehmer from Mike Manatos summing up a meeting of the congressional leadership with the president noted that the leaders assured the president they would move speedily on 14(b) in the congressional session but that "Mansfield was not encouraging about 14(b)." Box 2, Legislative 1965, Jan.–Sept. folder, Office Files of Mike Manatos, LBJL.

75. Conversation with Reuther recounted by Larry O'Brien to President Johnson, memo, Dec. 5, 1965, WHCF-LE, box 6, 10/9/65–12/19/65 folder, LBJL

76. Andrew Biemiller, Alexander Barkan, and Albert Zack to President Meany, memo, Oct. 25, 1965, Office of the President, George Meany Files, box 100, folder 17, GMMA.

77. Meeting summed up in a Feb. 3, 1966, memo from Mike Manatos to President Johnson. Senator Pell, for example, noted that "14(b) was not like Civil Rights when an aroused nation forced the issue." Box 3, Legislative-General-1966, Jan.–Mar. folder, Office Files of Mike Manatos, LBJL.

78. Only two Democrats actively participated in the filibuster. Copy of a newspaper article (Robert Allen and Paul Scott, "Mansfield Infuriates Labor," *The State*, Sept. 20, 1965) found in Legislation Department, Congressional Correspondence, box 70, folder 2, GMMA.

79. A Nov. 25, 1966, memo from Secretary of Labor Willard Wirtz to President Johnson noted that the election results made a range of labor bills less likely to pass. He also suggested that there was likely to be a bill introduced in Congress to prohibit union-shop contracts unless states passed legislation specifically allowing such contracts, and he noted that Republican gains in the state legislatures would likely mean renewed efforts to pass more right-to-work laws. WHCF-LE, box 134, 9/29/65 folder, LBJL.

80. A Mar. 23, 1966, memo from George Reedy to President Johnson noted that while the national leadership of the AFL-CIO might have a good relationship with the president, there was dissatisfaction at the secondary level of labor leadership and among other labor legislative representatives in Washington regarding 14(b) and issues of access to the administration. WHCF-CF, box 60, Labor Management Relations folder, LBJL. The Texas AFL-CIO, which of course had a long-standing relationship with Johnson, was particularly critical. A Feb. 12, 1966, letter to President Johnson from the president of the Odessa Central Labor Council was representative of the sentiment in noting, "We are deeply shocked and disappointed at the failure of the Administration and the Democratic Party to keep its promise on repeal of Section 14B of the Taft-Hartley Act. We have supported the Party and its program as long as I can remember. Every Democratic President has had our support when he needed it. While we have supported others, not a *single one* of our own legislative goals have been enacted by your Administration. We are just plain angry about it." WHCF-LE, box 137, 2/16/66–4/26/66 folder, LBJL.

81. The Lyndon Johnson archives show repeated requests by Meany for meetings with the president on short notice during the 14(b) fight, and all were granted by Johnson.

82. July 30, 1965, memo from the vice president to Larry O'Brien outlining his activities on lobbying for 14(b) in the House. Of forty-two members he was assigned, all but two voted for repeal. WHCF-LE, box 134, 9/29/65 folder, LBJL.

83. Joe Califano to President Johnson, memo, Feb. 16, 1966, WHCF-CF, box 60, Labor Management Relations folder, LBJL.

84. Transcript, Lawrence F. O'Brien Oral History Interview XIII, Sept. 10, 1986, by Michael L. Gillette, Internet copy, LBJL, 13.

85. Box 8, 14(b) folder, Office Files of Mike Manatos, LBJL.

86. Marvin Watson to President Johnson, memo, Feb. 15, 1966, box 6, 1/15/65–2/15/65 folder, Handwriting File, White House Special Files, LBJL.

87. Quoted in Robinson, *George Meany*, 244.

88. Secretary of Labor Willard Wirtz to President Johnson, memo, Dec. 1, 1964, WHCF-LA, box 1, LA 2/2 folder, LBJL.

89. Willard Wirtz to President Johnson, memo, Feb. 9, 1965, WHCF-LA, box 1, LA 2/2 folder, LBJL.

90. If votes in the Senate are weighted for population, comparable to the proportional representation in the House, the support for cloture increases from 52% to 60.7%, indicating that senators from low-population states were more likely to oppose cloture and senators from higher-population states were more likely to support cloture.

91. Quoted in Robinson, *George Meany*, 247.

92. "Common-Site Picketing," CQ Press Electronic Library, CQ Almanac Online Edition, cqal66–1300498; originally published in *CQ Almanac 1966*.

93. Willard Wirtz to Lawrence O'Brien, undated memo, WHCF-LE, box 7, LE 1/1/66–2/3/66 folder, LBJL.

94. Willard Wirtz to President Johnson, memo, Aug. 4, 1965, WHCF-CF, box 63, LE/HI-LE/LE 3 folder, LBJL.

95. "Expansion of Minimum Wage Law Approved," CQ Press Electronic Library, CQ Almanac Online Edition, cqal66-1300503; originally published in *CQ Almanac 1966*.

96. Ibid.

97. The garment workers' unions had the most interest in the bill and wanted a minimum wage increase to $1.60 to be effective in 1967, whereas the administration stood firm at an effective date of 1968. AFL-CIO president Meany grudgingly conceded to the later date, in part because it was more feasible in Congress. Issues with the effective date covered in Willard Wirtz to President Johnson, memo, Feb. 12, 1966, WHCF-LE, box 134, LE/LA 9/29/65 folder, LBJL. Negotiations over details reviewed in Willard Wirtz to President Johnson, memo, Mar. 9, 1965, WHCF-LA, box 16, LA 3 folder, LBJL; and Henry Wilson to President Johnson, memo, Mar. 9, 1966, White House Special Files, Legislative Background Minimum Wage Increase 1966, box 1, LBJL.

98. Noted in Henry Wilson to President Johnson, Mar. 8, 1966, White House Special Files, Legislative Background Minimum Wage Increase 1966, box 1, LBJL. The memo noted, "This probably will be the toughest fight all year. But Ways and Means is a basically favorable Committee, Mills is a great Chairman, and I am sure that we can bring out a bill and can convince labor of our sincerity."

99. Andy Biemiller's optimism noted in Joe Califano to President Johnson, memo, Mar. 8, 1966, WHCF-CF, box 60, Labor Management Relations folder, LBJL. Meany quote in "Unemployment Compensation Changes Die in Conference Committee," *CQ Almanac 1966*.

100. Willard Wirtz to President Johnson, memo, Nov. 10, 1966, WHCF-LA, box 19, Strikes–Work Stoppages folder, LBJL.

101. Quoted in Barefoot Sanders to President Johnson, memo, July 20, 1967, WHCF-LE, box 170, LE5 9/7/66–6/30/67 folder, LBJL.

102. Discussion of conflict found in copy of article from *Inside Labor* attached to

May 17, 1968, memo from Joe Califano to President Johnson, WHCF-LA, box 31, LA 7 folder, LBJL.

103. After attending several union conventions, Willard Wirtz observed in May 1966 that the Vietnam issue was becoming a concern and that the guidelines were attacked in every speech. He noted, "What I find is *support*, but a shortage of *enthusiasm;* and the reasons for the shortage are 5% 14(b), 20% guidelines, and 75% Vietnam. Willard Wirtz to President Johnson, memo, May 25, 1966, WHCF-CF, box 60, Labor Management Relations folder, LBJL.

104. Greenstone, *Labor in American Politics.*

CHAPTER FOUR: Changing the Rules of the Game

1. For discussion of this coalition and its activities, see Zelizer, *On Capitol Hill,* chap. 3.
2. Karol, *Party Position Change,* 109.
3. Schickler, *Disjointed Pluralism,* chap. 5.
4. Report from Emil Mazey, secretary-treasurer of the UAW, addressed to "Officers, Board Members and International Representatives," Feb. 16, 1956, box 577, folder 8, UAW President's Office, Walter P. Reuther Collection, WSU.
5. For discussion of labor's goals in the South, see Draper, *Conflict of Interests,* chap. 4.
6. King speech to AFL-CIO Convention in *Proceedings of the Fourth Constitutional Convention of the AFL-CIO,* vol. 1, Dec. 7–13, 1961, 287.
7. Gall, *Politics of Right to Work,* 142–44.
8. Quoted in Allen P. Sindler, "The Unsolid South: A Challenge to the Democratic Party," in Allen Sindler, ed., *The Uses of Power: Seven Cases in American Politics* (New York: Harcourt, Brace, and World, 1962), 233, cited in Feinstein and Schickler, "Platforms and Partners," 16.
9. Feinstein and Schickler, "Platforms and Partners," 16.
10. Ibid.
11. Chen, Mickey, and Van Houweling, "Explaining the Contemporary Alignment."
12. Schickler, "Public Opinion."
13. Quoted in Foner, *Organized Labor,* 310.
14. Schickler, Pearson, and Feinstein, "Congressional Parties," 6.
15. Ibid., 14.
16. C. P. Trussell, "Poll Tax Repealer Taken Up in Senate," *New York Times,* May 10, 1944; Chen, *Fifth Freedom,* 67.
17. The Republican Party was becoming less supportive of civil rights over this period in part because of business opposition to fair employment practices legislation. Chen, *Fifth Freedom;* Karol, *Party Position Change.*
18. Berman, *Bill Becomes a Law,* 125.
19. Quoted in Robinson, *George Meany,* 236–37.
20. Noted in John Herling's Labor Letter from June 13, 1964, found in box 430, folder 13, UAW President's Office, Walter P. Reuther Collection, WSU. Biemiller discussed the strategy for getting the fair employment provision included and passed in oral history interview with James R. Fuchs, July 29, 1977, HSTL.
21. Multiple references in Legislation Department, Legislative Reference Files, box 9, folder 13, GMMA.

22. Letter, Feb. 5, 1964, in Legislation Department, Legislative Reference Files, box 9, folder 15, GMMA.

23. Andrew Biemiller to various senators, Mar. 13, 1964, Legislation Department, Legislative Reference Files, box 9, folder 16, GMMA.

24. "Civil Rights Act of 1964," CQ Press Electronic Library, CQ Almanac Online Edition, cqal64-1304542; originally published in *CQ Almanac 1964.*

25. Draper, *Conflict of Interests*, chap. 1.

26. Report from Emil Mazey, secretary-treasurer of the UAW, addressed to "Officers, Board Members and International Representatives," Feb. 16, 1956, box 577, folder 8, UAW President's Office, Walter P. Reuther Collection, WSU.

27. Foner, *Organized Labor,* 317.

28. Draper, *Conflict of Interests*, 26.

29. Ibid., 34.

30. Claude Ramsay to Meany, June 9, 1961, Office of the President, George Meany Files, box 31, folder 16, GMMA.

31. Draper, *Conflict of Interests*, 92.

32. Ibid.

33. Ibid., 104.

34. Meier and Rudwick, *Black Detroit*, 219–21.

35. Foner, *Organized Labor*, 323

36. Ibid., 348.

37. Ibid., 325.

38. Ibid., 335.

39. Draper, *Conflict of Interest*, 3–5.

40. Foner, *Organized Labor*, 349.

41. The emerging black radical wing of the civil rights movement continued to criticize organized labor, but the relationship between mainstream civil rights leaders and organized labor was cooperative.

42. Clarence Mitchell, director of Washington Bureau of the NAACP, to Andrew Biemiller, Feb. 24, 1964, Legislation Department, Legislative Reference Files, box 9, folder 15, GMMA.

43. Organized labor also organized "sympathy rallies" in other cities. Levy, *New Left and Labor*, 42.

44. Foner, *Organized Labor*, chap. 24.

45. Lichtenstein, *State of the Union*, 82.

46. Greenstone, *Labor in American Politics*, 16.

47. Report of James McDevitt, national director of COPE, to Administrative Committee of COPE, Feb. 10, 1960, Office of the President, George Meany Files, box 98, folder 8, GMMA.

48. Hank Brown, president of Texas AFL-CIO, and Roy Evans, secretary-treasurer of AFL-CIO, to Walter Reuther, May 26, 1964, box 430, folder 13, UAW President's Office, Walter P. Reuther Collection, WSU.

49. Report of McDevitt to COPE Administrative Committee, June 1961, Office of the President, George Meany Files, box 98, folder 8, GMMA.

50. Ibid.

51. An Oct. 23, 1964, memo from Larry O'Brien to President Johnson noted that the

"Negro vote could well mean the difference between victory or defeat in South Carolina, North Carolina, Georgia, and Florida. It is possible Virginia and Tennessee could also be added to this list." Box 3, Memos to President—O'Brien trip folder, Office Files of Henry Wilson, LBJL.

52. Quoted in Boyle, *UAW*, 200.

53. The AFL-CIO continued to contribute two thousand dollars a month to the institute, and while the organization also obtained outside funding, it was very closely allied with the AFL-CIO.

54. Don Slaiman to President Meany, memo, May 6, 1966, Office of the President, George Meany Files, box 49, folder 16, GMMA.

55. Al Barkan to President Meany, memo, Nov. 12, 1974, Office of the President, George Meany Files, box 98, folder 19, GMMA.

56. Edsall and Edsall, *Chain Reaction*, chap. 4.

57. Battista, *Revival of Labor Liberalism*, chap. 3.

58. Excerpts of letter in "To Clear the Record," Supplemental Report No. 1 of the AFL-CIO Executive Council on the disaffiliation of the UAW to the Eighth Constitutional Convention, 1969.

59. Lichtenstein, *Most Dangerous Man*, 353.

60. Chen stresses that the civil rights movement did not suddenly set its sights on the North after the mid-1960s legislative victories but had been active there since the 1940s. Chen, *Fifth Freedom*.

61. A July 13, 1967, memo from Marvin Watson to President Johnson included the labor memo as an attachment. Author is not noted. WHCF-Political Affairs, box 87, 6/3/67–8/22/67 folder, LBJL.

62. Quoted in Haynes Johnson and Nick Kotz, "Presidents Come and Go, but Labor's Might Stays," *Washington Post*, Apr. 13, 1972.

63. Dark, *Unions and the Democrats*, 81.

64. Victor Riesel, "New 'Party'? Union Chiefs Fight to Elect First Labor President of U.S.," *Inside Labor*, Aug. 27, 1968, found in box 437, UAW President's Office, Walter P. Reuther Collection, WSU.

65. Preliminary COPE report on 1968 elections, Office of the President, George Meany Files, box 98, folder 16, GMMA.

66. Ibid. In Pittsburgh, pro-Humphrey sentiment among union members rose from 69% on Oct. 25 to 80.7% on Oct. 31. In Baltimore, Humphrey support more than doubled, from 30% in September to 65% by the end of October. In Binghamton, New York; Cleveland, Ohio; and Connecticut, Humphrey support was increased by more than 10% in the last weeks of the campaign.

67. Battista, *Revival of Labor Liberalism*, 47–52.

68. The UAW, CWA, IAM, and AFSCME went on record in support of the reforms to open up the nominating system.

69. Dark, *Unions and the Democrats*, 87–92.

70. Scammon and Wattenberg, *Real Majority*, 2.

71. Battista, *Revival of Labor Liberalism*, chap. 3.

72. Noted in an attachment to an Aug. 5, 1952, memo from Don Montgomery to Walter Reuther. Box 430, folder 22, UAW President's Office, Walter P. Reuther Collection, WSU.

73. Poston cites Wall Street and big business pressure on several New York Republi-

cans, who had previously voted for adoption of the twenty-one-day rule, to vote against it at the opening of Congress in 1951. Ted Poston, "Truman Seeks Help of NY Congressmen in House Rules Fight," *New York Post*, Jan. 18, 1950.

74. "Limitation of Debate," *CQ Almanac 1949*.

75. Ibid.

76. J. A. Beirne to Senate Majority Leader Scott Lucas, Mar. 10, 1949, WHCF-OF, box 1106, #407, Mar.–Oct. 1949 folder, Truman Papers, HSTL.

77. An undated, unsigned report entitled "The Record of the 82nd Congress" noted, "The Dixiegop coalition had been riding high ever since March 17, 1949 when it worked out a two-point program for 1) stifling Civil Rights by the threat of filibuster under the new Rule 22 adopted to satisfy the Southern Democrats, and 2) blocking repeal of Taft-Hartley, to satisfy Taft and heavy contributors to the Republican Party including employers from all sections of the country." Box 430, folder 23, UAW President's Office, Walter P. Reuther Collection, WSU.

78. An Aug. 5, 1952, memo from Don Montgomery to Walter Reuther outlined issues to raise with Adlai Stevenson including cloture reform and reinstatement of the twenty-one-day rule. Box 430, folder 22, UAW President's Office, Walter P. Reuther Collection, WSU. A June 10, 1952, memo from William H. Oliver to Walter Reuther notes strategy on getting cloture reform included as part of the civil rights plank in the 1952 Democratic platform. Box 430, folder 20, UAW President's Office, Walter P. Reuther Collection, WSU.

79. The memo is undated but is after the 1954 and before the 1956 elections. Found in box 24, folder 23, UAW Political Action Department, Roy Reuther Files, WSU.

80. A November 1964 collection of typewritten and handwritten "Notes on Democratic Party Organization" presumably prepared for and by Walter Reuther suggested a number of proposals for strengthening the party organization, including a year-round director of organization for the Democratic National Committee and a review of "the working relationship between the DNC and the various Senatorial and Congressional Committees and other specialized committees." Handwritten notes stressed the "party responsibility on congressional reform" and the need to make the Democratic policy committees more representative in both houses and to strengthen the party caucus. Box 434, folder 5, UAW President's Office, Walter P. Reuther Collection, WSU.

81. Copy of speech by Senator Clark on Senate floor, June 22, 1959, found in Office of the President, George Meany Files, box 98, folder 8, GMMA.

82. Zelizer, *On Capitol Hill*, 55.

83. Sundquist, *Decline and Resurgence of Congress*, 392–94.

84. "Rule 22: An Unconstitutional Roadblock to Democratic Legislation. A Concrete Plan submitted by the UAW-CIO to the U.S. Senate Committee on Rules and Administration." Box 416, folder 13, UAW President's Office, Walter P. Reuther Collection, WSU.

85. Draft of Walter Reuther's speech given to the NAACP in advance of the 1953 fight over cloture reform, box 430, folder 20, UAW President's Office, Walter P. Reuther Collection, WSU.

86. Quoted in UAW news release from June 28, 1957. Box 577, folder 9, UAW President's Office, Walter P. Reuther Collection, WSU.

87. Conversation was relayed in a Jan. 16, 1959, letter from Frank McCulloch, a high-level Senate staffer, to Walter Reuther, box 409, folder 8, UAW President's Office, Walter P. Reuther Collection, WSU

88. Bolling, *House Out of Order*, 205.

89. Discussion drawn from Stevens, Miller, and Mann, "Mobilization of Strength," 668.

90. Ibid.

91. Kofmehl, "Institutionalization," 265.

92. Figure arrived at by comparing DSG membership speculated on in a Jan. 5, 1960, Congressional Quarterly Fact Sheet, "On Democratic Study Group," and the listing of union contributions in another Congressional Quarterly Fact Sheet, "On Labor's Campaign Spending," in the *CQ Almanac 1959*, 806–7. Prior to the 1970s there were very loose requirements on the reporting of campaign contributions, and these figures likely underestimate the number of DSG members who received union support.

93. Stevens, Miller, and Mann, "Mobilization of Strength," 670.

94. "Congressional Report," prepared by the National Committee for an Effective Congress," Dec. 2, 1965, WHCF-Federal Government Organizations, box 332, House of Reps. 11/23/63–3/17/66 folder, LBJL.

95. Stevens and colleagues found that there was greater cohesion among DSG members even when compared with other non-Southern, non-DSG members. Stevens, Miller, and Mann, "Mobilization of Strength."

96. Quoted in Jones, "Joseph G. Cannon," 640.

97. Discussion drawn from "House Enlarges Rules Committee," *CQ Almanac 1961*, 402–6.

98. Bolling, *House Out of Order*, 210.

99. "House Enlarges Rules Committee," 402–6.

100. Ibid.

101. The Leadership Conference on Civil Rights assigned the AFL-CIO and member unions certain House members to lobby on the rules changes. William H. Oliver to Walter P. Reuther, memo, Dec. 16, 1964, box 493, folder 32, UAW President's Office, Walter P. Reuther Collection, WSU.

102. Sheppard, *Rethinking Congressional Reform*, 40–41.

103. Ibid., 43.

104. Douglass Cater to President Johnson, memo, Nov. 25, 1966, WHCF-LE, box 45, 400 folder, LBJL.

105. Rohde, *Parties and Leaders*, 21.

106. Sheppard, *Rethinking Congressional Reform*, 62.

107. Zelizer, *On Capitol Hill*, 99–105.

108. The exception is the reforms in the presidential nomination process first used in the 1972 election.

109. Zelizer, *On Capitol Hill*, chaps. 6 and 7.

110. Sinclair, *Majority Leadership*, 5. Poole and Rosenthal find a slight shift to the left among Democrats outside the South in the mean nominate score on the liberal-conservative dimension. Poole and Rosenthal, *Ideology and Congress*, 84

111. Platform posted on the American Presidency Project's Web site at www.presidency.ucsb.edu/ws/index.php?pid=29605.

112. Schickler, *Disjointed Pluralism*, chap. 5.

113. Sheppard, *Rethinking Congressional Reform*, 195.

114. Because of other proposed jurisdictional changes, the maritime unions and various government workers unions also strongly opposed the proposal. Zelizer notes that the

UAW and the Steelworkers did not take a stand on Bolling's recommendations. Zelizer, *On Capitol Hill*, 148.

115. "Labor Looks at the 93rd Congress," 1975, Support Services Department, AFL-CIO Publications, Series 1, GMMA.

116. Schickler, *Disjointed Pluralism*, 201.

117. "Congressional Reforms Made in 1975," CQ Press Electronic Library, CQ Almanac Online Edition, cqal75-1210820; originally published in *CQ Almanac 1975*.

118. Rohde, *Parties and Leaders*, 22.

119. Zelizer, *On Capitol Hill*, 168.

120. One of these chairs, Wright Patman (D-TX), was an old-style populist, and he was actually defended by many liberals. At eighty-one years old, regardless of his policy preferences, he was viewed by the freshmen as ineffective and entrenched.

121. Quoted in Sheppard, *Rethinking Congressional Reform*, 206.

122. McCubbins and Schwartz, "Congress, the Courts, and Public Policy," 391.

123. Cox and Katz, "The Reapportionment Revolution."

124. Zelizer, *On Capitol Hill*, chap. 4.

125. Ibid., 72.

126. Vogel, *Fluctuating Fortunes*, 211.

127. Office of the President, George Meany Files, box 99, folder 3, GMMA.

CHAPTER FIVE: **Postreform Stalemate on Labor's Agenda**

1. Edsall, *New Politics of Inequality*; Berman, *America's Right Turn*; Lichtenstein, *State of the Union*; Moody, *Injury to All*.

2. Vogel, *Fluctuating Fortunes*, 150–59, and Edsall, *New Politics of Inequality*, 148–50.

3. Davis, *Prisoners of the American Dream*, 135.

4. Dark reaches a similar conclusion in his discussion of the failure of labor law reform. Dark, *Unions and the Democrats*, 109–13.

5. Vogel, *Fluctuating Fortunes*, 59.

6. Boyle, *UAW*.

7. Vogel, *Fluctuating Fortunes*; Battista, *Revival of Labor Liberalism*, 46.

8. For example, the mine workers bill preserved a role for the states in distributing black lung benefits; the Occupational Safety and Health Administration (OSHA) bill took three years to pass and involved a compromise on adoption and enforcement of safety standards; the clean water bill in 1972 had to overcome Nixon's veto; and the creation of a consumer protection agency was repeatedly filibustered.

9. The AFL-CIO's COPE (as well as the unaffiliated UAW and UMW) endorsed more candidates and more challengers to incumbents in 1974 than normal but had a surprising 70% victory rate for endorsed candidates. "Labor and Manpower 1974: Overview," CQ Press Electronic Library, CQ Almanac Online Edition, cqal74-1224465; originally published in *CQ Almanac 1974*.

10. In 1975, the AFL-CIO won on 78% of the COPE-identified votes in the House and 74% in the Senate.

11. "Labor Looks at Congress 1975," Support Services Department, AFL-CIO Publications, Series 1, GMMA.

12. Ibid.

13. Dark, *Unions and the Democrats*, 103.

14. Ibid., 101–2; Halpern, "Jimmy Carter."

15. Binder and Smith, *Politics or Principle*, 10, 135; Sinclair, "New World of U.S. Senators," 7.

16. Palazzolo, "From Decentralization to Centralization."

17. Dodd and Oppenheimer, "Maintaining Order."

18. Rohde, *Parties and Leaders*.

19. Oppenheimer, "Process Hurdles," 292, and "Congress and the New Obstructionism."

20. Rudder, "Committee Reform"; Arnold, *Logic of Congressional Action*.

21. "Reflections on the People's Lobby: An Interview with Andrew J. Biemiller," *AFL-CIO American Federationist,* Jan. 1979, 15.

22. Quoted in Robinson, *George Meany*, 369.

23. Mike Gildea, formerly in the AFL-CIO Department of Legislation, interview by author, July 23, 1999.

24. Davis, "Legislative Reform," 475–76.

25. Vogel, *Fluctuating Fortunes*. As noted in the previous chapter, labor dominance of PAC contributions to Democratic candidates was overtaken by business in the late seventies. On the proliferation of new politics groups, see Berry, *New Liberalism*.

26. Stated in Aug. 8, 1978, press conference.

27. Davis, "Legislative Reform."

28. As computed by Congressional Quarterly, Johnson was supported by Congress on 93% of the roll calls on which he had a clear position in 1965 compared with 79% in 1966 and 1967 and 75% in 1968. Carter's success rate varied between a low of 75.1% in 1980 to a high of 78.3% in 1978.

29. "Nixon Signs Minimum Wage Increase" *CQ Almanac 1974*.

30. Ibid.

31. Quoted in Tim Nicholson, "Big Labor's Big Defeat," *Newsweek*, Apr. 4, 1977.

32. McCarty, Poole, and Rosenthal, *Polarized America*, 166–69. On the minimum wage and income inequality, see Lee, "Wage Inequality."

33. Background and votes in "Ford Vetoes Common-Site Picketing Bill," CQ Press Electronic Library, CQ Almanac Online Edition, cqal75-1214784; originally published in *CQ Almanac 1975*.

34. Vogel, *Fluctuating Fortunes*, 204.

35. "House Rejects Labor-Backed Picketing Bill," CQ Press Electronic Library, CQ Almanac Online Edition, cqal77-1201876; originally published in *CQ Almanac 1977*.

36. Ibid.

37. "Labor Lost to 'Intense' Targeted Lobby Effort," *CQ Almanac 1977*, 124.

38. Ibid.

39. Andrew Biemiller noted before retiring in 1979, "Very frankly, we have to do a better job of trying to excite the grass roots. I've been asked so many times that I've lost track, 'are you sure you are really representing the people back home?' " "Reflections on the People's Lobby," 16.

40. Gross, *Broken Promise*, 241.

41. Labor law reform was listed among twelve top-tier legislative priorities for Carter's first congressional session among other bills such as Carter's energy plan, the 1978 bud-

get, and countercyclical spending. Les Francis and Bert Carp to Frank Moore and Stu Eizenstat, memo, Apr. 15, 1977, Records of the Domestic Policy Staff, box 232, Legislation folder, JCL.

42. Stu Eizenstat to President Carter, memo, June 30, 1977, Records of the Council of Economic Advisers, box 47, Labor Law Reform (1) folder, JCL.

43. Summary of negotiations in ibid.

44. Robinson, *George Meany,* 376.

45. Quoted in "Labor Law Revision," *CQ Almanac 1977,* 145.

46. "Weekly Legislative Report" from Frank Moore to President Carter, Apr. 22, 1978, PHF, box 82, 4/24/78 folder 2, JCL.

47. Secretary of Labor Ray Marshall to President Carter, memo, May 12, 1978, PHF, box 87, 5/30/78 folder, JCL.

48. Landon Butler to President Carter, memo, Apr. 25, 1978, PHF, box 85, 5/10/78 folder, JCL.

49. Landon Butler to President Carter, memo, May 8, 1978, PHF, box 84, 5/9/78 folder, JCL.

50. Ibid.

51. A June 19, 1978, memo from Stu Eizenstat and Bill Johnson to President Carter finally sounded a note of pessimism about the prospects for labor law reform, noting, "As you know, the labor law bill is in trouble—it appears that it will be more difficult to get the additional two Senators needed to invoke cloture than had been originally thought. . . . The present circumstances do present us with an unusual opportunity to show the depth of our commitment to labor." PHF, box 91, 6/19/78 folder, JCL.

52. Frank Moore and Bob Thomson to President Carter, memo, May 24, 1978, PHF, box 87, 5/30/78 folder 2, JCL.

53. Also noted in Dark, *Unions and the Democrats,* 110.

54. Senators Charles Percy (R-IL), John Heinz III (R-PA), and Lowell Weicker (R-CT) supported cloture. Senator Ted Stevens (R-AK), a traditional labor supporter, tied his vote to postponement of consideration of an Alaskan public lands bill he opposed. Discussion of Stevens's maneuverings found in a May 16, 1978, memo from Frank Moore, Bill Cable, and Bob Thomson to President Carter, PHF, box 87, 5/30/78 folder 1, JCL.

55. Handwritten note from President Carter on June 19, 1978, memo from Stu Eizenstat and Bill Johnston indicates he called Hollings.

56. A June 22, 1978, memo from Hamilton Jordan, Frank Moore, and the vice president to President Carter requested a last-minute contact by Carter with the wavering Sparkman. PHF, box 92, 6/22/78 folder, JCL.

57. A June 19, 1978, memo from Frank Moore and Bob Thomson to President Carter alerted Carter that "we may ask you on short notice to meet with any or all of [these three senators] during the next 48 hours. Our trading stock is the equal access provision and a 'guarantee' that the final bill emerging from Congress will be no tougher than the Senate bill. On equal access, labor will push for weakening modifications, but in the final analysis will accept elimination of the provision entirely. As for the 'guarantee,' it appears that labor will agree to push for House acceptance of the Senate bill, thereby eliminating the need for Senate consideration of a conference report. If concessions are made on the bill, they should be made by labor in bargaining sessions with the target Senators. Our role should remain that of a catalyst. We must also be prepared to consider requests not

directly related to labor law reform. We are within one vote of defeating the most expensive and powerful lobby ever mounted against a bill in the nation's history. Our attitude should remain upbeat and positive. We still believe we are going to win." PHF, box 92, 6/19/78 folder 2, JCL.

58. "Filibuster Kills Labor Law Reform Bill," *CQ Almanac 1978*, 286.

59. Ibid.

60. Moreover, the senators voting for the bill reflected 62% of the population, suggesting that the balance of opposition of senators in small states was dragging down labor's support.

61. For discussion, see Fink, "Labor Law Revision," and Halpern, "Jimmy Carter."

62. Fraser to President Carter, Aug. 11, 1978, Records of the Domestic Policy Staff, box 232, Labor Law Reform folder 4, JCL.

63. Press conference transcript, Aug. 8, 1978.

64. Background for this discussion in Weir, *Politics and Jobs,* 132.

65. "The Coalition behind Full Employment," *Business Week,* July 12, 1976, 76.

66. Charlie Schultze, chairman of the CEA, to the Economic Policy Group, memo, Mar. 14, 1977, Records of the Council of Economic Advisers, box 108, EPG Meetings 1977 folder 1, JCL.

67. The Humphrey-Hawkins process set up a planning mechanism very similar to the way the budget process has functioned since the 1974 reforms but with the added factor of the independent Federal Reserve and the state and local governments thrown in the mix. The negotiating, compromise, and just plain horse-trading that goes into the process has not been, and would not be, very conducive to coherent, long-range economic planning.

68. Representative Augustus Hawkins to Charles Schultze, May 11, 1977, Records of the Council of Economic Advisers, box 108, EPG Meetings 1977 folder 3, JCL.

69. "Full Employment," *CQ Almanac 1977,* 176.

70. "Humphrey-Hawkins Full Employment Bill," *CQ Almanac 1978,* 275.

71. An October 9, 1978, memo from Anne Wexler, Louis Martin, and Frank Moore to President Carter noted, "We are working to get a fair hearing on the floor of the Senate. Although Senator Byrd is committed to obtaining this and is making extraordinary efforts, the situation is made very difficult by the opposition of certain Republican Senators." PHF, box 105, 10/10/78 folder, JCL.

72. Stu Eizenstat, Charlie Schultze, Frank Moore, Jerry Rafshoon, and Anne Wexler to President Carter, undated memo, PHF, box 105, 10/6/78 folder, JCL.

73. Anne Wexler and Louis Martin to President Carter, memo, Oct. 7, 1978, and Anne Wexler, Louis Martin, and Frank Moore to President Carter, memo, Oct. 9, 1978, both in PHF, box 105, 10/10/78 folder, JCL.

74. "Humphrey-Hawkins Full Employment Bill," *CQ Almanac 1978.*

75. Ibid., 279.

76. Quoted in ibid., 272.

77. "Plans for AFL-CIO Drive for National Health Insurance," Legislation Department, Legislative Reference Files, box 25, folder 26, GMMA.

78. "Health Insurance: No Action in 1974," *CQ Almanac 1974,* 386.

79. Ibid., 387; Wainess, "Ways and Means," 311.

80. Wainess, "Ways and Means," 311.

81. "Health Insurance: No Action in 1974," *CQ Almanac 1974*, 387.

82. "A New Approach to National Health Insurance," Apr. 1, 1974, Legislation Department, Legislative Reference Files, box 25, folder 35, GMMA.

83. This was reported in a "Washington-insider" type publication published by McGraw-Hill, "Washington Report on Medicine & Health," March 13, 1974, found in Legislation Department, Legislative Reference Files, box 25, folder 35 GMMA.

84. Starr, "*Social Transformation of Medicine*, 404.

85. "Health Insurance: No Action in 1974," *CQ Almanac 1974*, 387.

86. Ibid.

87. Noted in interview with Representative Roy, a Democratic physician from Kansas, in *American Medical News*, Dec. 1974.

88. Notes of Dec. 16, 1974, meeting, Legislation Department, Legislative Reference Files, box 25, folder 39, GMMA.

89. Ibid.; Dick Shoemaker to Bert Seidman, memo, Nov. 21, 1974, and draft of proposals considered by the Subcommittee of the Technical Committee meeting of the CNHI, Nov. 22, 1974, both in Legislation Department, Legislative Reference Files, box 25, folder 39, GMMA.

90. "Health Care for Unemployed," *CQ Almanac 1975*, 628.

91. Bert Seidman to President Meany, memo, July 28, 1978, Office of the President, George Meany Files, box 39, folder 2, GMMA.

92. Joe Califano to President Carter, May 30, 1978, PHF, box 90, folder 6/8/78, JCL.

93. Stu Eizenstat, Joe Onek and Peter Bourne to President Carter, memo, Apr. 6, 1978, PHF, box 79, 4/6/78 folder, JCL.

94. Joe Califano to President Carter, memo, May 15, 1978, PHF, box 85, 5/16/78 folder, JCL. A number of other important committee chairs and subcommittee chairs also opposed taking up a bill before the election. A May 31, 1978, memo from Stu Eizenstat to President Carter noted that the House and Senate caucuses opposed taking up a bill because it might hurt vulnerable members but had no chance of becoming law before the election. PHF, box 88, 6/1/78 folder, JCL.

95. Joe Califano and Stu Eizenstat to President Carter, memo, July 22, 1978, PHF, box 96, 7/24/78 folder 2, JCL.

96. "National Health Insurance," *CQ Almanac 1978*, 630.

97. Stu Eizenstat and Joe Onek to President Carter, memo, July 27, 1978, PHF, box 97, 7/27/78 folder, JCL.

98. Joe Califano to President Carter, memo, May 30, 1978, PHF, box 90, 6/8/78 folder, JCL (emphasis in original).

99. "House Kills Carter Hospital Cost Control Plan," *CQ Almanac 1979*.

100. Joe Califano, Stu Eizenstat, Jim McIntyre, Charlie Schultze to President Carter, memo, May 16, 1979, PHF, box 131, 5/16/79 folder 3, JCL.

101. Jody Powell to President Carter, memo, May 18, 1979, PHF, box 132, 5/23/79 folder 2, JCL.

102. "National Health Insurance," CQ Press Electronic Library, CQ Almanac Online Edition, cqal79-1185951; originally published in *CQ Almanac 1979*.

103. Marmor, *Politics of Medicare;* Quadagno, *One Nation Uninsured;* Starr, *Social Transformation;* Steinmo and Watts, "It's the Institutions, Stupid!"; Wainess, "Ways and Means."

104. Steinmo, "American Exceptionalism Reconsidered."

CHAPTER SIX: The More Things Change, the More They Remain the Same

1. 1996 State of the Union Address.

2. When the Social Security program faced a solvency crisis in the early 1980s, Reagan and Congress reached a bipartisan compromise to raise the retirement age for future retirees from sixty-five to sixty-seven.

3. However, NLRB rulings and court interpretations of existing labor laws have further constrained labor.

4. Pierson, *Dismantling the Welfare State.*

5. Quoted in Jay Nordlinger, "Our Splendid Cuss: The Likeable Phil Gramm," *National Review,* Oct. 1, 2001.

6. Senator Ben Nighthorse Campbell, a conservative Democrat from Colorado, also switched parties, indicating that the ideological purification of the parties went beyond the South.

7. Polsby, *How Congress Evolves,* 77. Dixiecrats are defined as Southern Democrats "who have a party support to party opposition ratio of less than 2:1." All other Southern Democrats are referred to as "mainstream Democrats."

8. Shafer and Johnston, *End of Southern Exceptionalism,* chap. 2.

9. Stephen Gettinger, "R.I.P. to a Conservative Force," *CQ Weekly,* Jan. 9, 1999, 82–83.

10. The regional average was 62.6% in 1990 and 80.7% in 2000; author's calculations from COPE scores.

11. The following members of the Congressional Black Caucus from the South all have 2007 lifetime COPE scores of 95% or above: Corrine Brown (D-FL), John Lewis (D-GA), Hank Johnson (D-GA), Bennie Thompson (D-MS), Melvin Watt (D-NC), James Clyburn (D-SC), Al Green (D-TX), Sheila Jackson-Lee (D-TX), and Robert Scott (D-VA).

12. Bartels, *Unequal Democracy,* 78.

13. Despite the low rates of unionization in Florida, labor has been effective at mobilizing retired union members and allied constituencies like African Americans.

14. Francia, *Future of Organized Labor,* chap. 3.

15. Based on exit surveys from the Voter News Service, Francia reports union household turnout rose from 19% in 1992 to 24% in 1996 and 26% in 2000. He cites AFL-CIO estimates that there were 4.6 million more voters from union households in 2000 than in 1992, while votes from nonunion households fell 15.5 million. Voters from union households are estimated to have represented 24% of the electorate in 2004. See ibid., 75, 158.

16. There are some exceptions. Alaska, for example, is one of the most heavily unionized states, but it trends Republican. There are also some New England states with low rates of unionization that consistently vote Democratic. But the Plains and Southern states with their low rates of unionization are the heart of Republican strength, while the Democrats' strength is in the heavily unionized areas of the Northeast and West Coast.

17. Of the twenty-seven states with union density over 10%, eighteen are represented by two Democrats and eight are represented by one Democrat and one Republican.

18. Black and Black, *Divided America,* 95. In 2004 exit polls, union members (as opposed to union households) were 18% of Northeastern voters and 17% of Pacific Coast voters, compared with 7% in the South and Plains states.

19. Ronald Brownstein, "For GOP, a Southern Exposure," *National Journal,* May 23, 2009.

20. Abramowitz and Saunders, "Exploring the Bases"; Levendusky, *Partisan Sort.*

21. Rohde, *Parties and Leaders.*

22. Sinclair, *Legislators, Leaders, and Lawmaking.*

23. Dark, *Unions and the Democrats,* 142–47.

24. Ibid., 146; Barry, *Ambition and the Power,* 279–80.

25. Mike Gildea, formerly in the AFL-CIO Department of Legislation, interview by author, July 23, 1999.

26. Sinclair, "New World."

27. It is difficult to quantify the number of filibusters over time because no formal request or petition must be filed to launch a filibuster and it is not always clear when a filibuster is under way. Barbara Sinclair estimates that the average number of filibusters per Congress has gone from 11.2 in the 1970s to 52 in the 110th Congress (2007–8). Ibid., 7.

28. David Nather, "Switching Parties: Great Expectations." *CQ Weekly,* May 4, 2009, 1024–32.

29. On the rise of gridlock, see Brady and Volden, *Revolving Gridlock.*

30. Dark, *Unions and the Democrats,* 141–42.

31. "A Report on Congress: 1986," Support Services Department, AFL-CIO Publications, Series 1, GMMA.

32. On the Reagan administration and organized labor, see Davis, *Prisoners of the American Dream,* 138–40; Ferguson and Rogers, *Right Turn,* 130–37; Gross, *Broken Promise,* chap. 13; and Moody, *Injury to All,* 139–42.

33. Ginsburg, *Full Employment,* 76; Ferguson and Rogers, *Right Turn,* 118–19.

34. Geoghegan, *Which Side Are You On?*

35. Edsall, *New Politics of Inequality;* Ferguson and Rogers, *Right Turn;* Phillips, *Politics of Rich and Poor.*

36. For a discussion of the relationship between organized labor and Clinton, see Dark, *Unions and the Democrats,* chap. 8.

37. Quoted in Helen Dewar and David Von Drehle, "Stimulus Stalled, White House Seeks New Deal," *Washington Post,* Apr. 7, 1993.

38. Quoted in Kollman, *Outside Lobbying,* 143.

39. Uslaner, "Let the Chits Fall."

40. Mike Synar (D-OK), the chairman of the DSG, pointed out the feebleness of this argument by noting, "The only people complaining are the same people who voted against reconciliation. If you don't like voting, you shouldn't be a congressman." Quoted in "Striker Replacement Bill Stalls in Senate," *CQ Almanac 1993,* 396.

41. The Democrats' majority had fallen to fifty-six seats in June 1993 in a special election to fill a Texas Senate seat.

42. For example, a March 1993 *Wall Street Journal*/NBC News poll found 74% of respondents supported an overhaul and 66% were willing to pay higher taxes to fix the system. Poll cited in "Clinton's Health Care Plan Laid to Rest," *1994 CQ Almanac.* Steinmo and Watts cite Roper polls with 70–82% support for universal health care. Steinmo and Watts, "It's the Institutions, Stupid."

43. Skocpol, *Boomerang,* 27.

44. On the development of the plan, see Hacker, *Road to Nowhere,* and Johnson and Broder, *System.*

45. Skocpol, *Boomerang,* 39.

46. Gottschalk discusses the evolution of labor's position. She is quite critical of labor's

willingness to give up on the single-payer option in the interest of political expediency, arguing that this concession prevented organized labor from building a viable political coalition in favor of comprehensive health care reform. Gottschalk, *Shadow Welfare State,* chap. 7.

47. Hacker, *Road to Nowhere,* 133.

48. Christina Del Valle, "Even Cheerleaders Get the Blues," *Business Week,* May 30, 1994, 60; Gottschalk, *Shadow Welfare State,* 143–46.

49. Kenneth Crowe, "Health Care Solidarity," *Newsday,* Feb. 22, 1994.

50. Ibid.

51. Bennett Roth, "Labor Is Cool to Compromise on Health Plan," *Houston Chronicle,* Feb. 22, 1994.

52. Steinmo and Watts, "It's the Institutions, Stupid,"366.

53. Skocpol, *Boomerang,* 98.

54. Explanations discussed in Hacker, *Road to Nowhere;* Johnson and Broder, *System;* and Skocpol, *Boomerang.*

55. "Clinton's Health Care Plan Laid to Rest," 320.

56. Ibid., 336.

57. This was necessary if the committee was to produce a bill at all. The committee was composed of nine Republicans and eleven Democrats, two of whom were adamantly opposed to the Clinton plan.

58. Quoted in "Clinton's Health Care Plan Laid to Rest," 320.

59. Skocpol, *Boomerang,* 145.

60. Quoted in "Clinton's Health Care Plan Laid to Rest," 355.

61. Skocpol, *Boomerang.*

62. Hager and Pianin, *Balancing Act.*

63. Noble, *Welfare As We Knew It,* 123–25.

64. Gimpel, *Legislating the Revolution,* 13.

65. Hager and Pianin, *Balancing Act,* 276.

66. The executive order was later invalidated by a federal appeals court.

67. In most of the cloture votes Republicans D'Amato and Specter joined all the Democrats in opposing cloture.

68. "Congress Clears Wage Increase with Tax Breaks for Business," *CQ Almanac 1996.*

69. Frank Swoboda, "Labor Believes It's Gotten a Lift," *Washington Post,* Oct. 25, 1996.

70. Steven Greenhouse, "Organized Labor Outlines Ambitious Goals for the Next Congress," *New York Times,* Dec. 17, 1996.

71. Masters, "Unions in the 2000 Election."

72. In the 91st Congress (1969–70) the House overwhelmingly passed a constitutional amendment to eliminate the electoral college, but cloture failed 54–36 to shut off a Senate filibuster.

73. "GOP Rejects Ergonomics Rules," *CQ Almanac 2001,* 133.

74. Background for this discussion in "Homeland Department Created," *CQ Almanac 2002.*

75. Harold Meyerson, "New Labor," *American Prospect,* Jan. 14, 2005, found at www .prospect.org.

76. Ultimately a bipartisan group of senators brokered a compromise to avert the change in Senate rules, and President Bush's two Supreme Court appointments were easily confirmed.

77. Steven Greenhouse, "Unions Protest against Bush's Social Security Proposal," *New York Times*, Apr. 1, 2005.

78. Lafer, "Neither Free nor Fair"; Friedman et al., *Restoring the Promise.*

79. In keeping with the practice that Speakers do not typically sponsor legislation, Speaker Pelosi joined these eight Democrats in not signing on as a cosponsor of the bill.

80. Bensel, *Sectionalism,* 253.

81. Quoted in Associated Press story by Tom Krisher, "Angry UAW Members Lash Out at Southern Senators," Dec. 12, 2008, found at www.abcnews.go.com/Business/wire Story?id=6447769.

82. McCarty, Poole, and Rosenthal, *Polarized America,* chap. 6.

83. Hacker, "Privatizing Risk."

84. Brady and Volden, *Revolving Gridlock.*

85. For theory on polarization and inertia, see Tsebelis, *Veto Players.*

86. McCarty, Poole, and Rosenthal, *Polarized America,* 177.

Conclusion

1. Lichtenstein, "From Corporatism to Collective Bargaining."

2. See, for example, Goldfield, *Decline of Organized Labor;* Lichtenstein, *Labor's War;* and Moody, *Injury to All.*

3. Orren and Skowronek, *Search for American Political Development,* 113.

4. Theriault, *Party Polarization.*

5. Zelizer, *On Capitol Hill,* 61.

6. Ware, *Democratic Party Heads North,* 255.

7. Steinmo, "Rethinking American Exceptionalism."

8. According to exit polls, Obama carried 95% of African Americans, 67% of Latinos, 60% of union members, and 59% of union households. Exit polls found at www .cnn.com/ELECTION/2008/results/polls/. The union vote was particularly important in states like Pennsylvania, Ohio, Wisconsin, Minnesota, and Michigan. Obama won an 18-point margin with white male union members, compared with a McCain margin among white, male nonunion members of 16 points. Steven Greenhouse, "Still with Obama but Worried," *New York Times*, Mar. 3, 2010.

9. The AFL-CIO and many of the affiliates are cooperating with environmentalists to back efforts to create "green" jobs, and they have also been heavily involved with consumer groups on financial regulation, often leading protests on Wall Street.

10. Hopkins, "2008 Election," 381–84. Adam Nossiter, "For South, a Waning Hold on National Politics," *New York Times*, Nov. 11, 2008.

11. Ronald Brownstein, "For GOP, a Southern Exposure," *National Journal,* May 23, 2009.

12. AFL-CIO 2009 Convention, Resolution 2.

13. Jack Calmes and Robert Pear, "Rift over Stimulus Embroils G.O.P." *New York Times,* Feb. 22, 2009.

14. AFL-CIO 2009 Convention, Resolution 4.

15. Matthew Murray, "Solidarity with Health Reform," *Roll Call,* Sept. 8, 2009.

16. Steven Greenhouse, "New Yorker Leads Labor Charge for Health Care Reform," *New York Times*, Aug. 27, 2009.

17. Various polls at www.pollster.com; Kaiser Health Tracking Poll, Jan. 2010. www.kff .org/kaiserpolls/8042.cfm.

18. Tracey D. Samuelson, "Brown, Coakley Try to Get Out the Vote," *Christian Science Monitor,* Jan. 19, 2010. In fact, a slim plurality of union members voted for Brown. Jacobs and Skocpol suggest confusion over the status of the tax on high-cost health care plans likely contributed to this result. Jacobs and Skocpol, *Health Care Reform,* 105.

19. Washington Post, *Landmark,* 52.

20. Richard Trumka, "Time for Hill to Get Health Care Right." *Roll Call,* Feb. 9, 2010.

21. Washington Post, *Landmark,* 52.

22. The AFL-CIO Executive Council did not officially endorse the bill until days before the House vote on the Senate bill because of divisions over the benefits tax. The International Association of Machinists was particularly strident in its opposition. But powerful affiliates, like AFSCME, came out for the bill much earlier, and the AFL-CIO mobilized behind reform throughout the entire debate, even though it had not given its official endorsement to any particular plan.

23. Kevin Bogardus, "Harkin: Kennedy's Illness Stalled Card-Check," *The Hill,* Sept. 11, 2009; Kevin Bogardus and J. Taylor Rushing, "Senate Democrats Pull Back on Specter's Card-Check Prediction," *The Hill,* Sept. 17, 2009.

24. Max Fraser, "Labor's Love Lost: Is the Battle for EFCA a Quixotic Crusade?" *New Labor Forum,* Fall 2009, 23–27.

25. Bennett Roth, "Lincoln's Victory Tests the State of the Unions," *Roll Call,* June 9, 2010.

26. U.S. Bureau of Labor Statistics, *Union Members in 2009,* Jan. 22, 2010.

27. Moody, "American Labor's Civil War," 8.

28. Quoted in Kirk Victor, "Letdown on the Left," *National Journal,* Dec. 5, 2009, 26.

29. Esther Kaplan, "A Rump Group at Labor," *Nation,* Apr. 12, 2010, 18–22; Steven Greenhouse, "Plan to Seek Use of U.S. Contracts as a Wage Lever," *New York Times,* Feb. 26, 2010.

30. Steven Greenhouse, "Deadlock Is Ending on Labor Board," *New York Times,* Mar. 31, 2010.

31. See, for example, Asher et al., *American Labor Unions;* Delaney, Fiorito, and Masters, "Effects of Union Organizational and Environmental Characteristics"; Delaney, Masters, and Schwochau, "Union Membership and Voting"; Francia, *Future of Organized Labor;* Greenstone, *Labor in American Politics;* Jacobson, "Effect of AFL-CIO's Voter Education Campaigns"; Masters, "Unions in the 2000 Election"; and Sousa, "Organized Labor in the Electorate."

32. In terms of the political orientation of union members, their support for Democratic presidential candidates has followed the ups and downs of the larger electorate, peaking with 85.9% support for Johnson in 1964 and falling to a low point of 43.1% support for McGovern in 1972, with support typically falling at around 60%. Union members have typically supported Democratic presidential candidates at rates 10–20% higher than those of the larger electorate. The contrast between white union and non-union members is even more pronounced. Union support for Democratic House and Senate candidates has been more consistent, averaging around two-thirds. Union membership has had an appreciable impact on voting behavior even if labor union members do not vote as a monolithic block. Sousa, "Organized Labor."

33. Al Barkan to William Kircher, director of Department of Organization, following 1966 elections, Department of Organization Files, box 49, folder 2, GMMA.

34. Edison Media Research exit polls reported at cnn.com.

35. Anjeanette Damon, "Working on Winning Union Vote in Nevada," *USA Today,* Oct. 30, 2008; John Nichols, "Repainting Statehouses Blue," *Nation,* Oct. 23, 2007, 27.

36. AFL-CIO 2009 Convention, Resolution 2.

37. Joseph Schatz, "Looking for Room to Maneuver," *CQ Weekly,* Apr. 19, 2010.

38. Hacker, "Privatizing Risk," 257.

39. U.S. Bureau of Labor Statistics, *Union Members in 2009,* Jan. 22, 2010.

40. Estimates from 1994 and 2000 studies by Kate Brofenbrenner, a 1998 study by James Rundle, and a 2005 study by Nik Theodore reported in Lafer, *Neither Free nor Fair,* 42.

41. Although SEIU president Andrew Stern came under increasing criticism for being too top-down, too conciliatory with employers, and making the addition of new members a priority at all costs, including the interests of existing members.

42. Bronfenbrenner and Hickey, "Changing to Organize," 54.

43. Ibid., 40.

BIBLIOGRAPHY

Abram, Michael, and Joseph Cooper. "The Rise of Seniority in the House of Representatives." *Polity* 1 (Autumn 1968): 52–85.

Abramowitz, Alan I., and Kyle L. Saunders. "Exploring the Bases of Partisanship in the American Electorate: Social Identity vs. Ideology." *Political Research Quarterly* 59 (June 2006): 175–87.

Arnold, Douglas R. *The Logic of Collective Action.* New Haven: Yale University Press, 1990.

Asher, Herbert, Eric S. Heberlig, Randall B. Ripley, and Karen Synder. *American Labor Unions in the Electoral Arena.* Lanham, MD: Rowman and Littlefield, 2001.

Bailey, Stephen Kemp. *Congress Makes a Law: The Story behind the Employment Act of 1946.* New York: Vintage Books, 1950.

Barry, John M. *The Ambition and the Power.* New York: Penguin Books, 1989.

Bartels, Larry M. *Unequal Democracy: The New Politics of the Gilded Age.* New York: Russell Sage Foundation, 2008.

Battista, Andrew. *The Revival of Labor Liberalism.* Urbana: University of Illinois Press, 2008.

Bell, Daniel. "The Problem of Ideological Rigidity." In John H. M. Laslett and Seymour Martin Lipset, eds., *Failure of a Dream?* Garden City, New York: Doubleday, 1974.

Bensel, Richard Franklin. *Sectionalism and American Political Development: 1880–1980.* Madison: University of Wisconsin Press, 1984.

Berkowitz, Edward. *Disabled Policy: America's Program for the Handicapped.* New York: Twentieth Century Fund, 1987.

Berkowitz, Edward, and Wendy Wolff. "Disability Insurance and the Limits of American History." *Public Historian* 8 (Spring 1986): 65–82.

Berman, Daniel. *A Bill Becomes a Law: Congress Enacts Civil Rights Legislation.* New York: Macmillan, 1966.

Berman, William C. *America's Right Turn, from Nixon to Bush.* Baltimore: Johns Hopkins University Press, 1994.

Bernstein, Barton J. "The Truman Administration and the Steel Strike of 1946." *Journal of American History* 52 (March 1966): 791–803.

Berry, Jeffrey. *The New Liberalism: The Rising Power of Citizen Groups.* Washington, DC: Brookings Institution Press, 1999.

Binder, Sarah A., and Steven S. Smith. *Politics or Principle: Filibustering in the United States Senate.* Washington, DC: Brookings Institution Press, 1997.

Black, Earl, and Merle Black. *Divided America: The Ferocious Power Struggle in American Politics.* New York: Simon and Schuster, 2007.

Bolling, Richard. *House out of Order.* New York: E. P. Dutton and Co., 1965.

Boyle, Kevin. *The UAW and the Heyday of American Liberalism.* Ithaca, NY: Cornell University Press, 1998.

Brady, David W., and Craig Volden. *Revolving Gridlock: Politics and Policy from Jimmy Carter to George W. Bush.* Boulder, CO: Westview Press, 2006.

Brandon, Henry. "Conversation with Reuther." In Charles M. Rehmus and Doris B. McLaughlin, eds., *Labor and American Politics: A Book of Readings.* Ann Arbor: University of Michigan Press, 1967.

Brecher, Jeremy. *Strike!* Cambridge, MA: South End Press, 1999.

Brinkley, Alan. *The End of Reform: New Deal Liberalism in Recession and War.* New York: Vintage Books, 1995.

Brody, David. *Workers in Industrial America: Essays on the 20th Century Struggle.* New York: Oxford University Press, 1980.

Bronfenbrenner, Kate, and Robert Hickey. "Changing to Organize: A National Assessment of Union Strategies." In Ruth Milkman and Kim Voss, eds., *Rebuilding Labor: Organizing and Organizers in the New Union Movement.* Ithaca, NY: ILR Press, 2004.

Brown, Michael K. "Bargaining for Social Rights: Unions and the Reemergence of Welfare Capitalism." *Political Science Quarterly* 112 (Winter 1997): 645–74.

Carmines, Edward G., and James A. Stimson. *Issue Evolution: Race and the Transformation of American Politics.* Princeton: Princeton University Press, 1989.

Caswell, Bruce. "The Presidency, the Vote, and the Formation of New Coalitions." *Polity* 41 (July 2009): 388–407.

Chen, Anthony. *The Fifth Freedom: Jobs, Politics, and Civil Rights in the United States, 1941–1972.* Princeton: Princeton University Press, 2009.

Chen, Anthony S., Robert W. Mickey, and Robert P. Van Houweling. "Explaining the Contemporary Alignment of Race and Party: Evidence from California's 1946 Ballot Initiative on Fair Employment." *Studies in American Political Development* 22 (Fall 2008): 204–28.

Cohen, Lizabeth. *Making a New Deal: Industrial Workers in Chicago, 1919–1939.* New York: Cambridge University Press, 1990.

Cooper, Joseph, and Gary Bombardier. "Presidential Leadership and Party Success." *Journal of Politics* 30 (November 1968): 1012–27.

Cox, Gary W., and Jonathan N. Katz. "The Reapportionment Revolution and Bias in U.S. Congressional Elections." *American Journal of Political Science* 43 (July 1999): 812–41.

Cox, Gary, and Matthew D. McCubbins. *Legislative Leviathan: Party Government in the House.* Berkeley: University of California Press, 1993.

Dahl, Robert. *How Democratic Is the American Constitution?* New Haven: Yale University Press, 2001.

Dark, Taylor E. *The Unions and the Democrats: An Enduring Alliance.* Ithaca, NY: Cornell University Press, 1999.

Davis, Eric L. "Legislative Reform and the Decline of Presidential Influence on Capitol Hill." *British Journal of Political Science* 9 (October 1979): 465–79.

Davis, Mike. *Prisoners of the American Dream: Politics and the Economy in the History of the U.S. Working Class.* New York: Norton, 2000.

Delaney, John Thomas, Jack Fiorito, and Marick F. Masters. "The Effects of Union Organizational and Environmental Characteristics on Union Political Action." *American Journal of Political Science* 32 (August 1988): 616–42.

Delaney, John Thomas, Marick F. Masters, and Susan Schwochau. "Union Membership and Voting for COPE-Endorsed Candidates." *Industrial and Labor Relations Review* 43 (July 1990): 621–35.

De Vyver, Frank T. "The Present Status of Labor Unions in the South—1948." *Southern Economic Journal* 16 (July 1949): 1–22.

Dodd, Lawrence C., and Bruce I. Oppenheimer. "Maintaining Order in the House: The Struggle for Institutional Change." In Lawrence C. Dodd and Bruce I. Oppenheimer, eds., *Congress Reconsidered*. 5th ed. Washington: CQ Press, 1993.

Douglas, Paul H., and Joseph Hackman. "The Fair Labor Standards Act of 1938." *Political Science Quarterly* 53 (December 1938): 491–515.

Draper, Alan. *Conflict of Interests: Organized Labor and the Civil Rights Movement in the South, 1954–1968*. Ithaca, NY: ILR Press, 1994.

———. *A Rope of Sand: The AFL-CIO Committee on Political Education: 1955–1967*. New York: Praeger, 1989.

Dubofsky, Melvyn. *The State and Labor in Modern America*. Chapel Hill: University of North Carolina Press, 1994.

Edsall, Thomas Byrne. *The New Politics of Inequality*. New York: Norton, 1984.

Edsall, Thomas Byrne, and Mary D. Edsall. *Chain Reaction: The Impact of Race, Rights, and Taxes on American Politics*. New York: Norton, 1992.

Ellwood, David T., and Glenn Fine. "The Impact of Right-to-Work Laws on Union Organizing." *Journal of Political Economy* (April 1987): 250–73.

Farhang, Sean, and Ira Katznelson. "The Southern Imposition: Congress and Labor in the New Deal and Fair Deal." *Studies in American Political Development* 19 (April 2005): 1–30.

Feinstein, Brian D., and Eric Schickler. "Platforms and Partners: The Civil Rights Realignment Reconsidered." *Studies in American Political Development* 22 (March 2008): 1–31.

Ferguson, Thomas, and Joel Rogers. *Right Turn: The Decline of the Democrats and the Future of American Politics*. New York: Hill and Wang, 1986.

Fink, Gary. "Labor Law Revision and the End of the Postwar Labor Accord." In Kevin Boyle, ed., *Organized Labor and American Politics, 1894–1994*. Albany: State University of New York Press, 1998.

Fiorina, Morris. *Retrospective Voting in American National Elections*. New Haven: Yale University Press, 1981.

Fleck, Robert K. "Opposition to the Fair Labor Standards Act of 1938." *Journal of Economic History* 62 (March 2002): 25–54.

Foner, Philip S. *Organized Labor and the Black Worker, 1619–1973*. New York: International Publishers, 1974.

Forbath, William E. *Law and the Shaping of the American Labor Movement*. Cambridge: Harvard University Press, 1991.

Francia, Peter. *The Future of Organized Labor in American Politics*. New York: Columbia University Press, 2006.

Fraser, Steven. *Labor Will Rule: Sidney Hillman and the Rise of American Labor*. New York: Free Press, 1991.

Friedman, Gerald. "The Political Economy of Early Southern Unionism: Race, Politics, and Labor in the South, 1880–1953." *Journal of Economic History* 60 (June 2000): 384–413.

Friedman, Sheldon, Richard Hurd, Rudolph Oswald, and Ronald Seeber, eds. *Restoring the Promise of American Labor Law*. Ithaca, NY: ILR Press, 1994.

Gall, Gilbert J. *The Politics of Right to Work: The Labor Federations as Special Interests, 1943–1979.* New York: Greenwood Press, 1988.

Geoghegan, Thomas. *Which Side Are You On? Trying to Be for Labor When It's Flat on Its Back.* New York: Plume, 1992.

Gimpel, James G. *Legislating the Revolution: The Contract with America in Its First 100 Days.* Boston: Allyn and Bacon, 1996.

Ginsburg, Helen. *Full Employment and Public Policy: The United States and Sweden.* Lexington, MA: Lexington Books, 1983.

Goldfield, Michael. *The Decline of Organized Labor in the United States.* Chicago: University of Chicago Press, 1987.

——. "Worker Insurgency, Radical Organization, and New Deal Labor Legislation." *American Political Science Review* 83 (1989): 1257–82.

Gottschalk, Marie. *The Shadow Welfare State: Labor, Business, and the Politics of Health Care in the United States.* Ithaca, NY: Cornell University Press, 2000.

Greenstone, J. David. *Labor in American Politics.* Chicago: University of Chicago Press, 1977.

Griffith, Barbara S. *The Crisis of American Labor: Operation Dixie and the Defeat of the CIO.* Philadelphia: Temple University Press, 1988.

Gross, James A. *Broken Promise: The Subversion of U.S. Labor Relations Policy, 1947–1994.* Philadelphia: Temple University Press, 1995.

——. *The Reshaping of the National Labor Relations Board.* Albany: State University of New York Press, 1981.

Hacker, Jacob. *The Divided Welfare State: The Battle over Public and Private Social Benefits in the United States.* New York: Cambridge University Press, 2002.

——. "The Historical Logic of National Health Insurance: Structure and Sequence in the Development of British, Canadian, and U.S. Medical Policy." *Studies in American Political Development* 12 (Spring 1998): 57–130.

——. "Privatizing Risk without Privatizing the Welfare State: The Hidden Politics of Social Policy Retrenchment." *American Political Science Review* 98 (May 2004): 243–60.

——. *The Road to Nowhere.* Princeton: Princeton University Press, 1997.

Hager, George, and Eric Pianin. *Balancing Act: Washington's Troubled Path to a Balanced Budget.* New York: Vintage Books, 1998.

Halpern, Martin. "Jimmy Carter and the UAW: Failure of an Alliance." *Presidential Studies Quarterly* 26 (Summer 1996): 755–77.

Harrington, Michael. *Socialism.* New York: Saturday Review Press, 1972.

Hartz, Louis. *The Liberal Tradition in America.* New York: Harcourt Brace, 1955.

Hattam, Victoria. *Labor Visions and State Power: The Origins of Business Unionism in the United States.* Princeton: Princeton University Press, 1993.

Hopkins, David A. "The 2008 Election and the Political Geography of the New Democratic Majority." *Polity* 41 (July 2009): 368–87.

Horowitz, Ruth. *Political Ideologies of Organized Labor.* New Brunswick, NJ: Transaction Books, 1978.

Howard, Christopher. *The Hidden Side of the American Welfare State.* Princeton: Princeton University Press, 1999.

——. *The Welfare State Nobody Knows: Debunking Myths about U.S. Social Policy.* Princeton: Princeton University Press, 2007.

Huber, Evelyne, Charles Ragin, and John D. Stephens. "Social Democracy, Christian Democracy, Constitutional Structure, and the Welfare State." *American Journal of Sociology* 99 (1993): 711–49.

Immergut, Ellen M. *Health Politics: Interests and Institutions in Western Europe.* New York: Cambridge University Press, 1992.

——. "Institutions, Veto Points, and Policy Results: A Comparative Analysis of Health Care." *Journal of Public Policy* 10 (October–December, 1990): 391–416.

Jacobs, Lawrence R., and Theda Skocpol. *Health Care Reform and American Politics: What Everyone Needs to Know.* New York: Oxford University Press, 2010.

Jacobson, Gary C. "The Effect of the AFL-CIO's Voter Education Campaigns on the 1996 House Elections." *Journal of Politics* 61 (February 1999): 185–94.

Johnson, Haynes, and David Broder. *The System: The American Way of Politics at the Breaking Point.* Boston: Little, Brown, and Co., 1997.

Jones, Charles O. "Joseph G. Cannon and Howard W. Smith: An Essay on the Limits of Leadership in the House of Representatives." *Journal of Politics* 30 (August 1968): 617–46.

Josephson, Matthew. *Sidney Hillman: Statesman of American Labor.* Garden City, NY: Doubleday, 1952.

Karol, David. *Party Position Change in American Politics.* Cambridge: Cambridge University Press, 2009.

Katznelson, Ira. *City Trenches: Urban Politics and the Patterning of Class in the United States.* Chicago: University of Chicago Press, 1988.

——. "Was the Great Society a Lost Opportunity?" In Steve Fraser and Gary Gerstle, eds., *The Rise and Fall of the New Deal Order, 1930–1980.* Princeton: Princeton University Press, 1989.

Katznelson, Ira, Kim Geiger, and Daniel Kryder. "Limiting Liberalism: The Southern Veto in Congress, 1933–1950." *Political Science Quarterly* 108 (Summer 1993): 283–306.

Katznelson, Ira, and John Lapinski. "Congress and American Political Development: Missed Chances, Rich Possibilities." *Perspectives on Politics* 4 (June 2006): 243–60.

Key, V. O., Jr. *Southern Politics in State and Nation.* New York: Knopf, 1949.

Klein, Jennifer. *For All These Rights: Business, Labor, and the Shaping of America's Public-Private Welfare State.* Princeton: Princeton University Press, 2006.

Kofmehl, Kenneth. "The Institutionalization of a Voting Bloc." *Western Political Quarterly* 17 (June 1964): 256–72.

Kollman, Ken. *Outside Lobbying: Public Opinion and Interest Group Strategies.* Princeton: Princeton University Press, 1998.

Krehbiel, Keith. *Pivotal Politics: A Theory of U.S. Lawmaking.* Chicago: University of Chicago Press, 1998.

Lafer, Gordon. *Neither Free nor Fair: The Subversion of Democracy under NLRB Elections.* Washington: American Rights at Work, 2007.

Lee, David. "Wage Inequality in the United States during the 1980s: Rising Dispersion or Falling Minimum Wage?" *Quarterly Journal of Economics* 114 (August 1999): 977–1023.

Lee, Frances E., and Bruce I. Oppenheimer. *Sizing Up the Senate: The Unequal Consequences of Equal Representation.* Chicago: University of Chicago Press, 1999.

Lee, R. Alton. *Truman and Taft-Hartley: A Question of Mandate.* Westport, CT: Greenwood Press, 1966.

Levendusky, Matthew. *The Partisan Sort: How Liberals Became Democrats and Conservatives Became Republicans.* Chicago: University of Chicago Press, 2009.

Levy, Peter B. *The New Left and Labor in the 1960s.* Urbana: University of Illinois Press, 1994.

Lichtenstein, Nelson. "From Corporatism to Collective Bargaining: Organized Labor and the Eclipse of Social Democracy." In Steve Fraser and Gary Gerstle, eds., *The Rise and Fall of the New Deal Order, 1930–1980.* Princeton: Princeton University Press, 1989.

———. *Labor's War at Home: The CIO in World War II.* Philadelphia: Temple University Press, 2003.

———. *The Most Dangerous Man in Detroit: Walter Reuther and the Fate of American Labor.* New York: Basic Books, 1995.

———. *State of the Union: A Century of American Labor.* Princeton: Princeton University Press, 2002.

Lipset, Seymour Martin. *American Exceptionalism: A Double-Edged Sword.* New York: Norton, 1997.

Lipset, Seymour Martin, and Gary Marks. *It Didn't Happen Here: Why Socialism Failed in the United States.* New York: Norton, 2001.

Lowi, Theodore. "Why Is There No Socialism in the United States? A Federal Analysis." *International Political Science Review* 5, no. 4 (1984): 369–80.

Lumsden, Keith, and Craig Petersen. "The Effect of Right-to-Work Laws on Unionization in the United States." *Journal of Political Economy* 83 (December 1975): 1237–48.

Marmor, Theodore. *The Politics of Medicare.* Chicago: Aldine Publishing Co., 1970.

Masters, Marick. "Unions in the 2000 Election: A Strategic Choice Perspective." *Journal of Labor Research* 25 (Winter 2004): 139–82.

McAdams, Alan K. *Power and Politics in Labor Legislation.* New York: Columbia University Press, 1964.

McCarty, Nolan, Keith T. Poole, and Howard Rosenthal. *Polarized America: The Dance of Ideology and Unequal Riches.* Cambridge, MA: MIT Press, 2006.

McClure, Arthur. *The Truman Administration and the Problems of Postwar Labor, 1945–1948.* Cranbury, NJ: Associated University Presses, 1969.

McCubbins, Mathew D., and Thomas Schwartz. "Congress, the Courts, and Public Policy: Consequences of the One Man, One Vote Rule." *American Journal of Political Science* 32 (May 1988): 388–415.

Meier, August, and Elliott Rudwick. *Black Detroit and the Rise of the UAW.* Ann Arbor: University of Michigan Press, 2007.

Mills, C. Wright. *The New Men of Power: America's Labor Leaders.* New York: Harcourt Brace, 1948.

Moody, Kim. "American Labor's Civil War: The Crisis and the Potential." *Against the Current* 145 (March/April 2010): 7–10.

———. *An Injury to All: The Decline of American Unionism.* London: Verso Press, 1997.

Noble, Charles. *Welfare As We Knew It.* New York: Oxford University Press, 1997.

Oestreicher, Richard. "The Rules of the Game: Class Politics in Twentieth-Century America." In Kevin Boyle, ed., *Organized Labor and American Politics, 1894–1994: The Labor-Liberal Alliance.* Albany: State University of New York Press, 1998.

Oppenheimer, Bruce I. "Congress and the New Obstructionism: Developing an Energy Program." In Lawrence C. Dodd and Bruce I. Oppenheimer, eds., *Congress Reconsidered.* 2nd ed. Washington: CQ Press, 1981.

———. "The Process Hurdles: Energy Legislation from the OPEC Embargo to 2008." In

Lawrence C. Dodd and Bruce I. Oppenheimer, eds., *Congress Reconsidered.* 9th ed. Washington: CQ Press, 2008.

Ornstein, Norman J., Thomas E. Mann, and Michael J. Malbin. *Vital Statistics on Congress.* Washington: Brookings Institution Press, 2008.

Orren, Karen. "Union Politics and Postwar Liberalism in the United States, 1946–1979." *Studies in American Political Development* 1 (March 1986): 215–52.

Orren, Karen, and Stephen Skowronek. *The Search for American Political Development.* New York: Cambridge University Press, 2004.

Palazzolo, Daniel J. "From Decentralization to Centralization: Members' Changing Expectations for House Leaders." In Roger H. Davidson, ed., *The Postreform Congress.* New York: St. Martin's Press, 1992.

Patterson, James T. *Congressional Conservatism and the New Deal.* Lexington: University of Kentucky Press, 1967.

———. "The Failure of Party Realignment in the South, 1937–1939." *Journal of Politics* 27 (August 1965): 602–17.

Phillips, Kevin. *The Politics of Rich and Poor.* New York: Harper Perennial, 1990.

Pierson, Paul. *Dismantling the Welfare State? Reagan, Thatcher, and the Politics of Retrenchment.* Cambridge: Cambridge University Press, 1994.

———. "Increasing Returns, Path Dependence, and the Study of Politics." *American Political Science Review* 94 (June 2000): 251–67.

———. *The New Politics of the Welfare State.* Oxford: Oxford University Press, 2001.

———. *Politics in Time: History, Institutions, and Social Analysis.* Princeton: Princeton University Press, 2004.

Piven, Frances Fox, and Richard A. Cloward. *Poor People's Movements: Why They Succeed, How They Fail.* Vintage Books, 1979.

Plotke, David. *Building a Democratic Political Order: Reshaping American Liberalism in the 1930s and 1940s.* New York: Cambridge University Press, 1996.

Poen, Monte M. *Harry S. Truman and the Medical Lobby: The Genesis of Medicare.* Columbia: University of Missouri Press, 1979.

"The Political Aims of Organized Labor." *Annals of the American Academy of Political and Social Science* 259 (September 1948): 144–52.

Polsby, Nelson. *How Congress Evolves: Social Bases of Institutional Change.* New York: Oxford University Press, 2004.

Poole, Keith T., and Howard Rosenthal. *Ideology and Congress.* New Brunswick, NJ: Transaction Publishers, 2007.

Quadagno, Jill S. *One Nation Uninsured: Why the U.S. Has No National Health Insurance.* New York: Oxford University Press, 2005.

———. "Physician Sovereignty and the Purchasers' Revolt." *Journal of Health Politics, Policy, and Law* 29 (August–October 2004): 815–34.

Quadagno, Jill, and Debra Street. "Ideology and Public Policy: Antistatism in American Welfare State Transformation." *Journal of Policy History* 17 (January 2005): 52–71.

Richter, Irving. *Labor's Struggles, 1945–1950: A Participant's View.* New York: Cambridge University Press, 1994.

Robinson, Archie. *George Meany and His Times.* New York: Simon and Schuster, 1981.

Rohde, David. *Parties and Leaders in the Postreform House.* Chicago: University of Chicago Press, 1991.

Rudder, Catherine. "Committee Reform and the Revenue Process." In Lawrence C. Dodd and Bruce I. Oppenheimer, eds., *Congress Reconsidered*. New York: Praeger, 1977.

Savage, Sean J. *Truman and the Democratic Party*. Lexington: University Press of Kentucky, 1997.

Scammon, Richard M., and Ben J. Wattenberg. *The Real Majority*. New York: Primus, 1992.

Schickler, Eric. *Disjointed Pluralism: Institutional Innovation and the Development of the U.S. Congress*. Princeton: Princeton University Press, 2001.

——. "Public Opinion, the Congressional Policy Agenda, and the Limits of New Deal Liberalism, 1936–1945." Presented at the August 2009 meeting of the American Political Science Association, Toronto, Canada.

Schickler, Eric, and Kathryn Pearson. "Agenda Control, Majority Party Power, and House Committee on Rules, 1937–1952." *Legislative Studies Quarterly* 34 (November 2009): 455–91.

Schickler, Eric, Kathryn Pearson, and Brian D. Feinstein. "Congressional Parties and Civil Rights Politics from 1933 to 1972." *Journal of Politics* 72 (July 2010): 1–18.

Schmitt, John, and Kris Warner. "The Changing Face of Labor, 1983–2008." Center for Economic Policy Research, November 2009.

Shafer, Byron E., and Richard Johnston. *The End of Southern Exceptionalism: Class, Race, and Partisan Change in the Postwar South*. Cambridge: Harvard University Press, 2006.

Shelley, Mark C., II. *The Permanent Majority: The Conservative Coalition in Congress*. University: University of Alabama Press, 1983.

Sheppard, Burton. *Rethinking Congressional Reform*. Cambridge, MA: Schenkman Books, 1985.

Sinclair, Barbara. *Legislators, Leaders, and Lawmaking*. Baltimore: Johns Hopkins University Press, 1995.

——. *Majority Leadership in the U.S. House*. Baltimore: Johns Hopkins University Press, 1983.

——. "The New World of U.S. Senators." In Lawrence C. Dodd and Bruce I. Oppenheimer, eds., *Congress Reconsidered*, 9th ed. Washington: CQ Press, 2008.

Skocpol, Theda. *Boomerang: Health Care Reform and the Turn against Government*. New York: Norton, 1996.

Skocpol, Theda, Kenneth Finegold, and Michael Goldfield. "Explaining New Deal Labor Policy." *American Political Science Review* 84 (December 1990): 1297–1315.

Sousa, David. "Organized Labor in the Electorate, 1960–1988." *Political Research Quarterly* 46 (December 1993): 741–58.

Starr, Paul. *The Social Transformation of Medicine: The Rise of a Sovereign Profession and the Making of a Vast Industry*. New York: Basic Books, 1982.

Steinmo, Sven. "American Exceptionalism Reconsidered: Culture or Institutions?" In Lawrence Dodd and Calvin Jillson, eds., *The Dynamics of American Politics: Approaches and Interpretations*. Boulder, CO: Westview Press, 1994.

——. "What Is Historical Institutionalism?" In Donatella Della Porta and Michael Keating, eds., *Approaches and Methodologies in the Social Sciences: A Pluralist Perspective*. New York: Cambridge University Press, 2008.

Steinmo, Sven, Kathleen Thelen, and Frank Longstreth. *Structuring Politics: Historical Institutionalism in Comparative Analysis*. New York: Cambridge University Press, 1992.

Steinmo, Sven, and Jon Watts. "It's the Institutions, Stupid! Why Comprehensive National Health Insurance Always Fails in America." *Journal of Health, Politics, and Law* 20 (Summer 1995): 329–69.

Stevens, Arthur, Jr., Arthur H. Miller, and Thomas E. Mann. "Mobilization of Strength in the House, 1955–1970: The Democratic Study Group." *American Political Science Review* 68 (June 1974): 667–81.

Stevens, Beth. "Blurring the Boundaries: How the Federal Government Has Influenced Welfare Benefits in the Private Sector." In Margaret Weir, Ann Shola Orloff, and Theda Skocpol, eds., *The Politics of Social Policy in the United States*. Princeton: Princeton University Press, 1988.

Sundquist, James L. *The Decline and Resurgence of Congress*. Washington: Brookings Institution Press, 1981.

Taft, Philip. "Political Activity of Organized Labor, 1948." In Charles M. Rehmus, Doris B. McLaughlin, and Frederick H. Nesbitt, eds., *Labor and American Politics: A Book of Readings*. Ann Arbor: University of Michigan Press, 1978.

Thelen, Kathleen. *How Institutions Evolve: The Political Economy of Skills in Germany, Britain, the United States, and Japan*. New York: Cambridge University Press, 2004.

Theriault, Sean M. *Party Polarization in Congress*. New York: Cambridge University Press, 2008.

Troy, Leo. "The Growth of Union Membership in the South, 1939–1953." *Southern Economic Journal* 24 (April 1958): 407–20.

Truman, Harry. *Memoirs*. Garden City, NY: Doubleday, 1955.

Tsebelis, George. *Veto Players: How Institutions Work*. Princeton: Princeton University Press, 2002.

Turner, Julius. *Party and Constituency: Pressures on Congress*. Baltimore: Johns Hopkins University Press, 1970.

Tynes, Sheryl. *Turning Points in Social Security*. Stanford: Stanford University Press, 1996.

Uslaner, Eric M. "Let the Chits Fall Where They May? Executive and Constituency Influences on Congressional Voting on NAFTA." *Legislative Studies Quarterly* 23 (August 1998): 347–71.

Vogel, David. *Fluctuating Fortunes: The Political Power of Business in America*. New York: Basic Books, 1989.

Wainess, Flint J. "The Ways and Means of National Health Care Reform, 1974 and Beyond." *Journal of Health Politics, Policy and Law* 24 (April 1999): 305–33.

Ware, Alan. *The Democratic Party Heads North, 1877–1962*. New York: Cambridge University Press, 2006.

Washington Post. *Landmark: The Inside Story of America's New Health-Care Law and What It Means for Us All*. New York: Public Affairs, 2010.

Wawro, Gregory, and Eric Schickler. *Filibuster: Obstruction and Lawmaking in the U.S. Senate*. Princeton: Princeton University Press, 2006.

Weaver, R. Kent, and Bert A. Rockman, eds. *Do Institutions Matter? Government Capabilities in the United States and Abroad*. Washington: Brookings Institution Press, 1992.

Weir, Margaret. *Politics and Jobs: The Boundaries of Employment Policy in the United States*. Princeton: Princeton University Press, 1992.

Wilson, James Q. *The Amateur Democrat*. Chicago: University of Chicago Press, 1962.

Witwer, David. *Corruption and Reform in the Teamsters Union*. Urbana: University of Illinois Press, 2008.

Zelizer, Julian. *On Capitol Hill: The Struggle to Reform Congress and Its Consequences, 1948–2000*. New York: Cambridge University Press, 2006.

——. *Taxing America: Wilbur D. Mills, Congress, and the State, 1945–1975*. New York: Cambridge University Press, 1998.

Zieger, Robert. *American Workers, American Unions, 1920–1985*. Baltimore: Johns Hopkins University Press, 1986.

INDEX

Page numbers in *italics* indicate tables.